Unions in AMERICA

Gary Chaison
Clark University

SAGE Publications
Thousand Oaks ▪ London ▪ New Delhi

For information:

Sage Publications, Inc.
2455 Teller Road
Thousand Oaks, California 91320
E-mail: order@sagepub.com

Sage Publications Ltd.
1 Oliver's Yard
55 City Road
London EC1Y 1SP
United Kingdom

Sage Publications India Pvt. Ltd.
B-42, Panchsheel Enclave
Post Box 4109
New Delhi 110 017 India

Printed in the United States of America

Library of Congress Cataloging-in-Publication Data

Chaison, Gary N.
Unions in America / Gary N. Chaison.
        p. cm.
Includes bibliographical references and index.
ISBN 1-4129-2671-8 (cloth)—ISBN 0-7619-3034-5 (pbk.)
    1. Labor unions—United States. 2. Industrial relations—United States. I. Title.
HD6508.C384 2006
331.88'0973—dc22   2005019005

This book is printed on acid-free paper.

05   06   07   08   09   10   9   8   7   6   5   4   3   2   1

Acquisitions Editor:	Al Bruckner
Editorial Assistant:	MaryAnn Vail
Production Editor:	Diane S. Foster
Copy Editor:	Kate Peterson
Typesetter:	C&M Digitals (P) Ltd.
Proofreader:	Scott Oney
Cover Designer:	Michelle Kenny

Contents

Tables and Figures

Tables

Figures

Introduction

E verybody has something to say about labor unions. We all have opinions about the power of unions, the vices or virtues of union offi- cers, and the impact of unions on our economy and society. Some believe that unions are too powerful, while others worry that unions have become too weak to confront large, multinational employers. Some call unions anti- quated organizations without a future in the modern industrial world. Others insist that only by forming unions can workers deal with their employers as equals. We hear that union officers are corrupt and unions are undemocratic. But some say that union officers are more honest than busi- ness leaders and unions are run more democratically than companies.[1]

We are surrounded by discussions of labor unions, but what we hear and read is often based on erroneous information, unsupported general- izations, and romanticized notions about what unions can or should do. This book is intended to raise the level of that discussion by providing a concise, unbiased and up-to-date portrait of unions in America.

Describing unions is not easy because they are so complex and diverse. All unions are essentially organizations formed or joined by workers to negotiate terms and conditions of employment with their employers. But there is no typical union. Some unions are local in scope and represent only a hundred or so workers at a single plant; others are huge organiza- tions, representing more than a million members at thousands of plants owned by hundreds of companies. And unions that use the modifier *national* or *international* come in all sizes, from the International Brother- hood of General Workers with its nine members to the National Education Association with 2.5 million members.[2]

The unions' internal structures also vary greatly. The Atlantic Independent Union, with 500 members, has only three local branches, but the American Federation of State, County and Municipal Workers has 1.3 million members in 3,500 locals. The National Education Association has

13,000 locals. The Writers Guild of America has no locals; rather it is divided into two distinct organizations—one is the Writers Guild–East and the other is the Writers Guild–West.[3]

There are unions of retail, hotel, and health care workers that have members who earn little more than the minimum wage. There are also unions of professional athletes that represent more than a few millionaires.

Most unions have diverse memberships; for example, there are social workers and prison guards among the members of the Communications Workers of America, and there are professional writers and assembly line workers in the United Auto Workers.[4] All big unions, no matter what they call themselves, represent some service and government workers. The International Brotherhood of Teamsters reserves the right to organize all workers in all industries.[5] But there are also many unions that limit their membership to particular occupations. Only flight attendants can join the Association of Flight Attendants, only actors are in Actors' Equity, only firefighters are in the International Association of Fire Fighters, and only horseshoers are in the International Horseshoers Union.

Some unions resemble labor federations because they have districts and local organizations that are self-governing, but other unions are highly centralized and require that important decisions be made at national headquarters. And for each union that is praised for being democratically run with high membership participation and a vibrant political system, there always seems to be another that is notorious for operating like a closed family business.

Unions also have to deal with some serious contradictions. For example, union officers always say that organizing is a top priority, but they seldom allocate sufficient financial resources for it.[6] Unions are proud to be in adversarial relationships with employers, but they know that their survival and their members' livelihoods depend on the financial health of those employers. Unions threaten to strike during negotiations to pressure management to agree to their demands, but they also know that if they strike too effectively and inflict severe economic harm, management will be unable to meet their demands.

Despite their daunting complexity, we need a full and clear understanding of labor unions. Unions are not obscure, inconsequential organizations— what they do can affect all of us. For instance, recall the 2002 dispute on the West Coast docks between the International Longshoremen's and Warehousemen's Union and an association of employers. When the employers locked out the workers during negotiations, the backlog of shipments drained the economy of nearly $1 billion per day. The country would have fallen into a deep and long recession if the president had not invoked emergency disputes legislation to force the resumption of work (and the eventual resolution of the dispute).[7] That year, a subway strike was avoided at the last minute in New York City by intense negotiations. No doubt, a strike would have paralyzed the city and dragged down the national economy.[8]

We should also know about unions because they pursue objectives that we value. Through political action as well as collective bargaining, unions seek to reduce poverty, end discrimination, ensure safer workplaces, give workers a voice in running the enterprise, and cushion the impact of foreign competition on wages and job security. If we understand how unions operate, we will know how they define and pursue priorities important to us and why they are successful or unsuccessful.

Finally, without any exaggeration, unions are at a crucial juncture in their history. A quarter of a century of severe membership losses and declining economic and political influence have forced unions to reconsider what they are doing. There are intense debates within unions about whether greater resources should be devoted to organizing or political action; whether part-time, temporary, or self-employed workers should be recruited in large numbers; and whether coalitions with community organizations are needed to strengthen bargaining and organizing.[9] Only those who understand unions as organizations can appreciate the importance of these debates in shaping the future of unionism.

This book presents a broad portrait of unions in seven chapters. First, I describe the evolution of unions, including their earliest activities, the major union federations, the opposition of employers and the government to unions, and the legal framework of labor relations. Major themes are the widening scope of union membership and the extreme reluctance of employers to accept the presence of unions at the plant and the bargaining table. In the second chapter, I describe union structure and growth. The discussion covers the types of unions, relations between unions, internal union structures, and the causes of union growth and decline. The third chapter deals with union government and administration, including the links between union structures, union self-governance, and union democracy and corruption. In the fourth chapter, I examine the most basic of union activities—collective bargaining. There is a discussion of recent concessionary bargaining, the declining use of the unions' strike weapon, and the content, interpretation, and enforcement of collective bargaining agreements. Union political action is described in the fifth chapter. I emphasize forms of political action such as the endorsement of candidates and the mobilization of the membership, and some recent political campaigns in which unions had varying degrees of success. In the sixth chapter, I examine the common features of recent proposals for union revival, asking whether plans for reversing union decline are realistic or simply too little, too late. In the concluding chapter, I speculate about the unions of the future by presenting three possible scenarios—retreat, rebound, and renew. These seven chapters present an overview of American unionism by asking where unions came from, where they are right now, and where they might be heading.

Notes

1. For a brief review of public opinion regarding unions and union officers, see Chaison, G., and Bigelow, B. (2002). *Unions and legitimacy.* Ithaca, NY: ILR Press, pp. 15–17.

2. Gifford, C. (2002). *Directory of U.S. labor organizations, 2002.* Washington, DC: Bureau of National Affairs.

3. Gifford (2002).

4. Smallwood, S. (2003, January 17). United academic workers. *Chronicle of Higher Education,* pp. A8–A10.

5. For a review of the diversity of union membership and the unions' practice of organizing outside traditional jurisdictions, see Chaison, G. N. (1987). The recent expansion of union organizing jurisdictions. Working Paper no. 87–102, Graduate School of Management, Clark University, Worcester, MA; Chaison, G. N., and Dhavale, D. G. (1990). The changing scope of union organizing. *Journal of Labor Research,* 11, pp. 307–320.

6. Chaison and Dhavale (1990).

7. Sanger, D., and Greenfield, S. (2002, October 9). President invokes Taft-Hartley Act to open 29 ports. *New York Times,* pp. A1, A14; Sappenfield, M., and Scherer, R. (2002). West Coast dock strike cost $1 billion a day. http:www.csmonitor .com/2002/1001/s03/p01.

8. Mahler, J. (2002, December 13). The ghost of walkouts past. *New York Times,* p. A32; McFadden, R. (2002, December 9). Amid holiday glow, the real chill in the air is the fear of a transit strike. *New York Times,* p. A25.

9. Turner, L., Katz, H., and Hurd, R. (Eds.). (2001). *Rekindling the labor movement: Labor's quest for relevance in the twenty-first century.* Ithaca, NY: ILR Press; Century Foundation Task Force on the Future of Unions. (2000). *What's next for organized labor?* New York: Century Foundation Press.

Acknowledgments

This book is my attempt to present a concise, unbiased, up-to-date, and readable portrait of labor unions in America. Because it is based on the books and articles that I have written over the past three decades, it is impossible to thank everyone who has helped me. What I know and think about unions has been shaped by discussions with my colleagues and research collaborators, students, editors and reviewers, news reporters, research assistants, industrial relations practitioners, and union members, staff, and officers. But there are a few who deserve special mention for their help with this book.

Al Bruckner, my editor at Sage Publications, was always kind and encouraging. MaryAnn Vail, editorial assistant at Sage, along with Diane Foster, production editor, and Kate Peterson, copy editor, processed the manuscript with impressive skill. They are an outstanding group of professionals and I enjoyed working with them. The six anonymous reviewers selected by Sage examined the manuscript and proposal with care and imagination, and I thank them for their suggestions. I hope they are pleased with the revisions I have made. My research assistant, Julia Abakaeva, was simply extraordinary—smart and determined, but always a woman of good judgment and good humor. *Spasiba balshoye.* Finally, I thank my wife, Joanne, for her patience and understanding, and (as I have said so many times before, but never really enough) I thank her for much, much more.

One

The Evolution of Labor Unions

This chapter briefly traces the evolution of labor unions and lays the foundation for subsequent discussions of union structure, administration, and activities. Obviously, it is not written as a comprehensive history of unions or labor-management relations. Rather, it highlights the forces that shaped what unions do in our economy and society, with a particular emphasis on the debate within the union movement over the appropriate union mission and structure and the employers' acceptance or rejection of unionism.[1]

The Early Years

Prior to 1800, those few workers who were organized usually joined guilds for their crafts so they could restrict competition among tradesmen and enforce work standards. Some workers formed unions, but these organizations were usually short-lived reactions to employers' attempts to cut wages or reduce job skills. A union of shoemakers was established in 1782 in Philadelphia and lasted less than a year. Another Philadelphia shoemakers' union was chartered in 1794 as the Federal Society of Cordwainers and negotiated with employers, struck, and remained active until 1806. New York cabinetmakers organized into a union in 1796.

New York printers formed a union in 1799 and negotiated over wages and work rules.

Most early unions could not withstand attacks from employers who claimed that they were illegal conspiracies to raise wages above the rates accepted by individual workers. For example, in 1806, the Journeyman Cordwainers of Philadelphia were found guilty of a conspiracy in restraint of trade when they struck over wages. By the middle of the century, however, an important decision (*Commonwealth v. Hunt*) by the highest court in Massachusetts freed unions from the harsh application of conspiracy doctrine. Unions were not engaged in an illegal conspiracy if their objectives were lawful.[2] This decision set the tone for courts elsewhere and created a favorable climate for the development of national unions.

Most early unions were formed on a citywide or regional basis because they could best exercise their economic power at that level. Goods were produced for local market and there was little if any competition between producers. By the mid-19th century, however, some national unions were created for the wider product competition caused by improved transportation and marketing and the emerging factory system. If employers were starting to compete successfully in an expanded market, they had to find ways of cutting costs. This usually meant lowering wages or increasing productivity. Employers redesigned and simplified jobs so that they could be performed more productively and by lesser skilled workers. If unions wanted wages, hours, and working conditions taken out of competition by organizing the workers of competing employers, they had to operate on a wider basis than the local community or company.

In the 1860s, American national unions began to organize members in Canada. The Iron Molders and the Printers were among the earliest unions to absorb Canadian unions that were citywide. During the next two decades, American unions launched organizing drives in Canada in metal trades, building trades, and railroads. By the start of the 20th century, the majority of union members in Canada were in international unions. International unionism is discussed in the next chapter, on union structure, although it is important at this point to mention that on the Canadian side of the border international unionism has been a serious concern because these U.S.-based unions restricted Canadian section autonomy in administration and bargaining.[3] In the United States, international unionism seemed like a natural extension of the union movement to where many American employers operated and American workers found jobs. For unions of the time, the greatest concern was *what* unions should do rather than *where* they should do it.

In 1866, a group of union leaders, led by William Sylvis of the Iron Molders, created the National Labor Union (NLU). The NLU opened its membership to both skilled and unskilled workers and considered politics to be its primarily role. It supported the eight-hour workday, restrictions on immigration, abolition of convict labor, monetary reform, and equal rights for woman. Early labor historian Norman Ware described the NLU with undisguised contempt for its broad political agenda and diverse membership: "It was a typical American politico-reform organization, led by labor leaders without organizations, politicians without parties, women without husbands, and cranks, visionaries, and agitators without jobs."[4]

The NLU held its last convention in 1872, when it became the National Labor Reform Party, and sought, unsuccessfully, to play a major role in national politics.[5] Despite its political goals, the NLU was never entirely divorced from representation at workplaces, and it was able to organize and negotiate in railways, coal mines, shoe factories, and textile mills. But within the NLU, there was no consensus about how national unions should promote the interests of their members. The next major union, the Knights of Labor, offered a unique brand of unionism that was neither purely political nor workplace oriented.

The Knights of Labor

The Noble and Holy Order of the Knights of Labor (the Knights) was founded in Philadelphia in 1869 by Uriah Stevens and other leaders of the Garment Cutters Unions. The Knights was initially formed as a secret society so employers would not fire its members. Stevens held office until 1879, when he ran for Congress and lost, and was succeeded by Terence Powderly.

The Knights grew rapidly in its early years. In 1879, it had 9,000 members, 28,000 in 1880, and 111,000 in 1885. After winning some major strikes, including an important victory with the Wabash Railroad, membership in the Knights exceeded 700,000 in 1886.[6]

Although the Knights was initially a union of craft workers, under Powderly's leadership it became an all-inclusive organization—nearly anyone could belong—with an equally broad mission of reforming the American economy and society and the moral and intellectual betterment of its members. The Knights believed that the system of industrial production was incompatible with the workers' sense of pride and personal accomplishment. The wage system should be abolished. Every worker should be his or her own master. As the conditions of employment were reformed, workers would inevitably benefit morally and intellectually.

According to the Knights, there were several paths leading to economic reform. Members could be educated about the faults of industrial production and shown ways to change it. Political pressure could be applied to limit the import of foreign labor and increase funding for schools. Producer and consumer cooperatives owned by workers could be created to make workers their own masters and avoid the inevitable conflict between labor and capital.[7] Workers could also go on strike, but only during their direct dealings with employers, not for political causes, and when other approaches failed.

The Knights structure was composed of trade assemblies with members confined to a particular trade and mixed assemblies with a variety of workers and even some employers.[8] It accepted members regardless of their industry or craft, including clerical and professional workers along with production workers. Manufacturers and merchants were also admitted if they "showed respect for the dignity of labor" by employing the Knights' members. This union's jurisdiction reflected its belief in the unity of workers and their common predicament under the economic system. The real division in society was between those who produced and the moneyed interests rather than between employers and employees, or between employees themselves.

Despite its spectacular growth, the Knights of Labor was unstable because its goals were so vague and its membership so diverse. Leo Wolman, an early observer of the union movement, concluded that the Knights had "all the characteristics of an unstable and impermanent organization."[9] Its mission of workers' moral betterment through education and the reform of the economic system overstated the degree to which employees and employers have common interests and understated the extent to which the two were motivated by self-interests. The Knights assumed that the same national union and even the same local body of that union could effectively represent all workers, regardless of their skill level, occupations, or industries. It had lofty goals—the unity of workers' interests—but it was weak on pragmatic issues. For example, although it advocated the eight-hour workday, it would not support the May 1, 1886, general strike to reduce hours. It won several big strikes that brought it notoriety and thousands of new members, but it could not create local organizations capable of maintaining attachments to these members.

Ironically, a decisive factor in the Knights' decline was an affair in which it was not even a major participant. In May 1886, there was a rally in Chicago's Haymarket Square in support of a series of strikes for the eight-hour day. Twelve hundred people attended, but by the concluding speech rain began to fall and only about 300 remained. When the police tried to break up the rally before the last speaker was done, a bomb was thrown, killing 7 and wounding 60 officers. The police responded by opening fire on the crowd, killing one and wounding several. The Haymarket Affair, as it was called, came around the time of several major strikes and demonstrations and it heightened public hysteria about labor radicalism and union violence. Although the Knights of Labor was not directly involved in Haymarket, it was the biggest and best-known union of the time, and it took the brunt of the criticism for the riot.[10] In addition, as word spread of the bargaining gains of traditional labor unions, members left the Knights to join them. Confronted with a hostile public, a dissatisfied membership, and rival unions, the Knights' officers proved ineffective. Terence Powderly was generally considered to be inept,[11] and the union's other officers were mostly poor negotiators and incapable of pronouncing a coherent union policy on strikes that could relieve public pressure and attract more members.[12]

The Haymarket Affair may have marked the beginning of the end for the Knights,[13] but its most severe and persistent problem was defining exactly what it stood for.

> The [Knights] started on their national career in 1878 with a brave platform, but for a long time it was impossible to discover what they were doing. They were in sympathy with everything and involved in nothing. An assembly would organize, go through the founding ritual, elect officers, initiate new members with due solemnity, pay the tax, do a little charity work and employment-finding for the brothers, and pass out.[14]

At its height of power in 1886, the Knights had more than 700,000 members. By 1890, the Knights had 100,000 members and only 75,000 in 1893.[15] The lesson that the national unions saw in the decline of the Knights was how a vague reform agenda combined with a mixed membership could bring down the largest of unions. When national unions created the American Federation of Labor, they were careful to narrowly define union mission and membership.

The American Federation of Labor

Within the Knights, trade assemblies and the regional craft unions had to coexist with groups of unskilled and semiskilled workers. In the 1880s, there were several disputes over organizing jurisdiction (which unions should recruit which workers) between the Knights and national unions. In reaction to the unsatisfactory settlement of jurisdictional disputes as well as the Knights' sudden decline after the Haymarket Affair, national unions such as the Bricklayers, the Iron Molders, and the Cigarmakers founded a new union federation, the American Federation of Labor (AFL), in 1886.[16] Samuel Gompers, one of the federation's founders and the leader of the Cigarmakers Union (a union that left the Knights), became first president of the AFL and remained in office until his death in 1924.[17]

Gompers was undoubtedly the "chief architect of the modern American trade union movement."[18] Philip Taft, the preeminent historian of the AFL, wrote of Gompers, "No man in his time or since has had his pervasive influence upon organized labor in North America."[19] Gompers did not control any large unions, always faced opposition to his policies within the AFL, and lacked a commanding presence, but his "influence was founded upon his intelligence and consuming loyalty to the trade union movement, his ability to devote endless hours in its service, his remarkable capacity to work; his knowledge of the needs of labor and his power to express them in writing; his talent for compromise and negotiation; and, finally, his acceptance of the limited power which he and the federation could exercise upon affiliates."[20]

Although Gompers was first attracted to socialist politics and radical unionism, through his experiences in the labor movement, particularly with the rampant ideological factionalism within his own Cigarmakers, he developed a pragmatic perspective of unionism. Gompers was critical of the Knights' reformist mission and open membership as well as the power of its top officers. He believed that unions should avoid long-run utopian goals and should seek to improve the workers' conditions in the existing economy. What works best is collective bargaining backed by strikes. The unions' political role should be one of rewarding friends and punishing enemies. Changes in laws should be aimed at strengthening rather than replacing collective bargaining. Management and labor might have some common concerns at the workplace, but they would inevitably disagree about the workers' fair share of the profits, and this would have to be resolved through direct negotiations. This perspective was called *pure and simple unionism* because it was so straightforward, pragmatic, and work related.[21] Gompers wrote:

> The trade unions not only discuss economics and trade union problems, but deal with them in a practical fashion calculated to bring about better conditions of life today. . . . The ground-work principle of America's labor movement has been to recognize that first things must come first. The primary essential in our mission has been the protection of the wage-worker, now; to increase his wages; to cut hours off the long workday, which was killing him; to improve the safety and the sanitary conditions of the work-shop; to free from the tyrannies, petty or otherwise, which served to make his existence a slavery. These, in the nature of things, I repeat, were and are the primary objectives of trade unionism. . . . Our great Federation has uniformly refused to surrender this conviction and to rush to the support of any one of the numerous society-saving or society-destroying schemes which decade upon decade have been sprung upon this country.[22]

The AFL set forth some principles to avoid the structural weaknesses of the Knights. First, affiliated unions were assigned exclusive jurisdictions—each had a type of membership described in its charter that would not overlap with others.[23] Second, the federation was designed as an association of autonomous unions—a "rope of sand" in the words of its leaders—in which power flowed from the affiliated unions to the federation. Gompers and the federation, however, did assist in the organization of local craft unions in the hope that many would combine to form national unions in their craft and be chartered as affiliates. Because of this policy, the number of affiliates increased from 58 in 1897 to 120 in 1904.[24]

Confrontations With Employers

Soon after the AFL's creation, the national unions had to prove their mettle in some intense labor-management conflicts. Two big strikes during the 1890s show the depth of employer antiunion sentiment and the unions' struggle for survival.

In 1892, a dispute broke out between an AFL affiliate, the Amalgamated Association of Iron, Steel and Tin Workers, and the Carnegie Steel Works in Homestead, Pennsylvania. Negotiations between the union and the company had turned acrimonious as the company tried to drive down operating costs. The employer was determined not to be caught unprepared for a strike, so it built a 12-foot-high fence around its plant, for a length of three miles, and hired 300 Pinkerton detectives to protect the company's property and act as strikebreakers.

By the end of June, the company had made its final offer—a wage cut and a change in work rules—and took the offensive by locking out 750 union members, who were soon joined by about 3,000 other workers at the plant. The workers maintained a continuous surveillance of the plant and the Monongahela River that ran by it so as to prevent it from being reopened with strikebreakers. On July 5, 300 Pinkerton guards reached the plant by river barge but were met by workers and townspeople. In the fight that followed, 40 strikers were shot with 9 killed, and 20 Pinkertons were shot with 7 killed. The guards were eventually disarmed by the townspeople. After further attempts by the company to use guards and strikebreakers were met with violence, the state militia was brought in to take control of the town. Five months later, the defeated union lifted its ban on members returning to work and the strike ended. Only 800 of the original employees at Homestead got their jobs back, and the union was destroyed nationally—membership fell from 24,000 in 1892 to 8,000 in 1894. The employer introduced machinery to increase productivity and reduce the workforce by 25 percent.[25] The Homestead plant was able to operate without a collective bargaining agreement for the next 45 years.[26]

A second major strike of the decade was also a stinging defeat for unions. In response to an economic recession in 1893, the Pullman Palace Car Company in Pullman, Illinois, a major manufacturer of railway cars, laid off more than half of its 5,800 workers and cut wages 25 to 45 percent. These drastic measures were taken in the ultimate company town: in Pullman, the company owned all buildings, including the workers' homes, and provided all basic services. The workers' rents were not reduced when wages were cut. After several unsuccessful attempts to have wages restored, the workers walked off their jobs on June 11, 1894.

The Pullman workers belonged to the American Railway Union (ARU), an organization formed in 1893 to represent all railway workers regardless of their craft.[27] The ARU was a rival to the AFL's railway unions. Its president, Eugene Debs, asked the Pullman strikers to consider the dispute as a response to the company's overbearing employment policies rather than the pursuit of purely economic gains. The ARU's other locals began a boycott by refusing to operate any trains that carried Pullman sleeping cars. But Pullman's allies, the railways, responded by hiring strikebreakers and carrying mail in their trains, thus opening the way to get a court order against the boycott. The continuation of the strike and boycott of railway cars, along with the destruction of railway property, resulted in court injunctions, the intervention of federal troops, and the loss of public support. Debs appealed to Gompers to call a national strike in support of the Pullman workers, but his pleas were rejected. Gompers was wary of such mass sympathy strikes, opposed the ARU's practice of broad-based unionism, and considered the ARU and Debs as rivals to AFL unions and his leadership of the labor movement.[28]

The strike continued until early August when a conference of union delegates finally declared it ended, and the company resumed operations. The strikers were unable to withstand the combination of a powerful and determined employer and an injunction backed up by federal troops. Debs was subsequently convicted of violating antitrust legislation and imprisoned, and the ARU quickly declined.

The unions at Homestead and Pullman were quite different from each other; the Iron Workers at Homestead was an exclusive organization of skilled workers, while the ARU was an inclusive organization of all workers in railroads. But both had limited objectives—to negotiate with the employers for collective agreements that would protect job security and wages—and both, despite the solidarity of the strikers and their allies, were overwhelmed by powerful employers. Within a decade, another union—one with radical objectives and an open membership—would battle powerful employers.

Industrial Workers of the World and Revolutionary Unionism

The Industrial Workers of the World (IWW or the *Wobblies*) was founded in 1905 in Chicago as a revolutionary general (all-inclusive) union at a convention of delegates from 43 unions. The union's radical ideology, its belief in the inevitability of class warfare, was evident in the opening line of its constitution's preamble: "The working class and the employing class have nothing in common."[29]

The IWW's revolutionary unionism has been described by the industrial relations scholar Hoyt Wheeler as "a labor movement that is essentially protest. It rejects, or at least does not consider as a salient alternative, a continuing routinized relationship with employers such as exists under collective bargaining. Instead it aims to lash out at employers either simply out of anger or with the idea of eliminating the employer altogether and changing society."[30]

The IWW favored strike action rather than collective bargaining. It was a proponent of syndicalism—the view that a nationwide general strike would bring about the downfall of capitalism. Until that happened, strikes were to be used to compel employers to improve wages and working conditions. Formal collective contracts were avoided; the IWW simply posted its list of wages.[31]

The union's jurisdiction was simple. As the prototype of the radical all-inclusive "one big union" that would appear from country to country over the years, the IWW organized all workers regardless of trade or industry—factory workers, migratory farm workers, seamen and longshoremen, and practically anyone else who would join it. The IWW had several successful organizing drives and strikes in the textile, lumber, and longshoring industries, among others, but it could not build effective local organizations. Also, violence often accompanied its strikes and led the public to fear that a labor insurrection was brewing. When the IWW refused to support U.S. involvement in World War I, which it believed to be part of a capitalist plot, the government arrested and imprisoned many of its leaders.

Reliable membership figures do not exist beyond 1914, when the IWW claimed 120,000 members (the real figure was probably closer to 30,000 to 40,000).[32] Although it exists today as a few local branches in, for example, bookstores and food shops, and has perhaps a total of a thousand members, by 1918 the IWW was no longer a major union. In its time, however, it was a powerful experiment in revolutionary unionism and a major force during strikes and organizing.

Union Decline and Resurgence During the Years Between the Wars

Unions gained power during World War I because of the low unemployment and the government's pursuit of uninterrupted production. Union work standards were enforced in government contracts, and labor representatives were appointed to wartime labor boards created to reduce work stoppages and resolve bargaining impasses. During the war, union membership increased from 3.5 million to 4.1 million and, with this momentum, exceeded 5 million in 1920.[33]

The 1920s were extremely difficult for labor unions; their wartime gains in membership and power were obliterated as they faced intense employer resistance. The war had been followed by the release of pent-up pressure within unions for new bargaining gains. The number of strikes increased in the immediate postwar years as unions tried to catch up to the rising cost of living and faced stiff employer opposition negotiations. Among the major disputes were those of coal miners, longshoremen in New York City, and police in Boston, as well as the 1919 general strike in Seattle (a strike of all workers in the city to support striking metal trades workers in the shipyards).[34] The massive strike in the steel industry in 1919 vividly demonstrates the lengths to which employers would now go to break the hold of unions.

A national steel industry organizing committee of the AFL, composed of 24 unions that claimed jurisdiction in steel, attempted to gain recognition for bargaining from the U.S. Steel Corporation. The unions demanded the right to bargain, the end to an employer-dominated company union, better overtime pay, and an eight-hour workday. When the company rejected these demands, the unions set a strike deadline, took a strike vote, and then walked out on July 22. Nearly 350,000 workers went on strike.

The company fought the strike on all fronts. It joined with the press in branding the strikers unruly and radical foreigners (many of the strikers were East European immigrants) led by agitators from the IWW. The local authorities restricted the strikers' right to assemble. The company had its spies spread false information about the strike and its leaders. It also incited animosity between different immigrant groups in an attempt to destroy the strikers' solidarity. It hired 30,000 African American workers as strikebreakers. Facing this onslaught, the strikers could not keep up their morale, and eventually two-thirds returned to work. In January 1920, the unions declared the strike over. For nearly two decades, there would be no collective bargaining at U.S. Steel.[35] A huge and calamitous confrontation by any standard, the steel strike was a harbinger of the hard times and intense employer opposition that lay ahead for unions during the 1920s.

In the 1920s, unions lost 1.6 million members (about one in three members)[36] as a result of a widespread and well-organized employer offensive. Employers returned to their earlier practice of requiring that workers sign *yellow dog contracts* under which, as a condition of employment, workers promised not to join unions. In January 1921, a national conference of manufacturers associations proposed that industry adopt the *American Plan*, a pledge to strive to remain or become union-free.

Employers portrayed unions as alien to the nation's individualistic spirit, a drag on industrial efficiency, and a plot by foreign radicals. They hired spies to identify, fire, and then *blacklist* union supporters (i.e., add their names to do-not-hire lists). They reacted to organizing drives and strikes with violence and coercion, the discharge of union supporters, and the hiring of strikebreakers.

A few employers tried a kinder and gentler approach to win over the loyalty of workers and keep them indifferent to unions.[37] They adopted a paternalistic management style (called *welfare capitalism* by later critics) and gave workers a variety of employment benefits that included group life insurance plans, counseling, paid vacations, and pension plans. This was intended to show workers that they could do well without a union and that the employer, like a benevolent father, was concerned about their welfare. Workers did well, it was argued, when the company did well. Personal grievances should be subordinated to the good of the common enterprise.[38] Some employers even went so far as to form union substitutes, often called *employee representation plans,* so that workers would feel that they already had a representative. These organizations were not truly independent representatives; employers controlled the selection of plans officers, supported the plans financially, and determined the subjects for joint discussions.

The unions were helpless against the employers' offensive. Their organizing drives were lackluster, their leadership uninspired, and their membership fell sharply.[39] But the unions would suddenly rebound in the next decade by organizing new members on a huge scale as labor laws promoted collective bargaining and the workers had a new appreciation of unionization.

For many years, union leaders had disagreed about the best way to organize and represent workers. The earliest unions were usually formed among skilled workers in a particular craft (e.g., printers or shoemakers). The AFL had advocated strong craft exclusivity and chartered unions with clear and narrow definitions of their membership. But since World War I, the number of production workers, many of them semiskilled, had expanded and craft workers were no longer predominant. Most AFL unions were craft and highly critical of unions that organized on an industrial basis. They felt that industrial workers had less bargaining power and that the presence of a diverse group of workers in a single union would destroy cohesiveness and lead to factionalism. Large manufacturing plants, the craft unionists argued, should be organized by a separate union for each craft.

The issue of industrial versus craft unionism was debated at the AFL's 1935 convention. The federation's leaders supported craft unionism and John L. Lewis, president of the United Mine Workers, argued the case for industrial unionism. In convention votes, the delegates rejected industrial unionism. In November 1935, the Committee for Industrial Organizations, led by Lewis, was formed ostensibly to advise unions about industrial organizing but in reality to promote industrial unionization, particularly in mass production industries. Seeing this as a challenge to its core principles and its leadership, the AFL accused the new organization of *dual unionism*—supporting a rival and being divisive. The AFL ordered the committee to disband. Lewis rejected this. The AFL expelled seven unions with nearly 1 million members, which then formed a rival federation, the Congress of Industrial Organizations (CIO).[40]

The CIO unions launched successful organizing drives in steel, autos, rubber, textiles, and maritime industries, and the AFL unions responded with their own organizing among skilled trades workers in mass production industries.[41] Despite the expansion of the CIO, the AFL remained the larger labor federation. The rivalry between the unions of the federations occurred in the context of important changes in labor law and workers' attitudes about collective action. This combination set the stage for unprecedented union growth.

The legal framework of labor relations had evolved over the past century from weapons that could be used by employers to block organizing drives (the application of the conspiracy doctrine and antitrust legislation against unions, the use of court injunctions to halt strikes), to a brief period of neutrality (the Norris-LaGuardia Act of 1932, which greatly restricted the ability of federal courts to issue injunctions in labor disputes and prohibited their use to stop legal union activities[42]) to the explicit protection of workers' rights to unionize in 1933 and 1935.[43]

During the Great Depression, unemployment reached historical highs (from 3 percent in 1929 to 25 percent in 1933) and wages fell (the average hourly earnings went from 57 cents to 44 cents).[44] The centerpiece of President Franklin D. Roosevelt's New Deal program to move the nation out of the Great Depression was the National Industrial Recovery Act of 1933 (NIRA). This law established codes of fair practice under which employers could set wages and working hours for their industry or occupation without being stopped by federal antitrust laws. To be approved by the government, each code of fair practice had to have a clause recognizing the right of workers to bargain collectively through unions of their own choosing. The passage of the NIRA was followed by a surge in organizing along with a number of strikes as unions sought to pressure employers to recognize them as bargaining agents. The NIRA was "the spark that rekindled the spirit of unionism within American labor."[45] In 1933 alone, the AFL unions gained more than a million members. In the Mine Workers, under the forceful leadership of Lewis, membership went from 60,000 to 350,000 within six months of the passage of the NIRA. In the coalfields, the Mine Workers' organizers proclaimed with great effect: "The President wants you to join. Your government says 'Join the United Mine Workers.'"[46] But in 1935, the Supreme Court declared the NIRA to be an unconstitutional extension of federal power.[47] The workers' right to unionize was resurrected, however, in the core of new legislation passed later that year.

When Congress passed the National Labor Relations Act (the Wagner Act), it sought to even out the imbalance of power between workers and their employers. It reasoned that if workers did not have full freedom of association to form or join unions for dealing with their employers, there would be industrial strife as workers struck to compel their employers to recognize their unions. Accordingly, the preamble of the Wagner Act directly and unambiguously endorses collective bargaining:

> It is hereby declared to be the policy of the United States to eliminate the causes of certain substantial obstructions to the free flow of commerce and to mitigate and eliminate these obstructions when they have occurred *by encouraging the practice and procedure of collective bargaining* and by protecting the exercise by workers of full freedom of association, self-organization, and designation of representatives of their own choosing, for the purpose of negotiating the terms and conditions of their employment or other mutual aid or protection. (emphasis added)[48]

Section 7(a) of the Wagner Act echoed the workers' rights under the NIRA: "Employees shall have the right to self-organization, to form, join or assist labor organizations, to bargaining collectively through representatives of their own choosing."[49]

The act prohibited, as unfair labor practices, employers' conduct that interfered with the exercise of workers' rights, for example, discharging or otherwise discriminating against workers who support unions, refusing to bargain in good faith with unions selected by employees, and setting up company-dominated unions. Union and employee allegations of unfair labor practices could be filed with the National Labor Relations

Board (NLRB), a government agency established by the act. If the NLRB found that violations had occurred, employers would be ordered to cease and desist.

The Wagner Act also formalized the act of union organizing. Recognition strikes were no longer needed to compel employers to accept unions as bargaining agents. Instead, the NLRB would conduct union certification elections. Employers were required to recognize and bargain in good faith with unions receiving the majority of votes cast. The key section of the act stated:

> Representatives designated or selected for the purposes of collective bargaining by the majority of the employees in a unit appropriate for such purposes, shall be the exclusive representatives of all the employees in such unit for the purposes of collective bargaining with respect to pay, wages, hours of employment, and other conditions of employment.[50]

This clause was truly revolutionary and it still is. First, it made clear that whether a union would get to represent a group of workers would be determined by *the workers themselves* and not by their employers or unions. The unions' jurisdictional claims to industries or occupations did not give them automatic rights to represent workers. The principle of exclusive jurisdiction—only one union for each industry or occupation—was shattered forever. Labor historian Irving Bernstein concluded: "While the concept of jurisdiction remained alive in the American labor movement, it could no longer be exclusive. Competition replaced monopoly. In fact, with the passage of time, jurisdictions would become so fouled as to defy any unraveler."[51]

Second, union certification as bargaining agent became a simple matter of winning all or nothing. A union had to prove to the labor board that it was the majority's choice, and anything less than a majority—even a fifty-fifty tie for and against the union—meant the defeat of an organizing drive. There is no minority representation.

Third, unions that won certification became exclusive representatives—no other union could represent the workers at that workplace unless they displaced the incumbent union through another election. There was no room for multi-union representation; a *bargaining unit*—the group of workers who can vote in the certification election—can be represented by only one union at a time.

Fourth, the labor board determined the basis for union representation when it defined the so-called *unit appropriate for collective bargaining*. When it approved of units of production and maintenance workers, rather than of individual crafts, the unionization of the mass production industries became possible and the CIO's industrial unions had the inside track in organizing.

The Wagner Act was an incredible step forward for labor; not only did it give workers a right to organize, but it provided unions with a process for organizing, restricted employer conduct that interfered with the right to unionize, and compelled employers to bargain with the employees' choice.[52] It clearly endorsed the process of collective bargaining without dictating the outcomes of collective bargaining. The act was based on a belief, called *industrial pluralism*, that conflict between unions and management is enduring but controllable. Management has the right to manage and to promote efficiency by administering resources, including the human resources of the firm. Workers have the right to participate in decisions about the terms and conditions of their employment—that is, to negotiate the impact of management decisions. Society has the right to be free of the protracted labor disputes between unions and employers. "Since labor and management also share a common interest in building and maintaining a successful enterprise, means are needed for accommodating their diverse interests without inflicting excessive harm on either party or on the public."[53] This is the role of collective bargaining, which was considered by the act to be "the preferred mechanism to accommodate the partially conflicting and partially shared goals of the parties to the employment relationship."[54]

But bargaining was more than just periodic union-management negotiations. As it endorsed collective bargaining, the Wagner Act was promoting *job control unionism*—the negotiation of highly formalized and legally binding contracts that specified the union and management rights and obligations.

The passage of pro-collective bargaining labor law coincided with an important shift in workers' attitudes. The massive unemployment of the Great Depression had shown workers that job loss should not be blamed on the failings of individual workers, but rather on the failure of the entire economic system. Accordingly, self-organization for collective bargaining rather than relying on individual bargaining seemed completely appropriate. Unionism became an attractive way for individual workers to gain sufficient power to confront their employers on an equal basis.

Three forces converged in the 1930s: unions in the two federations devoted great energy and resources to organizing workers, the new law endorsed collective bargaining and provided unions with a process for organizing to bargain, and workers became more receptive to the collective power of unionism. From 1935 to 1940, union membership shot up 143 percent, a gain of 5 million members. New and important industrial unions emerged from successful organizing campaigns in the steel, auto, rubber, and chemical industries, and collective bargaining finally became firmly entrenched in American industry.

Unions During and After World War II

Union Solidarity and Power

During World War II, unions promoted cooperative efforts with management to reduce strikes and increase production, and they participated in government agencies such as the War Production Board that pursued these objectives. When the Mine Workers went on strike in 1942 over wages, President Roosevelt seized the mines until a settlement could be reached, but the overall incidence of strikes during wartime was low and reflected the unions' 1941 no-strike pledge.

Soon after the war ended, prices increased rapidly and the unions sought to protect their wartime bargaining gains. The unions were now free from bargaining and strike restraints and tried to make up lost ground by negotiating for job security and wage increases. Strike activity went up, and there were major disputes in auto, steel, railroads, and coal. This strike record combined with the union growth of the past decade to give the public and legislators the impression that unions were no longer underdogs in their dealings with management. The stage was set to correct what seemed to many to be the Wagner Act's tilt toward labor. The Labor-Management Relations Act (Taft-Hartley Act of 1947) introduced unfair labor practices of unions (e.g., the refusal to bargain in good faith with employers), the right of workers to *not* join unions, and the exclusion of supervisors from a protected right to unionize. It also gave the states the right to pass laws (the so-called *right-to-work laws*) that prohibited any collective agreement clauses requiring union membership as a condition of employment.[55]

Despite legal restrictions, the unions of the immediate postwar years and the 1950s wielded considerable power at the bargaining table. They focused their power on controlling the impact of new production technologies on their members' employment, raising wages to keep pace with inflation, and developing employee benefits systems that included pensions and health care plans. Collective agreements grew in complexity and length.

Unions thrived at a time of increased consumer demand and industrial production. Although employers occasionally tried to gain the initiative in bargaining, they usually accommodated unions, "buying [labor] peace by yielding to union demands for more generous terms and conditions of employment."[56]

The 1950s were a decade of union consolidation. Soon after the CIO's founding in the mid-1930s, the AFL and CIO had gone through a period of intense union *raiding* (i.e., attempts by one union to organize workers already represented by another). Organizing raids used up union financial resources and the time and energies of union staff, without producing significant membership gains. As unions campaigned against each other with name-calling, they tarnished the reputation of the entire union movement. The unions realized this, and the incidence of raiding gradually declined.[57] In 1954, the AFL and CIO affiliates entered into an agreement to end raids between each other's affiliates. This peace accord proved to be a precursor to eventual merger. Over the years, the differences in the jurisdictions of the unions in the two federations had lessened; many AFL unions began recruiting semiskilled workers while some CIO unions organized the skilled craft workers traditionally represented by AFL affiliates.

In 1952, William Green, president of the AFL, and Phillip Murray, president of the CIO, both died. The new leaders of the two federations, Walter Reuther of the CIO and George Meany of the AFL, were never close friends but they did not have the mutual animosity of their predecessors. They believed that a consolidated union movement would wield greater political power because of its size. With its combined resources and the end to interunion rivalry, a new federation might revitalize sagging organizing campaigns. The AFL and the CIO merged in 1955 to form the AFL-CIO, and Meany became the president with Reuther as vice president. At the time of the merger, the AFL was twice as large as the CIO, with 4.6 million members.

After the merger of the federations, there was no revival of organizing as expected and union membership fell by about 200,000 over the next decade. Structural changes in the labor force (i.e., employment shifts to less unionized sectors such as services, and away from union strongholds, most notably manufacturing) caused some loss of private sector union membership. But within a decade, the government sector would become the new engine of union growth.[58]

Revelations of Union Corruption

Although leadership corruption was present to some degree since the earliest days of unions, by the late 1950s it seemed rampant, at least according to news reports. The wrongdoings of union officers received tremendous publicity over two years during the hearings before the Congressional Committee on Improper Activities in the Labor Management Field, chaired by Senator John L. McClellan. The McClellan Committee found that the officers of several unions (e.g., those of truck drivers, bakery workers, and construction workers) were engaged in such corrupt activities as extortion from employers and union members and the embezzlement of union funds. In reaction to these revelations, Congress passed legislation in 1959 directed at both weeding out corrupt union officers within unions and encouraging democracy in union governance, under the belief that the absence of democratic union governance set the stage for the emergence and continuation of corruption. The Labor-Management Reporting and Disclosure Act (the Landrum-Griffin Act of 1959)[59] gave union members a bill of rights that included the right to vote in elections, to attend and vote at union meetings, and to participate in union deliberations. Members were also given freedom of speech and assembly, the right to vote on increases in dues, the right to sue their union, safeguards against improper disciplinary action by union officers, and the right to have copies of their unions' collective agreements.

Unions must file financial reports with the U.S. Department of Labor. Employers must report on payments or loans to union officials and expenditures for industrial relations consultants. Officer elections for national unions must occur no less than every five years, and for the union local no less than every three years. Union officers are restricted in their ability to place locals in trusteeship (i.e., to suspend the self-governance of locals) because this was a common tactic to stifle political dissent on the local level.

The Erosion of the Labor Accord

American managers never accepted unions as equals in the workplace or as valued partners in the employment relationship. Nonetheless, in the postwar years, an understanding evolved between unions and management about how they handle their relationship and their conflicting objectives. Essentially, employers weighed the relative costs and benefits of avoiding or accepting unions and often accepted unions, albeit reluctantly. From the 1950s through the 1970s, employers accommodated unions because unions were powerful and pervasive. They were too costly to avoid at nonunion plants or to displace them at unionized ones. This tacit understanding is called the *labor accord.*[60]

Unions accepted the right of the employers to manage the enterprise within the bounds set by law and the collective bargaining agreement, and employers accepted the right of unions to exist and negotiate collective agreements, also within the bounds set by law. As George Strauss, an experienced observer of labor relations, succinctly characterized the accepted roles, "Management's job is to manage, and the union's is to object" (i.e., to negotiate and enforce collective agreements).[61]

For about 40 years, unions and management lived under the accord, although management did reserve the right to oppose unions within legal bounds at unorganized workplaces. The government underwrote the labor accord by ensuring the right of employees to select their own bargaining agents and requiring that employers recognize and bargain in good faith with the employees' choice.

The union-management accord was clearly unbalanced with "management serving as a senior partner with largely unrestricted authority to run the enterprise, and the unions as junior partner with the right to bargaining over a narrow range of topics."[62] Also, the mutual acceptance underlying the accord was limited to the major industrial regions of the country (e.g., the Northeast and Midwest) and more heavily unionized industries (e.g., manufacturing and transportation). Here, the degree of unionization was so high that employers saw little to gain by fighting unions. Elsewhere, for example, in the South or among service workers, employers still fought unions.

By the late 1970s, the accord began to disintegrate. Faced with competitive pressures from foreign and domestic nonunion producers, "management retreated from its commitment to collective bargaining, seeking to repel unions during organizing drives and suppress them at unionized operations."[63] Management believed that the costs of dealing with unions had become too high and that collective bargaining greatly hampered their competitiveness. "An aggressive market oriented ideology ... emerged among managers that justified antiunion activity in terms of the preservation of managerial flexibility necessary in a highly competitive environment."[64] Beginning around the late 1970s, employers withdrew acceptance from unions and devoted their energies and resources to creating a nonunion environment. "The elaborate system of rules and understandings, compromise and consent, that had marked U.S. industrial relations for a generation was suddenly transformed."[65]

In the early 1980s, the erosion of union-management accord accelerated as employers fought against union organizing, hired strikebreakers during bargaining disputes, closed and relocated operations to avoid recognizing unions, and pressured unions to grant concessions during bargaining. Employer opposition made union organizing more difficult, time-consuming, and expensive. Unions retreated from the organizing field, preferring the status quo to the tough job of expanding the membership.[66] Organizing activity (i.e., new union members gained in organizing drives) dropped by nearly a half and never returned to prior levels. To most observers, the inescapable conclusion was that organizing was "approaching a state of collapse."[67]

Employer misconduct during organizing campaigns (e.g., discharges and intimidation of union supporters) reached new highs. Not since the 1920s had it been as socially and politically acceptable for American management to embrace publicly a "union free" approach. Many companies made avoiding unions or displacing unions their highest labor relations policy.[68] Total union membership dropped, as unions were unable to gain enough new members to offset loss from declining employment in unionized firms.[69] Dues income from members declined and unions had fewer resources to devote to organizing, and so membership continued to fall. Unions found themselves caught in a vicious circle of decline.[70] The extent of this historic decline is discussed in the next chapter, and its implications are reviewed in later chapters on union revival and unions of the future (Chapters 6 and 7).

Unions were not only finding it more difficult to organize, but in about a third of the time when they were successful organizing they were unable to achieve their first contracts because of employer opposition. A discouraging trend was becoming apparent. In first negotiations, employers would ask for major concessions backed by the threat of relocating their operations. When unions responded with strikes, employers would hire striker replacements and continue operations, and even ask the labor board to have the unions' bargaining status withdrawn. In short, "there developed an explosively expanding confrontation sector in the industrial relations system."[71] Employers were finding ways to escape unionization.

The erosion of the labor accord was also evident in the spread of concessionary bargaining during the 1980s. Employers pressed unions to cut costs and increase productivity in the environment of deregulation (in such industries as trucking and airlines) and domestic and foreign nonunion competition. To save their members' jobs, unions had to grant contract concessions in the forms of wage freezes or reductions, lump-sum payments (which are less costly than regular wage increases because they do not become part of the base wage), and two-tiered wage systems (employers save money when newly hired workers receive lower wages than present workers for doing the same jobs). In 1986, for example, nearly a quarter of collective agreements that were negotiated had wage freezes or reductions, a third had lump-sum payments, and one-tenth had two-tiered wage systems. Concessionary bargaining continued even after economic expansion—evidence that it was more than a reaction to economic difficulties of the times, but rather the "erosion of the bargaining strength of American unions."[72] By the end of the 1980s, there was a gradual lessening of concessionary bargaining, but negotiations remained highly confrontational. For the unions, collective bargaining became a process for defending past gains in wages, benefits, and work rules rather than advancing to new highs. We will see in later chapters how concession bargaining, after lessening for more than a decade, has now returned in full force.

The Rise of Public Sector Unionism

The 1960s and 1970s were years of explosive growth for unions of government workers. The states and the federal government extended the protected right to join unions and bargaining collectively to most of their employees (though the right to strike was often curtailed). Fraternal orders of police and firefighters became bargaining agents for their members. State civil service associations and teachers associations became huge unions. Public employee associations vied with traditional labor unions over the rights to represent city hall workers, hospital staff, maintenance crews, and garbage collectors.

Public sector unionism expanded at the same time that private sector union membership was starting its long decline (this trend is illustrated in the next chapter). Government workers wanting union representation were having a much easier time of it than private workers. Many were already in associations that could quickly become bargaining agents. Their employers could not resist unionization as fervently or effectively as private employers. Overtly antiunion conduct would be politically unwise for elected officials since public workers, their families, and their supporters are voters. Public employers could not discharge union supporters or threaten to relocate operations to avoid union representation. They also did not face the competitive pressures of the private sector employers; in the early days of public employee unionism, wages could be increased and covered by higher taxes. At the time that the union accord was disintegrating in the private sector, there seemed to be no end to what unions could accomplish in the public sector.

Public sector unions, however, had to face a harsher reality in the 1980s and 1990s. State and local budgetary officers came under pressure to cut costs because of reduced transfer payments from the federal government and declining tax revenues. They proposed cutbacks or contracting out to private companies for such services as prison operations, water treatment, or waste disposal. At the federal level, an initiative to reinvent government had government agencies and programs to identify what the government should not be doing. Unions responded to this restructuring in several ways: "public demonstrations, law suits, lobbying for restrictive legislation, collective bargaining or other less formal negotiations, participation in programs to increase efficiency and lower labor costs, competitive proposals, and general acquiescence."[73] No single approach was consistently adopted or successful, and most unions relied on a combination of tactics (e.g., public demonstrations and lawsuits to pressure employers to negotiate over contracting out).[74]

In the late 1960s and the 1970s, growth in public sector union membership was able to mask over the decline in private sector unions.[75] But as the public sector unionism slowed, overall union membership declined. In the 1980s and 1990s, public union membership increased by 1.3 million while private membership fell by 5.2, for a net decline of 3.9 million.[76] No one could deny that the labor movement was falling into a deep membership crisis.

The Search for Union Revival

Perhaps the most dramatic happening in today's unions is the search for a way out of the present crisis. The officers and staff of virtually all unions are asking how to stem membership losses, restart organizing, regain the initiative in bargaining, and use politics to rebuild the unions and better serve the members. The plans for union revival share some features: more organizing and greater budgetary allocations for that task, more effective and militant bargaining to protect members' wages and benefits and job security, and the development of alliances with other organizations on the national and local levels to improve all areas of union activity. In a deeper sense, plans for proposals may also call for exploring new forms of representation that could appeal to part-time workers, immigrants, the unemployed, and workers who often move from job to job.

Some see revival as nothing short of moving well beyond the job-control unionism of the Wagner Act model and turning unions into social movements capable of helping all workers, not just the membership or workers in bargaining units. To others, revival means using organizing and politics to strengthen unions at the bargaining table so they can get better collective agreements.[77]

Much of the drive for union revival began with the election of John J. Sweeney and his reform slate of officers to the leadership of the AFL-CIO in 1995. The change in leadership was a reaction of federation affiliates to the apparent malaise in the unions and their unimaginative leadership. Sweeney exhorted the affiliates "to rebuild the culture of organizing" by making organizing a top priority. Organizing must happen now so that the law of organizing can be changed later when unions are stronger; unions should not wait for labor law reform before organizing in earnest.[78] The proposals for union revival are so varied and important that they are discussed in a separate chapter—Chapter 6—but it is worth noting here that union leaders and supporters are now nearly obsessed with finding a way to reverse the decline in the proportion of the workforce in unions (presently at 9 percent in the private sector) and regaining bargaining power. But even the most optimistic proponents of union revival see little chance of a repeat of the 1930s surge in union growth.[79]

Conclusions

This chapter is not a comprehensive labor history, but rather a brief review of the fundamental forces that have shaped contemporary unions. Two broad trends were apparent.

First, we saw that unions have had to constantly struggle for recognition from employers and the state. They were never accepted as valued partners at the workplace or as the voice of workers in our economy and society. The litany of long and violent strikes for recognition illustrates the forcefulness of employer opposition to collective bargaining. The erosion of the labor accord over the past two decades shows management deciding that bargaining relationships with unions had become too costly in an extremely competitive environment.

Unable to build on a solid foundation of management acceptance and legal protection, unions now find themselves in a crisis of organizing and bargaining that is even worse than that of the 1920s. And the public sector can no longer be counted on to serve as the engine for union growth. For most unions, bargaining is now defensive as they seek to protect past gains in the face of intense employer opposition and the competitive pressures of a huge nonunion sector in whatever their industry.

Second, the unions' mission and the best way to structure themselves to achieve that mission have always been controversial within the labor movement. As unions evolved, they adopted different objectives and jurisdictions. The Knights of Labor, for example, practiced a vaguely defined type of reform unionism premised on worker self-help. Nearly everyone could join the Knights. The unions of the AFL promoted pure-and-simple, job-control unionism that valued incremental gains at the bargaining table. The IWW, in sharp contrast, was a revolutionary union that sought the overhaul of the economic system and admitted all types of workers, including many who could find no place in other unions (e.g., migratory workers and unskilled immigrants).

Contemporary unions carry the double legacy of the AFL's pure-and-simple unionism and the Wagner Act model that confines unions to their narrow role as negotiators and enforcers of collective agreements. Rather than taking the reformist or revolutionary paths, unions evolved into bargaining agents that represent workers at their workplaces and negotiate legally binding agreements with employers over wages and hours and conditions of employment.

The burning issues of union jurisdiction, once so powerful they could tear apart a labor federation, have become much less important. We will see in the next chapter that a few unions remain highly exclusive, but in these lean times, most unions will admit to membership any workers who want to be represented.

Notes

1. Most of this discussion of the evolution of the labor unions is derived from Wolman, L. (1924). *Growth of American trade unions, 1880–1923.* New York: National Bureau of Economic Research; Wolman, L. (1936). *Ebb and flow in trade unionism.* New York: National Bureau of Economic Research; Ware, N. J. (1959). *The labor movement in the United States, 1860–1895.* Gloucester, MA: Peter Smith; Taft, P. (1964). *Organized labor in American history.* New York: Harper & Row; Bernstein, I. (1969). *Turbulent years: A history of the American worker, 1933–1941.* Boston: Houghton Mifflin; Galenson, W. (1986). The historical role of American trade unionism. In S. M. Lipset (Ed.), *Unions in transition: Entering the second century.* San Francisco: ICS Press, pp. 39–73; Brecher, J. (1997). *Strike!* Cambridge, MA: South End Press; Chaison, G., and Bigelow, B. (2002). *Unions and legitimacy.* Ithaca, NY: Cornell University Press; Lichtenstein, N. (2002). *State of the union: A century of American labor.* Princeton, NJ: Princeton University Press; Wheeler, H. N. (2002). *The future of the American labor movement.* New York: Cambridge University Press.

2. In *Commonwealth v. Hunt*, Chief Justice Lemuel Shaw of the Massachusetts Supreme Court concluded: "We cannot perceive that it is criminal for men to agree together to exercise their own acknowledged rights, in such a manner as to best subserve their own interests." Taft (1964, p. 11) commented on the importance of the decision: "For emerging labor organizations, the decision was a charter and a landmark. It gave voice to the new understanding of the position and significance of labor organizations and their activities. Even though a decision of the Massachusetts court was not controlling in other states, the eminence of its author gave it an influence beyond the borders of Massachusetts."

3. Crispo, J. (1967). *International unionism: A study in Canadian-American relations.* Toronto: McGraw-Hill.

4. Ware (1959), p. 11.

5. The NLU supported the reform of the federal monetary system (the so-called green-back program) under which paper currency would be a source of low-cost capital and would enable workers, among others, to form cooperatives free of the control from capitalists and bankers.

6. Ware (1959), p. 66. This is the most comprehensive study of the Knights and its times. The strike against the Wabash Railroad was particularly impressive to unorganized workers because it was against a powerful employer, the financier Jay Gould, and it produced one of the earliest collective agreements with a large company.

7. By the end of 1887, the Knights had created 135 cooperatives in industries as diverse as mining and the manufacture of shoes. While the Knights promoted the idea of cooperatives, it did little to establish and support them, and most of those established failed because of poor administration and insufficient funding. For a discussion of the producers' cooperatives, see Ware (1959), pp. 320–333.

8. Wheeler (2002), p. 90. At its peak in 1886, the Knights had 1,088 trade assemblies and 1,279 mixed assemblies.

9. Wolman (1924), p. 29.

10. For an analysis of the Haymarket Affair including its impact on the Knights, see David, H. (1958). *The history of the Haymarket Affair.* New York: Russell & Russell (2nd ed.), pp. 535–540; Ware (1959), pp. 313–319.

11. Ware (1959), p. xvi, described Powderly as "a windbag whose place was on the street corner rousing the rabble to concert pitch and providing emotional compensation for their dull lives. They should have thrown him out, but they did not. Instead, with the stupid loyalty of a dog for an abusive master, they clung to him as a savior."

12. Wheeler (2002), pp. 97–102, analyzes the strengths and weaknesses of the Knights and speculates how well it would do in the current environment.

13. Wolman (1924), p. 30.

14. Ware (1959), p. xv.

15. Wolman (1924), p. 32.

16. The immediate predecessor of the AFL was the Federation of Organized Trades and Labor Unions of the United States and Canada, established in 1881. Taft (1964), pp. 92–96.

17. Gompers served continuous terms as AFL president with the exception of 1895.

18. Taft (1964), p. 115.

19. Taft (1964), p. 115.

20. Taft (1964), p. 116.

21. Pure and simple unionism is also called "business unionism" because the union is run as an effective enterprise, like a business, with goals of attaining specific gains for its members, as opposed to social unionism, which seeks to benefit workers in general.

22. Gompers, S. (1919). *Labor and the common welfare.* New York: Dutton, pp. 7–8.

23. It proved impossible to eliminate all overlap between jurisdictions, and some affiliates had a few members that fell under the charter of another, for example, the carpentry workers in coal mines were represented by the Mine Workers, not the Carpenters. Where jurisdictional overlap appeared to be expanding because of new technologies or work processes, and could lead to organizing disputes, the federation tried to persuade affiliates to merge. Chaison, G. (1986). *When unions merge.* Lexington, MA: Lexington Books.

24. Wolman (1936), p. 17.

25. Brecher (1997), pp. 69–80.

26. Taft (1964).

27. Workers at Pullman joined the ARU in 1894. Though manufacturing workers and not within the union's jurisdiction, they were organized because the company owned some railroad track. See Brecher (1997), p. 97.

28. The leadership of the AFL also believed that "a head-on struggle between labor and capital should be avoided at all costs" (Brecher, 1997, p. 110). Taft (1964, p. 158) concluded that the strike was lost because of the power of the employers rather than the lack of support in the form of a boycott from other unions. "The American Railway Union made the decision to risk everything on the Pullman boycott. It did not go down because it lacked support. Gompers had no power to call a general strike even if he had favored such a step. Moreover, there was scant assurance that the heads of the affiliates would have followed him. In addition, with unemployment rampant, it is likely that the enlargement of the strike would have led only to increasing the size of the disaster."

29. Taft (1964), p. 290.

30. Wheeler (2002), p. 20.

31. Galenson (1986), p. 46.

32. Wolman (1924), p. 119.

33. Wolman (1936), p. 16.

34. For a discussion of these strikes, see Brecher (1997), pp. 115–157.

35. Brecher (1997), pp. 133–144.

36. Wolman (1936), p. 16.

37. Wolman (1936).

38. Galenson (1986).

39. Samuel Gompers died in 1924, and his successor, William Green, was not aggressive enough to counter the employer offensive.

40. The expelled unions were the United Mine Workers, the Amalgamated Clothing Workers, the Ladies Garment Workers, the Typographical Union, the Textile Workers, the Oil Field, Gas Well and Refining Workers, and the Mine, Mill and Smelter Workers (along with the Cap and Millinery Department of the United Hatters). For a discussion of the events leading up to the schism within the AFL and the formation of the CIO, see Taft (1964), pp. 463–483.

41. Employers often preferred the AFL unions, believing them to be more predictable and easier to deal with than the CIO unions.

42. Norris-LaGuardia Act 47, Stat. 70 (1932). The employers' use of court injunctions to stop organizing campaigns and picketing was one of their major weapons against unions.

43. A protected right to union membership and collective bargaining was extended to railway employees in 1926 under the Railway Labor Act, the oldest collective bargaining legislation (44 Stat., Part II, 577). Under that law, mediation by the National Mediation Board assists the parties to settlements, and arbitration is offered later if the parties reach an impasse. It also specifies the workers' right to "organize and bargain collectively through representatives of their own choosing." The National Mediation holds elections and certifies representatives. The airlines have been covered under the act since 1936.

44. Galenson (1986), p. 52.

45. Bernstein (1969), p. 37.

46. Galenson (1986), p. 53. For a review of union growth under the NIRA, see Wolman (1936), pp. 43–75.

47. *A. L. Schechter Poultry Corp. v. United States*, 295 U.S. 495 (1935).

48. National Labor Relations Act, 49 Stat. 449 § 1 (1935).

49. National Labor Relations Act, 49 Stat. 449 § 7 Rights of Employees.

50. National Labor Relations Act, 29 Stat. 449 § 9(a) Representatives and Elections.

51. Bernstein (1969), pp. 772–773.

52. Lichtenstein (2002, p. 35) commented on the revolutionary character of the Wagner Act: "The law was a radical legislative initiative because it was designed to put in place a permanent set of institutions situated within the very womb of private enterprise which offered workers voice, and sometimes a club, with which to resolve their grievances and organize themselves for economic struggle."

53. Kochan, T. A., Katz, H. C., and McKersie, R. B. (1986). *The transformation of American industrial relations.* New York: Basic Books, p. 23. The authors make the point that the labor market was no longer assumed to be operating in such a way as to protect the interests of all parties and that the imbalance of power between employer and worker is resolved through collective bargaining.

54. Kochan, Katz, and McKersie (1986), p. 24.

55. The Taft-Hartley Act also permitted states to prohibit requirements in collective agreements that employees join unions as a condition of employment (§ 14(b)). The requirements are called *union security clauses* and the states prohibiting them are *right-to-work law* states.

56. Jarley, P. (2002). American unionism at the start of the twenty-first century: Going back to the future? In P. Fairbrother and G. Griffin (Eds.), *Changing prospects for trade unionism: Comparisons between six countries.* London: Continuum, p. 201.

57. See Taft (1964), pp. 656–657, for a summary of the federation report indicating very small membership gains as a result of organizing raids between affiliates of the AFL and those of the CIO.

58. Chaison, G., and Rose, J. B. (1991). Continental divide: The direction and fate of North American unions. *Advances in Industrial and Labor Relations*, 5, pp. 169–205.

59. The Labor-Management Reporting and Disclosure Act, 73 Stat. 519 (1959).

60. One of the earliest and most influential discussions of the accord is Edwards, R., and Podgursky, M. (1986). The unraveling accord: American unions in crisis. In R. Edwards, P. Garonna, and F. Todtling (Eds.), *Unions in crisis and beyond: Perspectives from six countries.* Dover, MA: Auburn House, pp. 14–60.

61. Strauss, G. (1995). Is the New Deal collapsing? With what might it be replaced? *Industrial Relations*, 34, p. 342.

62. Chaison and Bigelow (2002), p. 22.

63. Chaison and Bigelow (2002), p. 22.

64. Chaison, G. N., Bigelow, B., and Ottensmeyer, E. (1993). Unions and legitimacy: A conceptual refinement. *Research in the Sociology of Organizations*, 12, p. 152.

65. Rogers, J. (1993). Don't worry, be happy: The post-war decline of private sector unionism in the United States. In J. Jensen and R. Mahon (Eds.), *The challenge of restructuring: North American labor movements respond*. Philadelphia: Temple University Press, p. 59.

66. Rose, J. B., and Chaison, G. N. (1985). The state of the unions: United States and Canada. *Journal of Labor Research*, 6, pp. 97–111.

67. Chaison, Bigelow, and Ottensmeyer (1993), p. 142.

68. Kochan, T. A., McKersie, R. B., and Capelli, P. (1984). Strategic choice and industrial relations theory. *Industrial Relations*, 23, p. 18.

69. Chaison, G. N., and Dhavale, D. G. (1990). A note on the severity of the decline in union organizing. *Industrial and Labor Relations Review*, 4, pp. 366–373; Chaison and Rose (1991).

70. Rose, J. B., and Chaison, G. N. (1996). Linking union density and union effectiveness: The North American experience. *Industrial Relations*, 35, pp. 78–105.

71. Chaison and Rose (1991), p. 182.

72. Rose and Chaison (1996), p. 89.

73. Rose, J. B., Chaison, G. N., and de la Garza, E. (2000). A comparative analysis of public sector restructuring in the U.S., Canada, Mexico and the Caribbean. *Journal of Labor Research*, 21, pp. 601–625.

74. Rose, Chaison, and de la Garza (2000).

75. Kochan, Katz, and McKersie (1986), p. 39.

76. Hirsch, B. T., and Macpherson, D. A. (2004). Union membership. www.unionstats.com.

77. Rose, J. B., and Chaison, G. N. (2001). Unionism in Canada and the United States in the 21st century: The prospects for revival. *Relations Industrielles/Industrial Relations*, 56, pp. 34–64.

78. Quoted in Rose and Chaison (2001), p. 42.

79. Jarley, P. (2002). The author concludes: "Few would dispute that American unionism is again on the verge of becoming an insignificant social force. There is serious concern among scholars and labor practitioners that American unions will fade into obscurity in the first few decades of the present century" (p. 203).

Two

Union Structure and Growth

W hen people talk about unions, they usually refer to them in the broadest terms. Their impressions of unions, whether favorable or unfavorable, are often about *national* union organizations, such as the Teamsters or the Steelworkers, rather than the thousands of local union branches where most union activities take place and members actually experience their unions. The public also likes to fit unions into categories, calling them manufacturing, government workers', or white-collar workers' unions, as if they each accepted only one type of member, although they clearly do not.

We hear a lot of half-truths about unions—for example, that the biggest unions are the most powerful ones or that unions are not growing because workers have lost interest in them—and we let these go unchallenged because they seem so plausible in a world of simplified unions. This chapter presents a portrait of the unions as complex and diverse, and asks why and how unions grow or decline. Although many like to think of unions as a family of broadly similar organizations, they are actually among the most complicated organizations in our society.

Union Structure

National Unions

National unions are labor unions that represent workers in several locations although they may not be truly national in scope and have members in all states. Many unions use the term *international* in their title (e.g., the Service Employees International Union or the International Longshore and Warehouse Union) to show that they have members outside of the United States. This is really a misnomer; *continental* would be better. The international unions' members are in the United States and Canada.

In 2004, there were 1.2 million Canadian members of 46 international unions, or 28 percent of all union members in Canada. Among the largest international unions operating in Canada were the United Food and Commercial Workers (188,000 Canadian members), the United Steelworkers of America (180,000), the International Brotherhood of Teamsters (110,000), and the Service Employees International Union (84,000). But many internationals have a small Canadian presence; about half have fewer than 10,000 Canadian members.[1]

National and international unions call themselves many things including *association* (e.g., the Air Line Pilots Association, National Association of Letter Carriers), *guild* (e.g., the Screen Actors Guild, the Writers Guild), *federation* (e.g., American Federation of Television and Radio Artists, American Federation of Teachers), and *brotherhood* (e.g., International Brotherhood of Teamsters, International Brotherhood of Electrical Workers). Some unions do not use any organizational terms in their titles (e.g., United Steelworkers of America, Communications Workers of America), although many refer to themselves simply as unions (e.g., the Amalgamated Transit Union, Service Employees International Union). Each union's title reflects its own history and traditions; for example, some early unions were formed as guilds or brotherhoods of skilled workers and this is reflected in their present names, while others joined together regional organizations and prefer the term *federation* rather than union. A few unions that were created by mergers have the term *amalgamated* in their title. Some unions list the industries or occupations of their members (e.g., International Brotherhood of Boilermakers, Iron Ship Builders, Blacksmiths, Forgers and Helpers), but others prefer simplicity (e.g., National Maritime Union). But no matter what they call themselves, any organization that acts as a bargaining agent for some or all of its members is a labor union.

The unions are highly fragmented as well as highly concentrated; there are many small unions but also a few very large unions that had a major share of total union membership. Table 2.1 shows the size distribution of national unions. In 2001, four unions had more than 1 million members; the Service Employees International Union (1.6 million), the International Brotherhood of Teamsters (1.4 million), the United Food and Commercial Workers (1.4 million), and the American Federation of State, County and Municipal Employees (1.3 million).[2] Together, these accounted for 5.7 million members, or one-third of all union members. But 28 of the 65 national and international unions had fewer than 50,000 members, and combined they had less than 4 percent of total membership.

Is there a size below which unions are no longer effective? Many argue that unions with fewer than 50,000 members have difficulty organizing and striking and lack economies of scale in operations (i.e., are too small to afford to provide a wide array of services to members).[3] Unless they can somehow grow through organizing (and most cannot), smaller unions should consider merging with each other to confront the power

Table 2.1   Size Distribution of National Unions (AFL-CIO Affiliates), 2001[a]

Union Size	Number of Unions	Percentage of Unions	Percentage of Members
Less than 10,000 members	8	12.3	0.2
10,000–24,999 members	9	13.8	1.1
25,000–49,999 members	11	16.9	3.0
50,000–99,999 members	12	18.5	6.8
100,000–499,999 members	17	26.2	29.2
500,000–999,999 members	4	6.2	22.4
1,000,000 members or more	4	6.2	37.4
Total	65	100.1[b]	100.1[b]

Source: Gifford, C. (Ed.). (2003). *Directory of U.S. labor organizations, 2002 edition*. Washington, DC: Bureau of National Affairs.

Note: The AFL-CIO affiliates provide a good approximation of the size distribution of the national unions. AFL-CIO affiliates are national unions except for the California School Employees Association (129,000 members), which is excluded from the figures above. The only major unaffiliated national unions in 2001 were the National Education Association (2,530,000 members) and the United Brotherhood of Carpenters (520,000).

a. Includes international unions, but union size is based on membership in the United States.

b. Does not equal 100.0 percent because of rounding.

of large employers. For example, Andrew Stern, the president of the Service Employees (the largest union) and one of the most influential labor leaders, has declared that smaller unions are ineffectual and should merge together into 15 to 20 mega-unions, each covering a major industry.[4]

But objections to smallness are not always justified. Small unions can be quite effective if they are not overextended (if they negotiate only a few collective agreements or represent small, specialized groups in narrow geographic areas), if they represent most workers in their industry or occupation, or if they have organized a key group of workers in a larger production or transportation process. There has been great power in the unions of airline pilots (46,000 members)[5] and musicians (12,000 members) because both have organized most of a type of skilled and irreplaceable work group. The various unions of police officers (patrolmen's benevolent associations) each has fewer than 50,000 members but are strong bargainers and lobbyists because they represent every police officer in their cities. Undoubtedly, one of the strongest of all unions is the Major League Baseball Players Association—with only 1,200 members, it has organized its entire industry and can shut it down with a strike. The labor dispute on the West Coast docks in September 2002 cost nearly a billion dollars a day, yet the union involved, the International Longshore and Warehouse Union, had only 35,000 members.[6]

In short, there are no hard-and-fast rules about union size—some small unions are strong just as some larger unions may be weak. For example, UNITE, the clothing and textile union, had roughly 200,000 members before its 2004 merger with the hotel and restaurant union, but had been severely weakened in organizing and bargaining by foreign and nonunion competition in its core industries. There are also several small unions that are boxed into declining industries or occupations and cannot expand into growing ones. Small size, with no chance of getting larger, led to the demise (through mergers) of such highly specialized unions as the Train Dispatchers, Coopers, Upholsterers, Potters, Hatters, and Jewelry Workers.[7]

Local Unaffiliated Unions
(or Local Independent Unions)

These unions (the terms are used interchangeably) are alternatives to national unions. They are formed on a regional, companywide, or plantwide basis, and are unaffiliated with the labor federation. Their exact number is unknown, but one union directory listed more than 1,200 in 1998, a figure that has probably changed little.[8]

Local unaffiliated or independent unions should not be confused with *company unions*—the designation for employer-dominated unions that are incapable of independent representation and arms-length bargaining. Many company unions were formed in the 1920s as employee representation plans or works councils for problem solving, grievance handling, and consultation with management, but *not* bargaining over wages or working conditions. More were created in the 1930s as employers responded to legislation that gave workers the protected right to join unions (the National Industrial Recovery Act of 1933) by forming "inside" unions that could be company controlled. By 1935, more than 2 million workers were in company unions. However, with the passage of the Wagner Act (National Labor Relations Act) in 1935, employer-dominated unions were banned if workers or national unions objected to their presence. Many were disestablished, but others became local unaffiliated unions by severing their ties with employers and negotiating collective agreements.[9]

Although many trade unionists consider local unaffiliated or independent unions to be only peripheral to the labor movement, these small unions are usually capable of effective workplace representation and pride themselves on being in close contact with their members. Some were even formed by workers to challenge large national unions. For example, in 2003, the flight attendants at Northwest Airlines voted to oust the Teamsters, their union for 26 years, and replaced it with a small, specialized union—the Association of Professional Flight Attendants. They believed that they would have greater influence over contract negotiations if they were in a smaller union composed only of flight attendants.[10] Around the same time, the mechanics at United Airlines replaced their representative, the International Association of Machinists, with a small, unaffiliated union—the Aircraft Mechanics Fraternal Association—because it seemed more attuned to their needs and willing to resist employer demands for concessions.[11]

Some unaffiliated unions are confined to a single employer or even a single plant (e.g., the International Brotherhood of DuPont Workers, the United Technologies Corporation Independent Fire/Security Officers Association, and the Association of Westinghouse Salaried Employees).[12] Others were created by workers who wanted unions exclusive to their industry or occupation or to their interests and beliefs (e.g., the Christian

Labor Association, with 1,800 members, and the National Association of Catholic School Teachers, with 4,600 members).[13]

Union Locals and Intermediate Bodies

Locals are the lowest-level branches of national unions. There might be a local for particular plant (e.g., United Automobile Workers Local 246 at the General Motors plant in Arlington, Texas) or in a geographic area (e.g., Carpenters Local 107, which covers all union carpenters in Worcester, Massachusetts). Some locals are the conglomerate or general type and include workers of several small plants or shops in an area, none of which are large enough to have their own local (e.g., Teamsters Local 170 with 3,900 members working for companies in the grocery, small-package delivery, construction, and beer and soft drinks industries, among others, and local government).

There are more than 33,000 locals in the United States.[14] Locals can vary in size from several thousand members (e.g., a local at a huge automobile assembly plant or steel mill) to fewer than 100 (e.g., at a small factory, store, or school). The number of locals in each union depends more on union tradition and the structure of the industry or occupation than on national union size. For instance, the Service Employees, with 1.6 million members, has only 305 locals; many cover all Service Employees' workplaces in a geographic area. The Steelworkers, with about 600,000 members, has 1,900 locals, mostly at individual plants and offices. With separate locals for schools or school systems, the American Federation of Teachers, with its 700,000 members, has 3,000 locals.[15]

Locals are the quintessential union structure. Members experience their unions at the local level. What they think of their own union and unions in general comes from their impressions of local union activities. If they believe their local is run effectively, they will usually believe all unions are run effectively; if their local leaders are inept or corrupt, they will think the same of all union leaders. Members attend meetings, sit on committees (e.g., to process grievances or prepare for bargaining), pay dues, and run for their first union offices at the local level.

Local autonomy, the ability of locals to decide how they will run themselves, is always a thorny issue. Local members and officers might want a great deal of self-control—"freedom from national union interference," as they call it—but the national headquarters might see the need for tight administration and coordination with close oversight of local affairs. In questions of local autonomy, it should always be remembered that locals are the creations of national unions, rather than the other way around. Some locals enjoy considerable freedom in bargaining and administration, but this is largely a matter of union tradition and the level of negotiations (e.g., locals exercise the most autonomy when negotiations take place on the local level as they would, for example, in the construction industry or local government). But national headquarters can always restrain local autonomy—they might not let locals go on strike without approval, or set dues or devise their own methods of electing officers. Collective agreements usually have to be approved by national headquarters so they do not deviate from general patterns. Locals are bound by their parent union's constitution. National union headquarters can place locals in *trusteeship*, that is, suspend their self-governance and replace their officers, if they believe the local leadership has been corrupt or grossly ineffective in representation, or violated the constitution (e.g., by calling the workers out on strike without authorization, or discriminating when admitting members).

Intermediate bodies are administrative structures situated between the national union headquarters and the locals. The United Steelworkers of America, for example, has 12 districts arranged geographically as well as two industry sections—the Rubber and Plastics Industry Conference (representing former members of the United Rubber Workers, which was absorbed by the Steelworkers) and the Aluminum, Brick and Glass Workers Division (also for unions absorbed by the Steelworkers).[16] The Service Employees has four divisions: Health Care, Public Services, Building Services, and Industrial and Allied.[17] The International Longshoremen's Association has districts according to the location of ports: Atlantic Coast, Great Lakes, South Atlantic and Gulf Coast, and Pacific Coast.[18] The Air Line Pilots Association is divided into "pilot groups," one for each of the 42 U.S. and Canadian airlines at which it represents pilots.[19]

Similar to locals, intermediate bodies can have a great deal of autonomy and their own officers and meetings. They may be responsible for setting negotiating priorities and approving strikes and collective agreements, especially when they are industrial or company divisions within their parent unions and they may be given the power to coordinate organizing and political activities. When intermediate bodies are formed to accommodate the officers, staff, and members of small unions after their mergers into large ones, they will be nearly autonomous organizations because these arrangements were enticements for approval of merger agreements. Large unions have found that they can absorb small unions easily by setting them up as intermediate bodies with their locals and officers unchanged.[20]

The Labor Federation

The labor federation—the American Federation of Labor and Congress of Industrial Organizations (AFL-CIO)—is a voluntary association of 56 national unions with more than 13 million members.[21] The AFL-CIO coordinates the activities of its affiliates in organizing, bargaining, and political action; prohibits organizing raids between affiliated unions; serves as the voice of workers in presentations and lobbying at state and national legislatures; maintains links with labor federations in other countries (primarily to enforce international work standards); promotes human rights and training programs for members and nonmembers; and develops and communicates the goals and priorities of the labor movement (e.g., reforming labor law, opposing unrestricted free trade between countries, reducing workplace discrimination). The AFL-CIO is not a bargaining agent; it does not represent members of affiliated unions in collective bargaining. It also does not carry the primary responsibility for organizing, although it will assist and encourage affiliated unions when they organize.

Workers do not belong to the AFL-CIO—they join AFL-CIO affiliates. Discussions of the limited role of AFL-CIO often use the analogy of the status of countries in the United Nations. Sloan and Witney's popular textbook made this comparison: "The relationship of the national unions to the federation is like the relationship of member nations to the United Nations. No nation *must* belong to the United Nations; any nation *may* withdraw from the international organization at any time and for any reason whatsoever. Nor does the United Nations have the power to determine the internal government of any of its affiliates, its tax laws, its foreign policy, the size of its military establishment, or any other national matters."[22]

Each month, the AFL-CIO collects a per capita tax from affiliated national unions of 53 cents for each member. The federation is governed by a convention of delegates selected by affiliates that meets every four years. The convention amends the constitution, passes resolutions, and sets broad policies and goals as well as elects officers—the federation president, the secretary-treasurer, the executive vice president, and 51 vice presidents. These officers, meeting as the AFL-CIO *Executive Council*, direct the daily work of the federation and make administrative and policy decisions. The AFL-CIO *General Board* is formed by the Executive Council members, the top officers of each affiliated union, the heads of the federation's trade and industrial departments, and four representatives of its state bodies. The board deals with matters referred to it by the Executive Council, such as the endorsement of national political candidates.[23] The AFL-CIO also has an executive committee composed of 17 union presidents that meets with the federation president every month to provide advice and support and help set the federation's policies and priorities. This body was created in 2003 to maintain closer and more frequent contact between union and federation officers than would be possible with the Executive Council and General Board.[24]

The AFL-CIO also has four regional offices (for the Midwest in Chicago, the Northeast in New York, the South in College Park, Georgia, and the West in Seattle). It also has 51 *state federations* (including Puerto Rico), which deal mostly with political activities, as well as 570 *labor councils*—local and regional organizations that coordinate branches of affiliated unions on a geographic basis. Labor councils in cities have become active in organizing, political action, and supporting strikes, often by working with community coalitions such as those promoting consumer boycotts, rights of immigrant workers associations, and local economic development committees.[25]

The federation has seven *trade* or *industrial departments* that coordinate affiliates' activities across unions and regions (e.g., Building and Construction Trades, Metal Trades, Food and Allied Services, and Professional Employees). It also has centers for specific services (e.g., providing group benefit programs to members, assisting unions in economic development and retraining, providing real estate investment opportunities for the pension plans of affiliates) as well as several affiliated organizations (e.g., a center for labor studies and training organizers and Union Privilege—an organization that provides group benefits programs such as legal aid and low-cost credit cards to workers).[26] In 2004, the federation formed an organization—Working America—that joins together union and nonunion workers and persons in community-based coalitions mostly for political mobilization with the stated goal of "good jobs, strong communities and the right set of priorities from government leaders."[27]

The issue of how much power the federation should have has never been completely resolved. On the one hand, the federation is expected to provide important services (e.g., preventing organizing raids, political lobbying) to affiliates to justify their payment of dues. But the federation must be careful to not appear to be usurping the role of its affiliates by directing organizing drives or interfering in bargaining. It must respect the autonomy of affiliates (e.g., it cannot prevent an affiliate from striking or compel it to accept a collective agreement), but it cannot tolerate behavior that hurts unions in general (e.g., the election of blatantly corrupt leaders).

There has been a great deal of tension within the AFL-CIO recently because of its activist leadership—president John J. Sweeney, secretary-treasurer Richard Trumka, and executive vice president Linda Chavez-Thompson. Sweeney is past president of the Service Employees, Trumka is past president of the United Mine Workers, and Chavez-Thompson is past vice president of the American Federation of State, County and Municipal Employees. They were elected as a reform slate, the New Voice Team, in 1995 in reaction to the perceived ineffectiveness and passivity of the incumbent federation officers. Since then, there has been considerable criticism of the federation's active promotion of greater organizing (many affiliated unions believe that organizing should remain an internal union matter with the federation, at most, coordinating union efforts), its close ties to the Democratic Party (particularly in light of the party's election losses in 2004), its inability to influence key legislation (mostly restrictions on foreign trade), and its neglect of key union issues such as the need to increase membership participation. In 2005, a group of five unions led by Andy Stern, president of the Service Employees, wanted a $50 million reduction in the AFL-CIO's budget with the funds going to affiliated unions for organizing. This challenge was initially beaten back by the federation's leadership, which presented its own plan for increased organizing and political activities and promised to cut the headquarters' budget and return funds to affiliates. But the dissident unions have repeatedly threatened to leave the AFL-CIO if the federation could not revive union growth and influence.[28]

Criticism of the federation's leadership should be expected; some will always believe the federation does too much, others will believe it does too little. But in times of severe membership losses, critics become more vocal. For example, many union officers have been very critical of federation proposals that small unions merge, seeing this as an inexcusable intrusion into affiliate autonomy, though others believe that mergers must be used to put an end to small ineffective unions that cannot organize and increase the quality of representation for all members.[29] At the other extreme, affiliates are joining together to challenge the federation's leadership and demand that it do more to reinvigorate the labor movement and increase the pace of organizing.[30] This challenge could split the federation between the large and growing service and government workers' unions (those pressing for major changes) and the older industrial unions (those more in favor of the status quo). Caught in the middle would be smaller unions that are under pressure to merge, lack the size to influence federation policy, and can only hope that the federation will continue to respect affiliate autonomy. If a new federation leadership emerges that seems too demanding and intrusive, there could be a deep division that might lead to the creation of a new federation by seceding unions. This would not be over the disagreements about jurisdictions that we saw split the AFL in Chapter 1, but over how best to achieve union revival.[31]

Union Jurisdiction

An organizing jurisdiction, as it was described in the preceding chapter, is a union's statement of the job territory that it claims the right to organize and represent in bargaining.[32] Descriptions of jurisdiction are usually found in union constitutions. Some are long lists of specific occupations or industries while others are broad statements that are nearly limitless. For example, the jurisdiction of the Laborers' International Union includes practically everyone; it lists the jurisdictions of all the unions that have merged into it over the years (six unions), any workers that have been included in the union by decisions of the AFL-CIO and labor boards, and workers who are members by its own organizing and bargaining. In other words, the Laborers' jurisdiction is everyone who is in it—or could be in it.[33] The International Brotherhood of Teamsters always comes to mind as the epitome of a general union—a union with an unlimited jurisdiction that claims the right to organize all workers in all industries. The Teamsters' mission statement begins: "The objectives of this International Union are to organize under one banner all workers engaged in industry."[34] Its statement of jurisdiction proclaims: "This organization has jurisdiction over all workers" and then lists some occupations and industries that the jurisdiction includes but is not limited to. Just to make sure that it is understood by everyone that all workers can be Teamsters, the clause ends with the inclusion of "office, technical and professional employees; health care employees; agricultural employees; public employees; and industrial employees."[35] The jurisdiction of the Communications Workers is also unlimited, but this is stated as directly and unequivocally as possible: "The union shall have jurisdiction over all communications work and of the persons engaged therein. The Union shall also include those workers who wish to become part of the Union regardless of their field of endeavor. There shall be no geographic limitation on the jurisdiction of the union."[36] The United Steelworkers of America simply extends membership eligibility to "all working men and women . . . for whom the union assumes or seeks to assume . . . collective bargaining and other responsibilities."[37] In contrast, the jurisdiction of the Bricklayers is relatively narrow and lists types of work (e.g., constructing, erecting, cleaning, repairing) and types of materials (e.g., brick, concrete, plaster, plastic) used for that work.[38]

The American Federation of State, County and Municipal Employees' jurisdiction flows beyond the public sector, but not too far beyond it. The union defines its membership as "an employee of any state, territory, commonwealth, county, district, school board, city, town, village, township, or other public authority or of any governmental subdivision of any such government or authority . . . or of any quasi-public agency or any non-profit or tax-exempt agency of a public, charitable, educational, or civic nature."[39] The Association of Flight Attendants is highly specialized, limiting its jurisdiction to "any person who is employed as a cabin crew member in commercial air transportation."[40] In contrast, the Office and Professional Workers, with its unlimited jurisdiction, has members in the public sector (e.g., employees of the Massachusetts court system and the Tennessee Department of Energy) as well as the private sector (e.g., professional and clerical workers at universities, nursing homes, and hotels). Also affiliated with it are organizations of "physicians, optometrists, pharmacists, podiatrists, clinical social workers, biofeedback practitioners, acupuncturists, hypnotists and helicopter pilots."[41]

Some union jurisdictions draw fine lines between their potential members and those of neighboring unions. For example, the Screen Actors Guild represents only actors making films in Hollywood studios or doing televised shows that are shot on film. This leaves the American Federation of Television and Radio Artists to represent actors on video-taped television shows along with television news reporters, sports announcers, and other broadcasters.[42]

In the previous chapter, we saw the historical importance of union jurisdiction. Unions often disagreed with each other over how workers should be organized; for example, AFL unions claimed workers in particular crafts, CIO unions claimed workers in particular industries regardless of their crafts, and the Industrial Workers of the World (IWW) claimed all workers regardless of craft or industry. Ironically, jurisdictions, once so controversial as to split the labor movement, have now lost most of their meaning. Jurisdictions are usually inflated claims of organizing intent rather than organizing accomplishment. Unions casually amend their jurisdictions to stake claim to growing industries or occupations (e.g., health care workers or clerical workers). They organize with little concern for each other's jurisdiction, responding instead to contacts from workers who want union representation.[43]

There still are a few unions that organize narrow jurisdictions (e.g., those of professional athletes and entertainers), but most unions will organize practically anyone. They only ask if it is worthwhile to represent a group: Are the workers so specialized that new staff will have to be hired to help them? Can the workers form a local that is not geographically isolated from the union's other locals so they can be serviced at a reasonable cost?[44]

For a century or more, union leaders have proclaimed the need for a streamlined union movement with only a few big unions, one for each major industry. This can never be achieved because too many unions already have broad and overlapping jurisdictions. A recent study found that in each of 13 major industrial sectors, at least four unions had a significant presence. In each of 9 sectors, there were six unions.[45]

Unions diversify their membership in much the same way that investors diversify their stock portfolios. They try to reduce risk by not having too many members in declining industries, or possibly in bargaining or going on strike at the same time. The diversification of membership is usually accomplished by creating affiliated bodies outside of the unions' core jurisdiction. For example, the local union seeking to represent teaching and research assistants at Yale University, the Graduate Student and Employees Organization, is an affiliate of HERE (Hotel Employees and Restaurant Employees International Union). Affiliates of the United Auto Workers have tried organizing at several university campuses, including New York University (successfully) and Cornell University (unsuccessfully), while the American Federation of State, County and Municipal Employees represents workers at Harvard University through its Harvard University Clerical and Technical Workers Union.[46]

The concept of exclusive jurisdiction—the principle that there should be only one union for each industry or occupation—was promoted by unions and federations during the early days of the labor movement to prevent wasteful inter-union competition. It was made meaningless during the 20 years of rivalry between AFL and CIO affiliates as the two federations created unions to challenge each other. When the federations merged in 1955 to form the AFL-CIO, they agreed that union jurisdictions would remain unchanged and mergers would be encouraged to reduce overlap, but mergers would not be forced. Today, jurisdictions have expanded so much that what were once craft unions and industrial unions are now multicraft and multi-industry unions (e.g., the Carpenters and the Steelworkers), and unions that were confined to the private sector have organized some public employees (e.g., the Auto Workers and the Teamsters).[47]

Union Mergers[48]

Unions merge for a variety of reasons: to end membership losses and reverse financial hardship; to diversify organizing jurisdictions and make quick inroads into new industries or occupations; to achieve economies of scale in operations and provide a full array of membership services such as political lobbying and legal assistance; to protect themselves from organizing raids by becoming parts of affiliated unions covered by the federation no-raid agreement; and to grow faster and less expensively than would be possible by traditional organizing.[49] When they promote mergers, unions often claim that bigger unions are simply better unions (we discussed this misconception earlier) and that merged unions will be more effective and powerful than their predecessors. For example, when the officers of UNITE (Union of Needletrades, Industrial and Textile Employees) and HERE announced their plans for a merger in 2004, the president of HERE remarked, "We think it makes sense to have like-minded unions join together to be bigger and stronger," and UNITE's leader observed, "The merged union will have tremendous financial resources and wherewithal so we can stand up to any employer." Both officers predicted that the merger would create a surge in organizing activity and union growth.[50] In a similar vein, when the United Steelworkers of America and PACE (Paper, Allied Industrial, Chemical and Energy Workers) announced that they were merging in 2005, the Steelworkers' president claimed, "We'll be able to bargain better agreements and better represent our members, and by doing that, we can do a better job organizing additional workers." The PACE leader added, "We believe we are creating the most powerful industrial organization in the United States, if not the world."[51]

National unions merge in either of two ways. In an *amalgamation*, two or more unions combine to form a new union. In an *absorption*, the more popular merger form, a small union (the *absorbed union*) merges into a larger union (the *absorbing union*). An absorbed union can become part of a larger union as a division or section; this entails little change in the union constitution, and most officers and staff are retained. Only the members of the absorbed union need vote to approve the merger agreement because the absorbing union usually authorizes its officers to explore merger opportunities and approve any merger agreements that do not entail major changes in its constitutions. Compare this to an amalgamation that creates a new union with its own officers, staff, constitutions, headquarters, and dues and fees. Because the merging unions are forming a new union by disbanding the old ones, the members of amalgamating unions have to approve the merger agreement.[52]

In a third type of merger, *affiliation*, regional unions such as state employee associations or local independent unions merge into national unions. Most large national unions negotiate affiliations, usually to establish their presence in areas where there is organizing potential. A particularly active union is the Service Employees, which affiliated 47 local and regional unions in its period of early major growth (1980 to 1993). Other important affiliating unions are the United Food and Commercial Workers and the American Federation of State, County and Municipal Workers.[53]

Unions affiliate for many of the same reasons that they agree to be absorbed. For example, in April 2002, the 1,700-member Professional Industrial and Trade Workers Union, a New Jersey-based union of workers from professional employment companies, agreed to affiliate with the International Association of Machinists. The union's officers claimed that the affiliation gave it name recognition and respect as part of the Machinists as well as help with legal and administrative costs. Typical of affiliations, the affiliating union became a local of the larger union with a promise that all new members in its industry would be members of that local regardless of where they worked.[54]

In industries where there are large numbers of local independent unions, national unions use affiliations to consolidate power. For example, the Air Line Pilots Association is involved in a campaign to affiliate the numerous unions of pilots at major carriers (e.g., Continental) and other companies (e.g., FedEx).[55]

Frequently, affiliations give a great a deal of autonomy to the smaller union as an enticement to merge. For example, when the Illinois Dental Hygienists' Association affiliated with the American Federation of Teachers (AFT) it retained its autonomy and bargaining role and paid a fee to the state chapter of the AFT in return for its lobbying assistance.[56]

Though the details of each merger differ, most merging unions go through a similar process.[57] There are informal initial discussions when officers believe that more might be gained than lost by merging their unions. If officers are in favor of the merger, they will ask their unions' executive councils to appoint committees for negotiating specific merger terms. Negotiations for amalgamations must resolve such issues as the composition and process for election of the amalgamated union's governing body, location of the new union's headquarters, merging of the unions' locals, employment and compensation of union staff, membership dues and fees, and autonomy granted to locals in bargaining and striking. Negotiations for absorptions and affiliations must determine the status of the absorbed or affiliating union in the larger union, titles and authority of its officers, continuation of the employment of staff, and changes in dues and fees.

Because there are so many contentious issues in any merger discussion, it is difficult to reach agreement unless there is strong pressure to merge, and this is usually caused by severe membership losses or financial hardship. Merger talks fail at least twice as often as they succeed (though it is difficult to know by exactly how much because unions do not publicize their unsuccessful merger negotiations).[58] There is always some opposition to mergers. Officers and staff will resist a merger that cuts short their careers and reduces their compensation and benefits. Merger campaigns can revive political opposition within unions. Opponents of the incumbent officers who favor merger will accuse them of forsaking union traditions and ending the union's existence for vague promises.[59] When there is political rivalry, elections for pro-merger officers or their antimerger challengers become de facto elections.

If the desire to merge is greater than the opposition to merge and consequently merger talks are successful, a proposal is presented to the union's members or convention delegates for approval. Officers try to persuade the members that the union's traditions and autonomy will be maintained if the merger is approved and that merger will lead to more effective bargaining and organizing. For example, in June 2003, the American Flint Glass Workers was absorbed by the United Steelworkers and became part of its new conference for the glass industry. The Steelworkers already had conferences for other unions it had absorbed over the years, including rubber and aluminum conferences. The Flint Glass Workers brought 12,000 members to the conference that already had 20,000 other members from the Aluminum, Brick and Glass Workers, the union absorbed by the Steelworkers six years earlier. At a special convention of the Flint Glass Workers, 92 percent of the delegates voted for merger. They believed their union had no other choice; in the 18 months before the merger, membership had fallen from 19,000 to 12,000 because of layoffs and plant closures. As a condition of the merger, there would be no staff cuts.[60] The union's leader declared: "Our membership is very excited about this opportunity to strengthen our bargaining position in the glass industry and enhance our ability to organize."[61]

Mergers have ended the independent existence of some of the oldest unions (e.g., the International Typographical Union, which was formed in 1852, merged into the Communications Workers in 1987); created some of the largest unions (e.g., the United Food and Commercial Workers with 1.2 million members was created by an amalgamation of two unions); and become an important way to expand membership outside of traditional organizing (e.g., the fast-growing Communications Workers, Service Employees, and American Federation of State, County and Municipal Employees absorbed or affiliated numerous small unions).[62] Despite their historic importance, mergers are based on pragmatic decisions—the officers' and members' impressions of probable gains and losses. Is there more to be gained by merger than lost? And the decision to merge is entirely voluntary. Mergers cannot be forced on unions by federations; that would violate affiliates' autonomy. The most that a federation can do is encourage mergers among small affiliates or those overlapping jurisdictions and provide assistance in negotiations and campaigns if the unions decide to merge. Grand plans to streamline the labor movement through a sequence of mergers, creating 12 to 20 industry-based megaunions, are always being proposed by scholars and labor leaders, but the decision to merge remains within the unions and is determined by the self-interests of officers and members.[63]

The form and frequency of mergers among national unions are shown in Table 2.2. Until the last period (2000–2004), there was a rising trend toward mergers because declining union membership and the limits to growth through expensive and time-consuming organizing have made larger unions turn to mergers as a growth strategy (essentially, organizing unions rather than workers). Small unions also began to doubt if they could ever stop their decline without becoming part of other unions.[64] Absorptions are the predominant merger form because it is far easier to negotiate the place of a small union in a large one than to create an entirely new union by dissolving two or more unions (the process of

Table 2.2   Frequency and Forms of National Union Mergers, 1955–2004

Period	Amalgamations	Absorptions	Total Mergers	Annual Average
1955–1959	3	6	9	1.8
1960–1969	5	19	24	2.4
1970–1979	6	21	27	2.7
1980–1989	4	31	35	3.5
1990–1999	2	36	38	3.8
2000–2004	1	6	7	1.4
Total	21	119	140	2.8

Source: 1955–1999: Chaison, G. (2002). Union mergers and union revival: Are we asking too much or too little? In L. Turner, H. C. Katz, and R. W. Hurd (Eds.), *Rekindling the movement: Labor's quest for relevance in the twenty-first century.* Ithaca, NY: Cornell University Press, pp. 238-255, Table 10–1; 2000–2004: Bureau of National Affairs, *Daily Labor Report,* various issues.

amalgamation).[65] In the most recent period, the number of mergers might have fallen because there were fewer potential merger partners among the remaining national unions (so many mergers had occurred in earlier years) and national unions may have increasingly turned to affiliations rather than absorptions for quick growth—affiliated unions are easily accommodated in postmerger unions as union locals.

Finally, we should recognize the limitations of union mergers. Despite the exhortations of union officers promoting merger plans, or stream-lined labor movements, mergers rarely resolve the problems that led to them.

> Mergers are a reaction to [union] crisis but not a determining force in its resolution. For example, mergers cannot revive declining industries, increase the propensity of workers to join unions, reverse foreign import penetration in manufacturing, or halt the employers' retreat from collective bargaining and their resistance to the spread of unionism. . . . For small [absorbed unions] merger was not selected from a lengthy list of options; it was usually the least costly, quickest alternative to slow decline, eventual disbandment and the loss of employment for union officers and representation for members. For large unions, amalgamating with each other or [absorbing] small unions meant having a better chance of weathering the hard times, gaining new members without organizing, and maintaining effective, solvent organizations for the days when circumstances improve.[66]

Union Growth and Decline

Union Membership and Density

Table 2.3 shows union membership and union density (the percentage of wage and salary workers in unions) by members' characteristics, industry, and occupation. Density is an indicator of union strength—how well unions have organized the workforce.[67]

Although there is a range in density rates, all figures are fairly low. Overall, only 12.5 percent of wage and salary workers are union members, although there are wide differences in private and public sector density; 7.9 percent of private workers are in unions compared to 36.4 percent of government workers. This is due to differences in the degree of employer opposition to union organizing. As described in the previous chapter, there is far greater resistance to unions by private sector employers who often face intense competitive pressures from nonunion firms than by public employers who are much less concerned about competition. Also, public employers are aware of the negative political consequences of discharging union supporters or threatening to close operations, and they cannot shift operations overseas, a common threat during private sector organizing.[68] However, public employers can avoid unionization by simply eliminating the rights of public workers to unionize. This was done by the governors in Indiana and Missouri in 2005, and if it happens in other states it would greatly accelerate the decline in public sector union membership and density.[69] Membership has been declining slowly, as public employers contract out government jobs (i.e., have some work such as maintenance or security done by private companies) or privatize operations (turn the operation of entire facilities, such as prisons, hospitals, or water treatment plants, over to private firms).

Unionism is certainly not a hallmark of our economy. There are no industries or occupations in which a majority of workers are union members. Density is greater for men than for women, but only 13.8 percent of men are unionized, compared to 11.1 percent for women. Black or African American workers have a higher density rate than White, Asian, or Hispanic workers but their percentage is also very low (15.1 percent for Black or African American, 12.2 percent for White, 11.4 percent for Asian, and 10.1 percent for Hispanic). In industries that we usually think of as the strongholds of unionism, density rates are surprisingly low—only

Table 2.3   Union Membership and Union Density, 2004

Characteristic	Membership (000s)	Density[a] (in Percentages)
Sex		
Male	8,878	13.8
Female	6,593	11.1
Total	15,472	12.5
Age		
16 to 24 years	890	4.7
25 to 34 years	2,982	10.6
35 to 44 years	4,173	13.7
45 to 54 years	4,771	17.0
55 to 64 years	2,390	16.8
65 years and older	264	7.5
Race		
White	12,381	12.2
Black or African American	2,130	15.1
Hispanic or Latino	1,676	10.1
Asian	603	11.4
Full- or part-time status		
Full-time workers	14,029	13.9
Part-time workers	1,406	6.4
Selected occupations		
Management	441	4.1
Education, training, and library	2,874	37.6
Health care practitioner and technical	762	12.6
Health care support	290	10.4
Sales	488	3.6
Office and administrative support	2,005	10.7
Production	1,485	16.3
Transportation and material moving	1,483	18.8
Protective services	1,059	37.3
Selected industries		
Private wage and salary workers	8,205	7.9

(Continued)

Table 2.3 (Continued)

Agriculture	23	2.2
Nonagricultural industries	8,182	8.0
Mining	57	11.4
Construction	1,110	14.7
Manufacturing	2,036	12.9
Durable goods	1,316	13.3
Nondurable goods	720	12.3
Transportation and public utilities	1,218	24.9
Transportation and warehousing	976	24.2
Utilities	241	28.4
Wholesale and retail trade	1,028	5.5
Wholesale trade	189	4.6
Retail trade	839	5.7
Financial activities	171	2.0
Professional and business services	246	2.3
Education and health services	1,405	8.3
Leisure and hospitality	319	3.1
Government workers	7,267	36.4
Federal	985	29.9
State	1,751	30.7
Local	4,532	41.3

Source: U.S. Department of Labor, Bureau of Labor Statistics. (2005). *Union members in 2004.* Press release USDL 05-112, Tables 1 and 3.

a. Density is union membership as a percentage of employed wage and salary workers.

11.4 percent in mining, 12.9 percent in manufacturing, and 14.7 percent in construction.

Table 2.4 shows covered nonmembers—workers who are covered by collective bargaining agreements but did not join the union that represents them.[70] Some pay partial dues called an *agency fee* that can range from 20 to 80 percent of regular dues for the services of their bargaining agents. Others pay no dues at all.[71] Unions are required by law to represent equally and fairly all workers covered by their collective agreements

Table 2.4   Nonmembers Covered by Collective Bargaining
                     Agreements, 2004

Sector	Nonmembers (000s)	Nonmembers as a Percentage of All Covered Workers
Private sector	751	8.4
Public sector	863	10.6
Federal	168	14.6
State	210	10.7
Local	485	9.7
Public and private	1,615	9.5

Source: U.S. Department of Labor, Bureau of Labor Statistics. (2005). *Union members in 2004.*
Press release USDL 05-112, Table 3.

whether or not they are union members. They often negotiate clauses in their collective agreement—*union security clauses*—requiring workers to join and pay dues as a condition of continued employment. Nonetheless, there are about 1.6 million covered nonmembers, or about 1 for every 10 union members. In the private sector, 8.4 percent of workers covered by collective agreements are not union members; the percentage is higher in the public sector (10.6 percent), where compulsory union membership is often prohibited, and it is highest in federal employment, where it is explicitly prohibited.[72]

Table 2.5 shows union density rates by state. New York State (25.3 percent) was the only state with more than a quarter of its workforce in unions. State size or the extent of its industrialization did not affect union density. Low and high density rates were found in large as well as in small states, and in states with manufacturing bases as well those that are agricultural or service oriented. The more heavily unionized states, aside from New York, were Hawaii (23.7 percent), Michigan (21.6 percent), Alaska (20.1 percent), and Washington (19.3 percent). The least unionized states were North Carolina (2.7 percent), South Carolina (3.0 percent), Arkansas (4.8 percent), Mississippi (4.8 percent), and Texas (5.0 percent). Union density was less than 10.0 percent in half of the states. Some states that we usually think of as bastions of union power actually have low density rates; for example, density was only 15.0 percent in Pennsylvania, 15.2 percent in Ohio, 16.5 percent in California, and 19.8 percent in New Jersey. Also, as we might expect, density rates are low in the Southern states, where there is little tradition of unionism and where union organizers are strongly

Table 2.5   Union Density by State, 2004

State	Density[a] (in Percentages)
Alabama	9.7
Alaska	20.1
Arizona	6.3
Arkansas	4.8
California	16.5
Colorado	8.4
Connecticut	15.3
Delaware	12.4
District of Columbia	12.7
Florida	6.0
Georgia	6.4
Hawaii	23.7
Idaho	5.8
Illinois	16.8
Indiana	11.4
Iowa	10.5
Kansas	8.4
Kentucky	9.6
Louisiana	7.6
Maine	11.3
Maryland	10.9
Massachusetts	13.5
Michigan	21.6
Minnesota	17.5
Mississippi	4.8
Missouri	12.4
Montana	11.7
Nebraska	8.3
Nevada	12.5
New Hampshire	9.9
New Jersey	19.8
New Mexico	6.7
New York	25.3
North Carolina	2.7
North Dakota	7.7
Ohio	15.2
Oklahoma	6.1
Oregon	15.2
Pennsylvania	15.0
Rhode Island	16.3
South Carolina	3.0

(Continued)

Table 2.5 (Continued)

South Dakota	6.0
Tennessee	6.7
Texas	5.0
Utah	5.8
Vermont	9.8
Virginia	5.3
Washington	19.3
West Virginia	14.2
Wisconsin	16.0
Wyoming	8.0

Source: U.S. Department of Labor, Bureau of Labor Statistics. (2005). *Union members in 2004.* Press release USDL 05-112, Table 5.

a. Density is union membership as a percentage of employed wage and salary earners.

resisted by employers, but they are also low throughout the Midwest and the Southwest.

Changes in union membership and density over the years are shown in Tables 2.6 and 2.7 and Figures 2.1, 2.2, and 2.3. The steep decline is obvious. Union membership expanded rapidly in the 1930s and through the 1940s, then stabilized, and fell sharply through the late 1970s, the 1980s, and the 1990s. The decline in private sector membership was initially masked by public sector growth, but it appeared when the public sector stabilized in the 1990s. Unions have lost more than 5 million members since 1980, and aggregate union density dropped from 23.2 percent to 12.5 percent. To put this in perspective, these tables and figures show losses that are equivalent to the disappearance of seven major unions, each the size of the Auto Workers.

The plight of American unions becomes even more apparent when we look at union density and collective bargaining coverage in other developed countries. Table 2.8 shows that the United States is not only near the bottom of the list (only France and Korea have lower density rates) but that it is possible for some countries to have low union density and still have influential union movements because large portions of the workforce are covered by collective bargaining agreements (e.g., France has a density rate of only 10 percent but 93 percent of the workforce is covered

Table 2.6   Union Membership and Union Density in the Private and Public
Sectors, 1975–2004

	Membership (000s)		Density[a] (in Percentages)	
Year	Private Sector	Public Sector	Private Sector	Public Sector
1975	13,177	3,601	21.5	24.8
1976	13,614	3,790	21.3	25.4
1977	14,341	4,995	21.7	32.8
1978	14,425	5,124	20.7	33.3
1979	15,118	5,868	21.2	37.0
1980	14,332	5,764	20.1	35.9
1981	13,944	5,190	18.7	34.3
1982[b]				
1983	11,980	5,737	16.5	36.7
1984	11,684	5.656	15.3	35.7
1985	11,253	5,743	14.3	35.7
1986	11,085	5,891	13.8	35.9
1987	10,857	6,056	13.2	35.9
1988	10,702	6,299	12.7	36.6
1989	10,536	6,424	12.3	36.7
1990	10,255	6,485	11.9	36.5
1991	9,937	6,632	11.7	36.9
1992	9,737	6,653	11.4	36.6
1993	9,580	7,018	11.1	37.7
1994	9,649	7,091	10.8	38.7
1995	9,432	6,927	10.3	37.7
1996	9,415	6,854	10.0	37.6
1997	9,363	6,747	9.7	37.2
1998	9,306	6,905	9.5	37.5
1999	9,419	7,058	9.4	37.3
2000	9,148	7,111	9.0	37.5
2001	9,141	7,148	9.0	37.4
2002	8,756	7,351	8.5	37.5
2003	8,452	7,324	8.2	37.2
2004	8,205	7,267	7.9	36.4

Source: 1975–2002: www.trinity.edu/bhirsch/unionstats.htm; 2004: U.S. Department of Labor, Bureau of Labor Statistics, *Union members in 2004*, www.bls.gov/news.release/union2htm.

a. Density is union membership as a percentage of employed wage and salary earners.

b. In 1982, union membership data were not collected in the survey.

Table 2.7   Union Membership and Union Density, Selected Years

Year	Membership (000s)	Density[a] (in Percentages)
1950	14,294	31.6
1955	16,126	35.1
1960	15,516	28.6
1965	18,269	30.1
1970	20,990	29.6
1975	22,207	28.9
1980	20,968	23.2
1985	16,996	17.4
1990	16,740	15.2
1995	16,360	14.9
2000	16,258	13.5
2004	15,472	12.5

Source: 1950–2000: www.trinity.edu/bhirsch/unionstats.htm; 2004: U.S. Department of Labor, Bureau of Labor Statistics. (2005). *Union members in 2004*. Press release USDL 05-112, Table 1.

a. Density is union membership as a percentage of employed wage and salary earners.

by collective agreements, and Spain has a density rate of 15 percent and coverage of 83 percent). Coverage can far exceed density when many nonunion employers voluntarily apply the terms of collective agreements to their workers, or when labor laws extend collective agreements to all workers in an industry or area regardless of their union membership. Where this is not done, low union density translates into low collective agreement coverage (e.g., Korea, Japan, and the United States).[73]

The high union density rates shown in Table 2.8 (in 5 of the 25 countries, density was over 50 percent, and it exceeded 30 percent in 10 countries) are the result of several factors. A comparative analysis by Bruce Western shows that countries with the highest rates of union density tend to have centralized collective bargaining systems (bargaining occurs on industry and regional levels, and therefore it is hard for employers to avoid dealing with unions); unions participate in the administration of unemployment insurance systems (so unions maintain links with unemployed members and also appear to play an important societal role beyond bargaining); and unions have close ties to political parties that promote workers' interests (ensuring that the laws or organizing and bargaining help rather than hinder unions).[74] American unions do not enjoy these conditions or the extension of collective agreements to

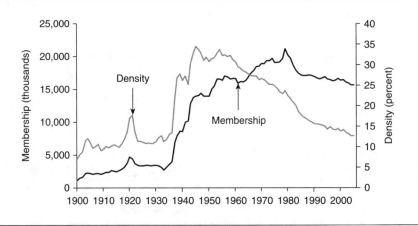

Figure 2.1   Union Membership and Union Density,[a] 1900–2004

Source: 1900–1995: Freeman, R. B. (1997). Spurts in union growth: Defining moments and social processes. In M. D. Bordo, C. Goldin, and E. N. White (Eds.), *The defining moment: The Great Depression and the American economy in the twentieth century.* Chicago: University of Chicago Press, pp. 291–293; 1996–2004: U.S. Department of Labor. *Union membership*, various years.

a. Density is the percentage of nonagricultural workers in unions.

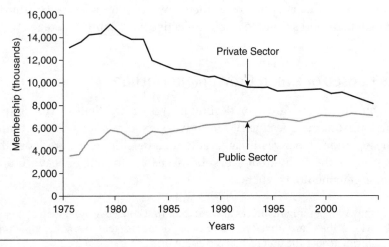

Figure 2.2   Union Membership in the Private and Public Sectors, 1975-2004

Source: 1975–2002: www.trinity.edu/bhirsch/unionststs.htm; 2003–2004: U.S. Department of Labor, Bureau of Labor Statistics. (2005). *Union members in 2004.* Press release USDL 05-112, Table 1.

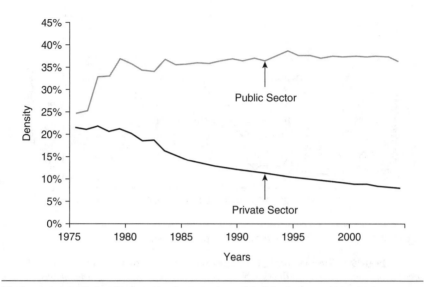

Figure 2.3   Union Density in the Private and Public Sectors, 1975–2004

Source: 1975–2002: www.trinity.edu/bhirsch/unionststs.htm; 2003-2004: U.S. Department of Labor, Bureau of Labor Statistics. (2005). *Union members in 2004*. Press release USDL 05-112, 2005, Table 1.

nonmembers; this is apparent in their low ranking in Table 2.8 (third to last in density and second to last in collective bargaining coverage).

The Causes of Union Growth and Decline

Why did unions grow or decline in the United States? This is quite different from the question, Why do workers join unions or select union representation? Changes in aggregate membership levels are more than the sum of the individual workers' decisions to join or leave unions. Unions gain members when

a. they win organizing drives and get their first collective agreements;
b. where there are already collective agreements, the covered nonmembers decide to join the unions that represent them;
c. employment expands in unionized firms and the newly hired workers join unions; or
d. unionized companies extend collective bargaining agreements to the workers at new operations.

Table 2.8   Union Density and Collective Bargaining Coverage
in Selected Countries, 2003 (in Percentages)

Country	Density	Collective Bargaining Coverage
Sweden	81	93
Finland	76	93
Denmark	74	83
Belgium	56	93
Norway	54	73
Austria	37	98
Slovak Republic	36	53
Italy	35	83
Luxembourg	34	63
United Kingdom	31	33
Canada	28	32
Czech Republic	27	28
Australia	25	83
Germany	25	68
Portugal	24	83
Netherlands	23	83
New Zealand	23	28
Japan	22	18
Hungary	20	33
Switzerland	18	43
Spain	15	83
Poland	15	43
United States	*13*	*14*
Korea	12	13
France	10	93

Source: Organization for Economic Cooperation and Development. (2004). *OECD employment outlook*. Chapter 3, Striking facts, chart 3.4, www.oecd.org/document/12/0,2340;en_2469.html.

Note: Figures are rounded to the nearest percent.

Unions lose members when

a. employment declines in unionized firms because of plant closures, the introduction of new production technologies, and transfers of work overseas or to domestic nonunion operations; or

b. workers decide to no longer be represented by their unions and decertify them as bargaining agents (essentially organizing drives in reverse).[75]

We can think of union growth as analogous to being on a treadmill; a person has to walk or run at a certain pace just to remain at the same place. For unions to expand, the factors contributing to union growth must more than offset those leading to union decline. Unions might organize many new members, but if this only offsets losses, unions will be at a steady state—neither growing nor declining. How fast do unions have to go just to stand still? Richard B. Freeman concluded: "To balance off the loss of members due to the normal birth and death of firms and changes in employment in union and nonunion workplaces . . . unions must add about 500,000 new members annually. To add a point of union density, unions must organize close to 1 million new members. The actual number of new unionists [added in each of recent years] was a bit over 150,000."[76]

There is a huge amount of research on union growth and decline, but the general consensus is that there are four primary causes: structural shifts in the labor force, employer opposition, the unions' lack of desire and ability to organize, and the failure of the law of organizing.[77]

Structural shifts in the labor force. Many blame shifts in employment for declining union membership. It seems perfectly logical that union membership should decline as employment falls in the highly unionized sectors and employment grows in traditionally nonunion areas. This has been stated in terms of occupations (fewer production jobs, more technical jobs), industries (fewer manufacturing jobs, more service jobs), gender (more women in the labor force), and part-time/full-time status (more part-time jobs). "Conventional wisdom asserts that some workers are simply union prone while others are not and that union density [and union membership] falls because of a lack of interest among the employees in emerging sectors of the labor force and the declining importance of traditional union strongholds."[78]

Despite its apparent logic and simplicity, the structural shift explanation is not very powerful. Analyses of union membership data show that structural shifts only account for a quarter to a third of the decline in union membership.[79] Moreover, this explanation is based on the unsupported assumption that workers in traditionally nonunion sectors have a deep and enduring antipathy toward unions. The historical record shows otherwise. We saw in the preceding chapter that there were spurts in the unionization of mass production workers in the 1930s and public sector workers in the 1960s and 1970s—two groups that were once assumed to be unreceptive toward unions. Among the most heavily unionized workers are teachers (53 percent unionized);[80] because teachers are professional, public sector workers who are mostly women, many once thought that they would be "union resistant." Also, surveys show that unionization has *not* fallen into disfavor with the contemporary workforce—a third of nonunion workers have consistently said that they would vote for union representation if given the chance.[81]

As an explanation of union growth and decline, structural shifts may not be particularly powerful, but it does give us a good sense of the enormity of the unions' organizing task. A 1998 AFL-CIO survey found that industries with declining employment were 20 percent unionized, but expanding ones were only 9 percent unionized. In the highest growth sectors—retail, business and personal services, and finance and insurance—the percentage of union members was 5 percent or less.[82] If unions are to grow, the report concluded, there must be a massive increase in organizing because the declining employment of union members is not being offset by membership gains in expanding sectors. Returning to the analogy we used earlier, unions are running slower than the treadmill is moving.

Structural shifts also suggest the tremendous impact of globalization on unions. Job losses are greatest in the more heavily unionized manufacturing sector as work is transferred overseas by American firms or lost to lower-cost foreign producers.[83] Thus, unions bear the brunt of the impact of globalization. The contraction of unionized employment makes the treadmill move faster.

Employer opposition. Researchers consistently identify employer opposition to unionization as a primary cause of union decline. Opposition, which reduces union organizing success while increasing organizing costs,[84] is now intense and widespread. About 80 percent of employers hire outside consultants to run campaigns against organizing unions and have their supervisors give antiunion messages to workers. Nearly a third of employers discharge union supporters during organizing drives.[85] It has also become fairly common for employers to threaten to close plants if unions are selected and to increase wages and benefits if unions are rejected, although law prohibits both tactics. A study of organizing by Bronfenbrenner and Hickey found that in 1997–2002 "the overwhelming majority of employers aggressively opposed union organizing efforts through a combination of threats, discharges . . . unscheduled unilateral changes in wages and benefits, and surveillance." For example, in half of the organizing drives employers made threats of partial or full plant closures, and in a quarter employers discharged workers for union activities. These tactics were largely effective. When employers were aggressively antiunion, the union win rate declined by 10 to 20 percent.[86]

Also, some employers choose to fight unionization in benign but nonetheless effective ways; they improve company communications, identify and resolve workers' grievances quickly, and adjust wages and benefits to the levels of unionized firms—all with the intent of reducing the attractiveness of unions to workers but without giving workers any legal status in decision making.[87]

Employers have intensified their opposition to union organizing over the past two decades because they believe that unions and collective bargaining hamper their ability to compete globally by imposing restrictive work rules, low productivity, and high labor costs. They justify fighting against unions by saying that only nonunion companies can survive in the long run in a highly competitive environment.

Unions' lack of desire and ability to organize. Although structural shifts and employer opposition contribute to union decline, there is no doubt that unions themselves have to shoulder part of the blame for their dilemma. Unions failed to respond to the employers' antiunion offensive of the 1980s and were too conservative and defensive in organizing and bargaining for nearly two decades.[88] They were concerned mostly with developing organizing tactics (ways to convince workers to vote for unions) rather than strategies for organizing industries and regions where they can maximize bargaining strength and attract additional members.[89]

The AFL-CIO's leadership has admonished its affiliated unions to "develop a culture of organizing," coordinate their organizing drives, and aim for a million new members each year.[90] Some union leaders have called for the creation of a special AFL-CIO organizing fund of $2 billion over five years.[91]

Very few unions, perhaps only a half dozen, are active and successful in organizing.[92] This is understandable given the high cost of organizing—about $2,000 for each new member, or about $1 billion simply to stabilize union density.[93] As their membership continued to decline, the unions were burdened with fixed costs (e.g., maintaining headquarters and holding conventions) as well as the costs of servicing the remaining members in bargaining and contract enforcement. Members were reluctant to approve of higher dues to increase organizing activity. As a result, unions were caught in a vicious circle—membership losses prevented unions from financing new organizing, and this failure to organize led to further membership losses.[94]

Failure of the law of organizing. Employer opposition makes organizing more difficult and costly, causing many unions to retreat from the organizing field. Changes in labor laws could break the vicious circle confounding unions. The law cannot cause union growth (unions themselves must do the organizing), but it can establish the conditions for it.[95]

Over the years, there have been many proposals for labor law reform based on the premise that the laws are not doing what they were intended to do.[96] Rather than encouraging collective bargaining and protecting workers who choose bargaining, labor laws "turned the process of unionization into a legalistic business, in which firms and union organizers battle before the NLRB [National Labor Relations Board] and courts as part of the election process."[97] The law should discourage employer misconduct during organizing campaigns, but by most accounts, this is not happening.[98] Union certification elections (discussed in detail in the next section) have become forums for employer opposition, and this increases the time and costs that unions must devote to organizing. Employers are not deterred from discharging union supporters during organizing because only minor remedies can be imposed—employers must merely reinstate workers with back pay, a small price for intimidating the workers so they reject unionism. Employers are required to bargain in good faith with newly certified unions but they are not compelled to reach agreements, and the animosity from the organizing drive often carries over into first-time bargaining (around a third of unions that are certified fail to get their first collective agreements).[99]

Proponents of labor law reform ask for tougher penalties for employer misconduct and faster organizing drives, for example, by having elections soon after unions file petitions.[100] Some union leaders demand labor law reform before there are renewed organizing efforts; others believe unions must first organize to achieve the political power needed to change the organizing process.[101] One thing that is clear in this debate is that union membership has fallen so far and so fast that unions must not only be more successful in organizing but also be much more active.

How Unions Organize

The union's goal in organizing is to gain sufficient support from workers to become their bargaining agent and start negotiations with employers. Essentially, unions must persuade workers that they could gain more than they could lose by being represented in collective bargaining.

Workers are attracted to union representation if they are dissatisfied with working conditions and wages and believe that as individuals they do not have the power to bring about improvement.[102] Most workers think about unionism in a pragmatic way—estimating and comparing its costs and benefits—so unions must point to bargaining achievements in similar workplaces.[103]

Employers have an inherent advantage during organizing campaigns because they are in constant contact with the workers and only have to persuade them to stay with the status quo—to reject union representation and to continue to let their employer make decisions. Recognizing that most workers are hesitant to choose change, employers call the union an "outside organization" that is only interested in collecting dues, creating a hostile relationship with managers, and going on irresponsible and calamitous strikes.[104] Employers also ask for a second chance; they admit that that their actions may have fueled the workers' interest in unionization and then say they are willing to set things straight if, and only if, the union is rejected.

During organizing campaigns, some workers will be early and fervent union supporters, some will oppose the union no matter what is said or done, and others will be undecided. The campaign focuses on the undecided workers who must be identified and converted to union supporters. To do this, organizers should do more than distribute leaflets and hold meetings; they must make personal contact with undecided workers and create a strong union presence at the workplace. Workers must sense that they are actually organizing themselves and determining what the union will demand in bargaining. The union cannot be seen as an outsider or an intruder in the workplace.[105] Furthermore, workers must favor unionization not only in principle but also in practice—they must think well of the specific union and its organizers. Organizing drives have been lost when workers felt that union organizers and union supporters had harassed them to vote pro-union or seemed too strike prone and disrespectful of the company.[106]

Union organizers coordinate organizing campaigns. Organizers are full-time union staff members who are trained in organizing tactics, labor law, communication skills, negotiations, and labor history. They are the contact persons for workers seeking union representation and the leaders of the in-plant organizing committees that collect union membership cards. Organizers encourage participation in campaigns by union members at nearby plants and pro-union activists in the local community (e.g., clergy and students).[107] But they and their allies cannot carry the whole campaign, and research has shown that there must be extensive participation by the workers themselves (selling the concept of unionism and getting out the vote) if the campaign is to be successful.[108]

There are four basic approaches to organizing workers and gaining the status of bargaining agent: *voluntary recognition, card check/neutrality, private elections,* and *labor board certification.*[109] At some point during most organizing drives, unions ask employers to voluntarily recognize them as bargaining agents and enter into negotiations. They do not expect to get recognition and employers rarely grant it unless the union already represents workers at most of the employer's other operations. The rejection of a recognition request places the burden on the union to prove it has majority support. There are several ways to do this.

In the card check/neutrality approach, unions try to get the most favorable conditions to demonstrate support from workers. They pressure employers to remain neutral during the organizing campaign; they can do this by threatening employers with strikes, consumer boycotts, negative publicity in the local community or among stockholders, and lawsuits over working conditions and pay discrimination. They ask employers to accept signed membership cards as proof of the workers' support for unionization, bypassing the certification election procedures of the labor board. Unions will argue that organizing is a matter between themselves and the workers—there is no need for employer involvement. Only unions have the burden of demonstrating majority support (employers do not have to), and they should be able to prove a majority with signed membership cards rather than elections.[110] Employers often respond to this request by arguing that secret ballot elections, not card checks, are free of coercion and good indicators of the workers' preferences and that workers can make an informed decision only after hearing the employers' side as well as the unions'. They may claim that they are being harassed into agreeing to neutrality and liken it to a "gag order" for one side only.[111]

If it looks like employers will not agree to card check/neutrality, unions may drop their demands for it and agree instead to have their majority support demonstrated through secret ballot elections conducted by a private neutral organization, such as the American Arbitration Association. Balloting can take place at work or through the mail.

Private elections and card check/neutrality account for roughly half of union organizing. They are often used when employers cannot resist them, for example, when employers (such as those in retailing and hotels) deal directly with the public and are sensitive to threats of consumer boycotts and adverse publicity.[112]

The final route for achieving bargaining status is the certification election process of the National Labor Relations Board.[113] When unions apply for certification as bargaining agents, the NLRB conducts preelection investigations to determine if it has jurisdiction (e.g., by asking whether the workers are covered by the National Labor Relations Act[114]), if the petition is filed in a proper and timely manner, if the bargaining unit (the jobs to be covered under a collective agreement) that is sought by the union is appropriate (e.g., do the workers share a community of interest?), and if workers have a substantial interest in union representation. A substantial interest is shown when at least 30 percent of the workers sign cards authorizing the union to represent them in collective bargaining.

After the NLRB accepts the petition and finds that adequate employee support is demonstrated, unions and employers may consent to elections, that is, agree to when and how elections will be conducted and who will be in the bargaining units. Elections will then be held in 30 to 45 days. But if employers contest election petitions, for example, by challenging the composition of bargaining units, hearings will be held on the undecided matters before the NLRB sets election dates.

Certification elections are secret-ballot contests usually held at workplaces and during work hours (though sometimes when workers are scattered they are conducted by mail). Voter turnout is high, often around 90 percent, because both management and the union try to get their supporters to vote so the outcome will be decisive. Workers are asked, "Do you wish to be represented for purpose of collective bargaining by XYZ union?" and they mark an x in one square for yes or in another for no. To win, unions must receive a simple majority—50 percent plus one—of those voting.[115] Unions and employers can file objections to election outcomes by charging misconduct (e.g., that their opponents seriously mislead or threaten workers) or by challenging the ballots of persons they believe should not have voted. When unions win elections, they are certified as collective bargaining agents and serve notice to the employers to commence bargaining.[116] If unions lose elections, they cannot petition again for at least another year.

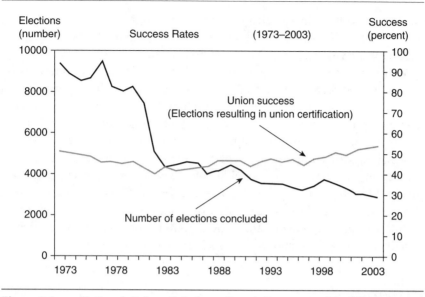

Figure 2.4   National Labor Relations Board Representation Elections and Union Success Rates, 1973–2003

Source: U.S. National Labor Relations Board, *Annual reports for the Fiscal Years 1983, 1993 and 2003*. Washington, DC: Government Printing Office.

Figure 2.4 shows the decline in union organizing activity through representation elections. The annual number of elections was fairly high through the 1970s, but fell sharply in the early 1980s, and remained low since. Union success rates varied within a fairly narrow range, about 40 to 55 percent, and did not fall when election activity suddenly dropped off. In all likelihood, unions found that the only way they could maintain their success rate was by having fewer election contests, that is, by moving organizing drives to the election stage only if they felt there was a good chance of winning. Despite this, union success is not very impressive. Unions are the proactive party in organizing—they pick where and when there will be certification elections, yet they win only around half of the elections.[117]

There is some evidence that election activity is also lower because unions have been bypassing elections, considering them too slow, costly, and contentious. One analysis found that two major organizing unions, UNITE and HERE, had 112 representation elections in 1997 but only 21 in

2003, despite their increased membership through new organizing. The leaders of both unions stated that they were relying on card-check certification for the vast majority of organizing drives.[118]

We need to put organizing gains in perspective. Over the past few years, unions gained fewer than 100,000 new members annually through representation elections. If unions could somehow match this figure with gains from other approaches, it would still be less than half the number needed (500,000 new members) to offset membership losses. The inevitable conclusion is that nothing short of a tremendous increase in organizing activity by whichever way possible could reverse union decline. Even a rebound to the pre-1982 level of representation elections would only stabilize union membership. For contemporary unions, this is the discouraging reality of union organizing and growth. After more than two decades of sustained losses, there may be too much ground to make up.

Conclusions

Our review of union structure and growth shows the two primary characteristics of the unions in America: complexity and decline. First, unions are complex, multilayered organizations that may belong to a federation, having alternative forms (i.e., national and local independent unions); undergo mergers that can range from amalgamations to absorptions or affiliations; and most often, are no longer confined in organizing by their membership jurisdictions. At the same time, unions in general have weathered severe membership losses; the tables and figures in this chapter show different faces of this decline. In later chapters, we ask what must be done for unions to revive themselves and what the unions of the future might look like.

Notes

1.   Manon, H. (2004). Union membership in Canada, 2004. *Workplace Gazette*, 5, pp. 42–78. Canadian sections of U.S.-based unions often enjoy autonomy in administrative and financial matters, much more so than in the past because of threats of secession over the past two decades. For example, see Chaison, G., and Rose, J. B. (1989). Unions: Growth, structure and internal dynamics. In J. C. Anderson, M. Gunderson, and A. Ponak (Eds.), *Union-management relations in Canada* (2nd ed.). Toronto: Addison-Wesley, pp. 125–154. Canadian membership is

not counted in the membership figures used in this chapter to show union growth and decline in the United States.

2. Gifford, C. (2002). *Directory of U.S. labor organizations, 2002.* Washington, DC: Bureau of National Affairs. Union membership figures are for 2001. The figures are for AFL-CIO affiliates and do not include the unaffiliated National Education Association (NEA). The NEA had 2,530,000 members in 1991. Although by far the largest union, the NEA does not represent all of its members in collective bargaining but serves as a professional association for about half of its members, representing their interests in consultations with school boards.

3. Shabecoff, P. (1980, May 11). Big labor, little labor. *New York Times,* p. 19; Chaison, G. (1995). Reforming and rationalizing union structure: New directions and unanswered questions. Paper presented at the Second International Conference on Emerging Union Structures, Stockholm, Sweden.

4. Bernstein, A. (2004, September 13). Can this man save labor? *Business Week,* pp. 80–88.

5. The recent loss of bargaining power by the pilots was the result of the serious financial difficulty of the major airlines and their recourse to concessionary bargaining and bankruptcy, discussed in Chapter 4, on collective bargaining, rather than their size.

6. Sanger, D., and Greenfield, S. (2002, October 1). West Coast ports prepare to reopen after Bush's intervention. *New York Times,* p. A1.

7. Strauss, G. (1993). Issues in union structure. In S. Bacharach, R. Seeber, and D. Walsh (Eds.), *Research in the sociology of organizations.* Greenwich, CT: JAI, pp. 1–49; Chaison (1995); Chaison, G. (1996). *Union mergers in hard times: The view from five countries.* Ithaca, NY: Cornell University Press.

8. Craft, D., and Peck, T. W. (1998). *Profiles of American labor unions.* Farmington Hill, MI: Gale Research.

9. For reviews of the evolution of company unions and the formation of local unaffiliated (independent) unions, see Jacoby, S. M. (1998). *Modern manors: Welfare capitalism since the New Deal.* Princeton, NJ: Princeton University Press; Jacoby, S. M. (2001). Unnatural extinction: The rise and fall of independent local unions. *Industrial Relations,* 40, pp. 377–404; Shostak, A. B. (1962). *America's forgotten labor organization.* Princeton, NJ: Princeton University, Department of Economics, Industrial Relations Section.

10. Northwest flight attendants to switch unions. (2003, June 20). *New York Times,* p. C4; Fedor, L. (2003, June 20). Northwest flight attendants break away from Teamsters. *Minneapolis Star Tribune,* pp. A1, A11.

11. Wong, E. (2003, June 15). Union sees opening in United's turmoil. *New York Times,* pp. C1, C4. This unaffiliated union also displaced national unions—the Machinists, the Teamsters, the Transport Workers—at other airlines.

12. For a discussion of the evolution of independent local unions, see Jacoby (2001). The classic study of independent local unions is Shostak (1962).

13.   Gifford (2002), p. 44.

14.   Craft and Peck (1998).

15.   Gifford (2002).

16.   www.uswa.org.

17.   www.seiu.org.

18.   www.ilaunion.org.

19.   www.alpa.org.

20.   Chaison, G. (1986). *When unions merge.* Lexington, MA: Lexington Books.

21.   For an updated and comprehensive description of the structure and activities of the AFL-CIO, see the federation's web page: www.aflcio.org.

22.   Sloan, A. A., and Witney, F. (2001). *Labor relations* (10th ed.). Upper Saddle River, NJ: Prentice Hall, p. 125. Although the federation does not organize and represent workers, it does charter local unions (called directly affiliated labor unions) that act as bargaining agents. Members of directly affiliated labor unions are usually transferred over to the affiliated national union that typically organizes workers in their industry or occupation.

23.   See the constitution of the AFL-CIO for details of fees and governing structures: www.aflcio.org/aboutaflcio/about/constitution.

24.   Bernstein, A. (2003, March 17). Palace coup at the AFL-CIO: In a rebuke to Sweeney, activists hope to reshape the federation. *Business Week*, p. 78; Greenhouse, S. (2003, March 9). Worried about labor's waning strength, union presidents form advisory committee. *New York Times*, p. 22. The executive committee is composed of the presidents of the AFL-CIO's 10 largest unions and the presidents of 7 smaller unions selected by the AFL-CIO president. It also includes the AFL-CIO president, vice president, and secretary-treasurer. The reported intent of the committee was to increase affiliates' influence over AFL-CIO policy, particularly in regard to organizing and politics.

25.   For example, see the discussion of the AFL-CIO's Union Cities program that encourages labor councils to play a central role in the revival of organizing, in Eckstein, E. (2001). Putting organizing back into labor councils. *WorkingUSA*, 5, pp. 124–125. Eckstein (2001, p. 124) quotes a union activist's appraisal of the role of labor councils: "A labor council, with its multiple relationships, can link politics and organizing, creating a better climate to win organizing drives. At the same time, organizing can electrify an organizing council, sparking it into action."

26.   For a description of the organization of the AFL-CIO, see the federation's web page: www.aflcio.org/aboutaflcio/about/howworks.

27.   www.workingamerica.org; Greenhouse, S. (2004, July 11). Labor federation looks beyond unions for supporters. *New York Times*, p. 18.

28.   Greenhouse, S. (2005, March 4). Labor chief emerges from meeting a winner, but for how long? *New York Times*, p. A13; Cummings, J. (2005, March 3). AFL-CIO leader beats back revolt. *Wall Street Journal*, p. A3; Edsall, T. B. (2005, January 4). AFL-CIO chief facing challenges from labor's left. *Washington Post*, p. A5;

Greenhouse, S. (2005, April 29). Facing dissent, labor chief offers a plan for growth. *New York Times*, p. A18; Greenhouse, S. (2005, June 16). Five top union leaders join forces, raising threat of labor rift. *New York Times*, p. A19. In July 2005, the leaders of the Service Employees, Teamsters, UNITE HERE, the Laborers International Union, and the United Food and Commercial Workers demanded that the AFL-CIO reallocate funds to revive organizing and reduce the number of small affiliated unions through mergers. These unions, formed in an alliance called the Change to Win Coalition, had about one-third of the AFL-CIO's members. Greenhouse, S. (2005, July 22). Among dissident union leaders, the backgrounds may vary but the vision is the same. *New York Times*, p. A15. The group's plan for union revival and its constitution are found in its website: www.changetowin.org.

29. Chaison (1996).

30. Bernstein (2004), p. 82. For examples of criticism of federation leadership, see Greenhouse. (2003, March 9); Slaughter, J. (1999). The new AFL-CIO: No salvation for the working stiff. In R. M. Tillman and M. S. Cummings (Eds.), *The transformation of U.S. unions: Voices, visions, and strategies from the grass-roots*. Boulder, CO: Lynne Rienner, pp. 49–60. For a review of the efforts of John Sweeney and the AFL-CIO under his leadership, see, for example, Aronowitz, S. (2001). Labor on trial: Assessing Sweeney's record. *WorkingUSA*, 5, pp. 10–31.

31. Greenhouse, S. (2004, August 1). Though united in politics, unions face internal turmoil. *New York Times*, p. A13; Greenhouse, S. (2004, November 10). Largest union issues call for major changes. *New York Times*, p. A16; Greenhouse, S. (2004, November 18). Unions resume debate over merging and power. *New York Times*, p. A24. The call for change in the federation was led by Andrew Stern, leader of the Service Employees International Union, and was derived from his union's proposal for union revival; Service Employees International Union. (2004, November). Unite to win: A 21st century plan to build new strength for working people. www.unitetowin.org. Strongly opposing the group of unions pressuring for change is Thomas Buffenbarger, leader of the Machinists. He complained: "The way they talk, it's my way or no way. If the rhetoric doesn't calm down, you'll see old alliances form and that might lead to recreating the old A.F.L. and old C.I.O." Greenhouse (2004, August 1), p. A13.

32. Barbash, J. (1956). *The practice of unionism*. New York: Harper and Row.

33. Article III, Jurisdiction, of the Constitution of the Laborers International Union of North America. www.liuna.org/Pages/legaldept/const/Consitution 2001/003.htm.

34. Article I, Objectives, of the Constitution of the International Brotherhood of Teamsters. www.teamster.org/about/constitution/article_ii_.htm.

35. Article II, Jurisdiction, of the Constitution of the International Brotherhood of Teamsters. www.teamster.org/about/constitution/article_ii_.htm.

36.   Article II, Jurisdiction. CWA Constitution as amended August 2002. (2002). Washington, DC: Communications Workers of America, p. 2.

37.   Article III, Eligibility, of the Constitution of the International Union. (2002). United Steelworkers of America. Pittsburgh, PA: United Steelworkers of America.

38.   Trade jurisdiction. www.bacweb.org/aboutbac/jurisdiction.htm.

39.   Article III, Membership, of the Constitution of the American Federation of State, County and Municipal Employees. www.afscme.org/about/const_04.html.

40.   Article II, Membership, of the Constitution of the Association of Flight Attendants. www.afanet.org/CB/ARTICLE_II.asp.

41.   Knight, D. M. (2002). The new paradigm of physician collective action. Shugharyt, Thomson, and Kilroy unpublished memo for the Office and Professional Employees International Union. www.lawmemo.com/emp/articles/physicians.htm.

42.   Lyman, R. (2003, June 18). It takes two for merger of actors' unions. *New York Times*, pp. B3, B8. The membership of the two unions overlap because many actors work on both filmed and videotaped productions. In 2003, the Screen Actors Guild had 117,000 members and the American Federation of Television and Radio Artists had 80,000 members—these figures include 45,000 members of both unions.

43.   Strauss (1993); Chaison (1995).

44.   Chaison, G. (1987). The recent expansion of union organizing jurisdictions. Working Paper no. 87–102, Graduate School of Management, Clark University, Worcester, MA; Chaison, G., and Dhavale, D. (1990). The changing scope of union organizing. *Journal of Labor Research*, 11, pp. 307–321.

45.   Service Employees International Union. (2003). *United we win.* Washington, DC: Service Employees International Unions, p. 5.

46.   Smallwood, S. (2003, January 17). United academic workers. *Chronicle of Higher Education*, pp. A8–A9; Smallwood, S. (2003, May 16). Organizers of TA union at Yale lose unofficial vote on representation. *Chronicle of Higher Education*, p. A12; Hoerr, J. (1997). *We can't eat prestige: The women who organized Harvard.* Philadelphia: Temple University Books. In contrast, the non–tenure track faculty (i.e., teaching assistants and adjunct or part-time teachers) at the University of Michigan voted in 2003 to be represented by a local organization affiliated with the Michigan Federation of Teachers and School Related Personnel, a section of the American Federation of Teachers. Their union is the traditional school staff representative in the state, with 34,000 members in school districts, community college, and universities, and includes the Detroit Public Schools. University of Michigan non–tenure track faculty vote yes for union. (2003, April 29). *PR Newswire.* It must be noted, however, that in July 2004, the National Labor Relations Board in the case of *Brown University* (342 NLRB No. 42, Brown University, 1-RC-21368) denied university teaching and research assistants the

protected right to join unions and bargain with their employers. A year later, the administration of New York University withdrew its recognition of the graduate students' union because the administration was no longer required to negotiate with it. Arenson, K. W. (2005, June 17). N.Y.U. moves to disband graduate students union. *New York Times*, p. B2.

47.   Chaison (1995, 1996). In May 1999, the AFL-CIO Executive Council adopted a statement calling on affiliated unions to focus their organizing efforts on the industry or occupation in which they are the major union. But the federation also had to recognize the extent of the affiliates' membership diversity and stated that although organizing in an industry should be used for long-term stability, it should not distract from organizing on a broader basis, particularly in those sectors where there was expanding employment and low union membership. Amber, M. (1999, May 10). Organizing: AFL-CIO urges affiliates to organize industries where they have density. *Daily Labor Report*, pp. A9–A10.

48.   For a description of the union merger process, see Chaison (1986). An international comparison of union merger causes, forms, frequency, and outcomes is found in Chaison (1996). A review of the state of research on union mergers is Chaison, G. (2004). Union mergers in the U.S. and abroad. *Journal of Labor Research*, 25, pp. 97–115.

49.   See Chaison (1986), pp. 43–90 for a review of the motivation to merge and the barriers to merger.

50.   Greenhouse, S. (2004, February 26). 2 key unions vote to accept plan to merge. *New York Times*, pp. C1, C6.

51.   Greenhouse, S. (2005, January 12). 2 large industrial unions plan to merge. *New York Times*, p. A18.

52.   This discussion assumes that each amalgamation combines two unions—the most common form. There are, however, some amalgamations that involve three, four, or even five unions, and these require extremely complex merger negotiations to combine several governing bodies and organizational structures. From 1955 to 1999, there were 20 amalgamations, including 2 of three unions and 1 of five unions. Chaison (1986, 1996), and Chaison, G. (2001). Union mergers and union revival: Are we asking too much or too little? In L. Turner, H. C. Katz, and R. W. Hurd (Eds.), *Rekindling the movement: Labor's quest for relevance in the twenty-first century*. Ithaca, NY: Cornell University Press, pp. 238–255.

53.   Chaison (1986).

54.   Bureau of National Affairs. (2002, April 26). New Jersey union affiliates with Machinists. *Daily Labor Report*, p. A12.

55.   Bureau of National Affairs. (2002, May 24). Merger of ALPA, FedEx pilots union scheduled to take effect on June 1. *Daily Labor Report*, p. A2.

56.   Bureau of National Affairs. (2002, October 10). AFT approves hygienist's group affiliation with the Illinois Federation of Teachers. *Daily Labor Report*, pp. A7–A8.

57. See Chaison (1986, 1996) for a review of the merger process and examples of the ways that mergers have been negotiated.

58. Chaison (1986).

59. For example, in the Screen Actors Guild (SAG) there was political opposition to its proposed merger with the American Federation of Television and Radio Artists (AFTRA) in 2003. The merger attempt failed when 57.8 percent of the SAG members voted in favor of merger (about 1,200 votes short of the 60 percent required by the union's constitution). The two unions had been discussing an amalgamation since the late 1930s. The merger was opposed mostly by the Hollywood-based members of SAG. AFTRA's compensation rates were lower than those of SAG, and merger opponents felt that the lower rates would prevail in a merged union. Bates, J. (2003, July 3). SAG, AFTRA may get another "take": The close vote provides hope for merger backers to consider new try. *Los Angeles Times*, sec. 3, p. 1.

60. Pakulski, G. (2003, June 4). Toledo, Ohio-based Flint Glass Workers vote to merge with Steelworkers. *The Blade* (Toledo), p. 1.

61. American Flint Glass Workers Union merges with the United Steelworkers. (2003, June 3). *Associate Press State and Local Wire*.

62. Chaison (1986, 1996, 2004).

63. Chaison (1996). For a plan to use mergers to streamline the labor movement while increasing union presence and strength in major industries, see Service Employees International Union (2003, 2004); Greenhouse (2004, November 18); Chaison, G. (2004, November 20). The union voice. *New York Times*. p. A20.

64. Chaison (1986).

65. Chaison (1986).

66. Chaison (1996), p. 496.

67. For a review of the concept of union density, see Rose, J., and Chaison, G. (1996). Linking union density and union effectiveness. *Industrial Relations*, 35, pp. 78–105.

68. Freeman, R. B. (1986). Unionism comes to the public sector. *Journal of Economic Literature*, 24, pp. 41–86; Freeman, R. B. (1988). Contraction and expansion: The divergence of private and public sector unionism in the United States. *Journal of Economic Perspectives*, 2, pp. 63–88.

69. Greenhouse, S. (2005, January 28). Membership in unions drops again. *New York Times*, p. A20.

70. Covered nonmembers have been called *free-riders* when they pay no dues and *cheap riders* when they pay partial dues. The partial dues cover the costs of representational activities (e.g., bargaining and grievance handling) as well as organizing in the same competitive market as the bargaining unit. McGolrick, S. (2002, November 13). Union dues: Organizing costs chargeable to nonmembers, Supreme Court says, letting ruling stand. *Daily Labor Report*, pp. AA1–AA2.

Chaison, G., and Dhavale, D. G. (1992). The choice between union membership and free-rider status. *Journal of Labor Research*, 13, pp. 355–369. The free-riders and cheap riders represent a tremendous organizing opportunity for unions because they are easy to locate and contact, they already work at unionized firms and are covered by collective agreements, and employers usually do not resist their union-ization because the union already has a presence at the workplace.

71.   The compulsory payment of partial or full dues is prohibited in the 22 states with right-to-work laws (Alabama, Arizona, Arkansas, Florida, Georgia, Idaho, Iowa, Kansas, Louisiana, Mississippi, Nebraska, Nevada, North Carolina, North Dakota, Oklahoma, South Carolina, South Dakota, Tennessee, Texas, Utah, Virginia, and Wyoming). In right-to-work law states, about one-fifth of the work-ers covered by collective agreements are not union members, compared to 9 per-cent in other states. Godard, J. (2003). Do labor laws matter? The density decline and convergence thesis revised. *Industrial Relations*, 42, pp. 458–492. In the 28 states *without* right-to-work laws, over 90 percent of collective bargaining agree-ments had union security clauses—clauses that require workers to join unions or pay dues as a condition of continued employment. Dau-Schmidt, K. G. (2001). Union security agreements under the National Labor Relations Act: The statute, the Constitution, and the Court's opinion in Beck. In S. Estreicher, H. C. Katz, and B. E. Kaufman (Eds.), *The internal governance and organizational effectiveness of unions*. New York: Kluwer Law International, pp. 199–227.

72.   Compulsory union membership may be prohibited, but surveys show that around 40 percent of workers did not know that they could refrain from being a union member and pay partial or no dues (Chaison and Dhavale, 1992).

73.   Organization for Economic Cooperation and Development. (2004). *OECD employment outlook*. Chapter 3, Striking facts. www.oecd.org/document/12/ 0,2340;en_6249.html. In Japan, workers who are union members, such as front-line supervisors, may not be covered by collective agreements; hence, density exceeds coverage.

74.   Western, B. (1997). *Between class and market: Post-war unionization in the capitalist democracies*. Princeton, NJ: Princeton University Press. For a discussion of union density in Europe and some concerns about how membership and density are measured, see European Foundation for the Improvement of Living and Working Conditions. (2005). *Trade union membership 1993–2003*. www.eiro .eurofound.eu.int/2004.html.

75.   Chaison, G., and Dhavale, D. (1990). A note on the severity of the decline in union organizing activity. *Industrial and Labor Relations Review*, 43, pp. 366–373.

76.   Freeman, R. B. (2004). The road to union renaissance in the United States. In P. V. Wunnava (Ed.), *The changing role of unions: New forms of representation*. Armonk, NY: M. E. Sharpe, pp. 3–4.

77.   For a review of research on the determinants of union growth and decline, see Chaison, G., and Rose, J. B. (1991). The macrodeterminants of union growth and

decline. In G. Strauss, D. G. Gallagher, and J. Fiorito (Eds.), *The state of the unions.* Madison, WI: Industrial Relations Research Association, pp. 3–46; Flanagan, F. (2005). Has management strangled U.S. unions? *Journal of Labor Research, 26,* pp. 33–61.

78.   Chaison and Rose (1991), p. 13.

79.   Chaison and Rose (1991).

80.   www.trinity.edu/bhirsch/unionstats.htm.

81.   Amber, M. (2002, August 30). Majority of nonunion workers say they would join unions, survey shows. *Daily Labor Report,* p. A11; Freeman, R. B., and Rogers, J. (1999). *What workers want.* Ithaca, NY: Cornell University Press. However, Freeman and Rogers (1999, p. 87) also found that the nonunion workers' preference for union representation declined when they were given a chance to join organizations that created less conflict with management than did unions. If given a choice between two hypothetical organizations, "one that management cooperated with in discussing issues but had no power to make decisions" and "one that had more power, but management opposed," 63 percent of respondents to a survey preferred the former (cooperation and no power) and only 22 percent selected more power but with management opposition. Apparently, the possibility of management opposition and conflict matters a great deal in the workers' decision, a point made later in this chapter's discussion of the forces behind the decline in union membership.

82.   Service Employees International Union (2003); Greenhouse, S. (1999, October 13). Union leaders see glum news in labor study. *New York Times,* p. A19. For a report on an organizing drive in a growth sector of the high-technology economy—the dot-com companies—see Greenhouse, S. (2001). The first unionization vote by dot.com workers is set. *New York Times,* p. C4. Apparently, employers in hi-tech use the same tactics as those in older declining sectors—intimidating and discharging union supporters during organizing drives—but they also claim that unions and collective bargaining deter the innovation, flexibility, and entrepreneurship needed to thrive in the industry and impose heavy costs on companies that have not even made profits.

83.   In the period 2001–2003, employment was down 15 percent in manufacturing and the majority of the 2.7 million jobs lost were in manufacturing, including 431,000 in the first eight months of 2003. Knowlton, B. (2003). Bush recognizes job losses and promises "better days ahead." www.nytimes.com/2003/09/01/politics/01 CND-Bush. Statement of Kathleen P. Utgoff, Commissioner, Bureau of Labor Statistics, before the Joint Economic Committee of the United States Congress. September 5, 2003. news@list.bls.gov.

84.   Chaison and Rose (1991), pp. 22–24. For a review of the factors causing the gap between private and public sector density, see Freeman (1986, 1988).

85.   Service Employees International Union (2003).

86.   Bronfenbrenner, K. and Hickey, R. (2003). *Blueprint for change: A national assessment of winning union organizing strategies.* Ithaca, NY: Cornell University, Office of Labor Education Research.

87.   Employer tactics, whether aggressively antiunion or apparently benign to workers, seem to be generally effective. Freeman and Rogers (1999, p. 9) observed that the demand for unionization has remained fairly stable over the years—in surveys, about one-third of nonunion workers expressed their desire for union membership. "The main reason these workers are not unionized is that the managements of their firms do not want them to be represented by unions." But for an analysis that suggests that employer opposition may *not* be a prime cause of union decline, see Lipset, S. M., and Meltz, N. M. (2004). *The paradox of American unionism: Why Americans like unions more than Canadians do but join much less.* Ithaca, NY: Cornell University Press. In contrast, a case study of successful employer opposition to union organizing, using a typical array of antiunion weapons, is Greenhouse, S. (2004, December 14). How do you drive out a union? South Carolina factory provides a textbook case. *New York Times*, p. A26.

88.   Clement, D. (2001). Labor pains. *Fedgazette* (May). http://minneapolisfed .org/pubs/fedgaz/labor.cfm

89.   For example, see Amber, M. (2003, January 1). Organizing: AFL-CIO convenes organizing summit to find new ways to expand membership. *Daily Labor Report*, pp. C1–C4.

90.   Burkins, G. (1997, February 19). Labor unions debate recruiting jurisdictions. *Wall Street Journal*, p. A20; Amber, M. (2003, February 28). AFL-CIO: Executive council adopts organizing plan emphasizing union partnerships, more staff. *Daily Labor Report*, pp. C1–C2; www.laborresearch.org/union_stats/1999_ density.

91.   Greenhouse (2004, November 10).

92.   The list of major organizing unions includes the Service Employees, HERE-UNITE, the Communications Workers, the American Federation of State, County and Municipal Employees, and the Auto Workers. Bronfenbrenner, K., and Hickey, R. (2004). Changing to organize: A national assessment of union strategies. In R. Milkman and K. Voss (Eds.), *Organizing and organizers in the new union movement.* Ithaca, NY: Cornell University Press, pp. 17–61.

93.   Freeman (2004). To add a percentage point to union density, unions would have to spend about 40 percent of their dues income on organizing.

94.   Rose and Chaison (1996). It was estimated that because of the high annual attrition of union membership (mostly the result of declining employment in unionized firms), unions would have to recruit 12 million new members in the years 1996–2000 to raise private sector union density from 11 percent to 18 percent. This task was beyond the financial resources of the union movement. Masters, M. (1997). *Unions at the crossroads: Strategic membership, financial and political perspectives.* Westport, CT: Quorum. In addition, when the unions' membership is low,

they not only have fewer resources to organize nonunion firms, but nonunion employers have a greater incentive to avoid unionization (they see their ability to compete in their industry hurt if they became one of the few unionized firms). But if union membership and density are high in the employers' industry, unions would have greater resources for organizing and the employers' costs of becoming a unionized firm would be lower and thus their resistance would be less. Freeman, R. B. (1998). Spurts in union growth: Defining moments and social processes. In M. D. Bordo, C. Goldin, and E. N. White (Eds.), *The defining moment: The Great Depression and the American economy in the twentieth century.* Chicago: University of Chicago Press, pp. 265–295.

95.   Godard (2003) argues that labor law matters in union growth. His review of evidence shows that the differences in the levels of union density in the United States and Canada can be traced to differences in the labor laws of the two countries, particularly the ways that labor boards certify unions as bargaining agents. Canadian provinces have mostly relied on membership cards and expedited elections for evidence of membership support while certification elections are used in the United States.

96.   For a review of the unsuccessful attempt at labor law reform in 1978, the first major attempt to reform the Wagner Act framework, see Gould, W. B., IV. (2004). *A primer on American labor law* (4th ed.). Cambridge, MA: MIT Press, pp. 129–138.

97.   Freeman (1988, p. 288) also argues that the Wagner Act has "locked the United States into an outmoded labor relations framework that does not fit labor market realities as the country moves into the twenty-first century. . . . [It] creates an institutional straightjacket that helps neither U.S. workers, nor firms, nor unions, but [is] one that has proven difficult to change, given the fears of labor and management that any shifts in the law will tilt the balance of power against their side." The law is faulted for failing to protect workers' rights to choose union representation, being unable to blunt employer opposition to union organizing, and for limiting the range of forms of union representation.

98.   This was concluded by leading critics of the law of union organizing, for example, Freeman, R. B. (1985). Why are unions faring poorly in NLRB representation elections? In T. A. Kochan (Ed.), *Challenges and choices facing American unions.* Cambridge, MA: MIT Press, pp. 45–64; Freeman, R. B. (1989). On the divergence in unionism among the developed countries. Working paper no. 2817. Cambridge, MA: National Bureau of Economic Research; Weiler, P. (1983). Promises to keep: Securing workers' rights to self-organization under the NLRA. *Harvard Law Review,* 96, pp. 1769–1827; Weiler, P. (1984). Striking a new balance: Freedom of contract and prospects for union representation. *Harvard Law Review,* 98, pp. 351–420.

Efforts to reform labor law culminated in the report of the Commission on the Future of Worker-Management Relations (Dunlop Commission), a committee created by the U.S. Departments of Commerce and Labor. The commission was chaired by John Dunlop of Harvard University and presented its report in 1994 (Commission on the Future of Worker-Management Relations. [1994]. *Report and recommendations.* Washington, DC: U.S. Department of Labor, U.S. Department of Commerce). It concluded, "The current labor law is not achieving its stated intent of encouraging collective bargaining and protecting workers rights to choose whether or not to be represented at the workplace" (xvii). Union certification elections were highly conflictual for workers, unions, and employers, and there was a high probability that workers would be discriminated against by their employers when they tried to exercise their right to choose a union. The commission recommended that the National Labor Relations Board expedite certification elections, provide injunctive relief to employees who are discriminated against by their employers for supporting unions, and offer arbitration if a newly certified union was unable to get its first agreement. The commission released its report just as elections brought about a conservative Republican House of Representatives. Its legislative recommendations were never acted upon.

99.   Commission on the Future of Worker-Management Relations (1994). This proportion of certifications that do not result in first collective agreements goes back to the 1970s and 1980s. See Pavy, G. (1993). *A question of fairness: Winning NLRB elections and establishing stable collective bargaining relationships with employers.* Washington, DC: AFL-CIO, Industrial Union Department.

100.   For example, see the review of the U.S. Senate hearings in Johnson, F. (2002, June 21). Senate committee explores difficulties workers face in organizing campaigns. *Daily Labor Review,* p. A1.

101.   Moberg, D. (1998, August 9). Organizing to win. *In These Times,* pp. 11–12. Efforts to reform the law of organizing often describe the workers' right to organize as basic civil rights and prime demonstrations of the freedom of association. Greenhouse, S. (2003, August 31). Unions to push to make organizing easier. *New York Times,* p. 16. A much stronger and more appealing case can be made that workers are being denied fundamental rights and this must be remedied rather than simply asserting that unions have a difficult time organizing under the present certification process and that this violates the spirit of the Wagner Act.

102.   Brett, J. M. (1980). Why employees want unions. *Organizational Dynamics,* 8, pp. 47–59.

103.   Chaison, G., and Bigelow, B. (2002). *Unions and legitimacy.* Ithaca, NY: Cornell University Press.

104.   For example, see Cohen and Hurd's (1998) discussion of the employers' use of fear and conflict during organizing drives. Cohen, L., and Hurd, R. W. (1998). Fear, conflict and union organizing. In K. Bronfenbrenner et al. (Eds.), *Organizing to win: New research on union strategies.* Ithaca, NY: Cornell University Press, pp. 181–196.

105.   For example, see the description of the organizing campaign at Harvard University in Chaison and Bigelow (2002), pp. 43–47.

106. For example, the union seeking to represent the graduate student assistants at Yale University lost a poll on the question of unionization when many of the assistants reacted against what they felt was an overly aggressive and undemocratic union. Greenhouse, S. (2003, May 2). Yale graduate students reject union, criticizing organizer. *New York Times*, p. A31.

107. Clergy have become increasingly involved in union organizing campaigns because they see unions as institutions that protect the weak and poor, promote the dignity of work, and preserve workplace rights. Clergy have helped in organizing through their sermons, meetings with employers, and communications with workers about the unions' mission. Greenhouse, S. (1999, September 6). Clergy and unions teaming up again, *New York Times*, p. A13.

108. For example, see Slaughter (1999); Nissen, B. (1998). Utilizing the membership to organize the unorganized. In K. Bronfenbrenner et al. (Eds.), *Organizing to win: New research on union strategies.* Ithaca, NY: Cornell University Press, pp. 135–149; Turner, L. (1998). Rank and file participation in organizing at home and abroad. In K. Bronfenbrenner et al. (Eds.), *Organizing to win: New research on union strategies.* Ithaca, NY: Cornell University Press, pp. 123–134; Bronfenbrenner, K., and Juravich, T. (1998). It takes more than house calls: Organizing to win with a comprehensive union-building strategy. In K. Bronfenbrenner et al. (Eds.), *Organizing to win: New research on union strategies.* Ithaca, NY: Cornell University Press, pp. 19–36.

109. All of these methods are legal even though they do not rely on the procedures of the labor board. Brody (2003, p. 17) observed, "Elections are not the only route to collective bargaining rights." Employers are required under the Wagner Act to bargain in good faith with representatives "designated or selected" by employees, and that can be done by means other than elections. However, over the years the case law has enabled employers to reject a union's showing of membership cards and force an election. Brody is critical of proposed legislation (the Norwood Bill, HR 4636) that would outlaw employer recognition of unions on the basis of membership card checks. Brody, J. (2003). Labor law reform: Taking a long view. *Perspectives on Work, 7*, pp. 16–18.

110. Greenhouse, S. (2003, May 31). Labor turns to a pivotal organizing drive. *New York Times*, p. 11.

111. For a rebuttal to the employers' criticism of card-check arrangements, see Eaton, A., and Kriesky, J. (2003). No more stacked deck: Evaluating the case against card-check union recognition. *Perspectives on Work, 7*, pp. 19–21. A discussion of the legal challenge to card check/neutrality is Cleeland, N. (2004, September 13). Labor board may rule on union tactics. *Los Angeles Times*, p. 13.

112. In 2001, about 80 percent of the workers organized by the Hotel Employees and Restaurant Employees were the result of card check/neutrality. Wessel, D. (2002, January 31). Some workers gain with new union tactics. *Wall Street Journal*, p. A1.

113.   For a brief description of the certification process, see the website of the National Labor Relations Board: www.nlrb.gov.

114.   This can be an important question because when workers are not covered by the National Labor Relations Act, they do not have protected rights to unionize and cannot use the board's certification election process. For example, graduate research and teaching assistants at universities were declared to be employees within the meaning of the act in 2000 but were then excluded by a 2004 decision that said they were essentially students and not employees. This means that they could not petition the labor board for a certification election to prove their majority support. When unions of these workers had already signed collective agreements, the employers could refuse to recognize and bargain with them after the agreements expired. Greenhouse, S., and Arenson, K. W. (2004, July 16). Labor board says graduate students at private universities have no right to unionize. *New York Times,* pp. AA14.

115.   If there are two or more unions in a certification election, a run-off election will be held if none of the choices (the union or the "no union" options) received a majority on the first ballot. Only about 5 percent of certification elections involve more than one union, primarily because rival organizing is restricted by the AFL-CIO among its affiliates.

116.   The employer must meet with the union and bargain in good faith but it is not required to make concessions or reach agreement. In about 30 percent of the first negotiations, newly certified unions are unable to negotiate collective agreements, usually because of employers' delays and failure to bargain in good faith. It seems only logical that the employers' fight against unions will carry over to the bargaining table. Therefore, despite the certification election outcome, organizing campaigns cannot be considered successful until the first collective agreement is signed and the union has established its role in the workplace.

117.   U.S. National Labor Relations Board. (2004). *Annual report, 2003.* Washington, DC: Government Printing Office. In 2003, there were 2,937 representation elections closed with unions winning 1,579 (53.8 percent).

118.   Cody, J. K. (2004). NLRB election statistics suggest new organizing strategies paying off for unions. News release. www.bna.com/press/2004/nlrb04.html.

Three

Union Government and Administration

W e cannot fully understand unions until we see them as political organizations. Unions have constitutions, elect officers and governing councils, and hold conventions. We expect unions to be run democratically and we are disappointed when they are not. We demand that union officers be responsive to the will of the members, and if they are not we call them union bosses.

But at the same time, unions are complex bureaucratic organizations that are expected to be run efficiently and operate within their financial means. Unions must manage millions of dollars in assets, maintain a stream of revenue from their members' dues, and meet the payroll for their staff. Unions function with organizational structures that are as intricate and multilayered as those of big corporations; they have headquarters and regional offices, and subordinate bodies, specialized departments, and committees. They hire managers and accountants for administration and organizers and negotiators for servicing the membership.

In short, unions must be governed but they must also be managed. In this chapter, we examine these two facets of unions and, in doing so, confront the controversial issues of union democracy, union corruption, and union efficiency.

Union Government

The Union Constitution

Although union constitutions vary in their length[1] and complexity, they all serve the same purpose—to establish the union as a legal, self-governing entity. The typical constitution has sections (called *articles*) on the union's name and mission; the oaths of officers and members; the qualifications for membership; the rights of regular and other members (e.g., retired, unemployed, honorary, and associate members); the duties of officers; the rules for holding conventions and amending the constitution; the method for electing officers; the procedure for hearing charges against members, staff, and officers; and the ratification of collective agreements and authorization of strikes.[2] Union constitutions may also describe the calculation of membership dues, the per capita fee (the amount that the local union must pay to the national organization), and the compensation of officers.

Union constitutions leave little doubt as to the subordinate position of locals. They usually have clauses giving national officers the right to charter locals, set local dues and fees, audit the locals' financial records, and suspend the self-governance of the locals when there is financial mismanagement or grossly ineffective collective bargaining. Local officers usually need permission from national headquarters before they can sign collective agreements or call strikes. The national union can even require that locals merge with each other if they are too small to be effective representatives.[3]

Constitutions set forth the rights of union members; these usually include the right to vote in democratic officer elections (e.g., with due notice of election, freedom to run for office, and the right to appeal the outcome if there are irregularities), and the rights to speak at union meetings and have access to union records. Members (as well as officers and staff) have the right to a fair trial and the presumption of innocence if charged with violating the constitution (e.g., for falsifying records, misusing funds, or slandering the union).[4]

Union Conventions

The heart of union government is the convention because it is at this meeting of delegates that the voice of the members is most clearly heard through debates and balloting. Indeed, technically, officers only have the authority to govern between conventions, although the period between conventions can be long and some officers manage to maintain tight control over what happens at conventions.

The frequency of conventions is a matter of union tradition and practicality (union conventions are expensive because of their set-up costs and the travel by delegates). For instance, the Communications Workers of America, a large union that prides itself on being run by its members, has a convention every year. The convention of the American Federation of State, County and Municipal Employees meets every other year. The Steelworkers has its convention every three years. The Auto Workers and the United Mine Workers meet every four years. The Teamsters, the Laborers, and the United Food and Commercial Workers (UFCW) have conventions every five years.[5]

Union constitutions invariably present formulas defining the number of convention delegates that a local union can send and the basis on which they are selected. For example, at the convention of Steelworkers, locals with 1 to 200 members have one delegate, those with 201 to 350 members have two delegates, those with 351 to 700 members have three delegates, and locals with 701 or more members send three delegates plus one for each additional 500 members or a majority fraction thereof (e.g., a 1,000-member local can send four delegates). Members elect delegates at local elections.[6]

Union constitutions describe the ways to present and approve resolutions at conventions and the procedures for amending the constitution. They may also contain the bylaws governing the convention, including the rules of order, the credentialing of delegates, the order of business, the nomination and election of officers, and rules of committees.[7]

Union Officers and Governing Bodies

The *president*, the highest union officer, presides over meetings of governing boards and conventions, chairs key union committees (e.g., committees for union finances and political activities), appoints staff members, acts as union spokesperson to the public, federation, and other unions, and frequently has the power to suspend the self-governance of locals. In some unions, such as the United Mine Workers of America, only the president can authorize a strike.[8]

Unions also have *secretary-treasurers* who are the chief financial and recording officers. Their duties include approving payments from their unions' general funds, setting dates and locations for conventions, overseeing convention balloting, preparing and distributing financial reports, enforcing local unions' standards for financial record keeping and reporting, and ensuring that proper procedures are followed for their unions' loans, pension plans, and investments.

Unions have *vice presidents* who either are elected by the members in geographic regions or industry conferences or hold their position at-large, that is, are elected by vote of all union members. Vice presidents sit with the president and secretary-treasurer on the union's governing board.[9] The Teamsters, for example, has 21 vice presidents, who are elected on a regional basis and serve for five years.[10] The Laborers has four vice presidents elected at-large and nine vice presidents elected in union districts; all vice presidents serve for five years.[11] The Communications Workers has an executive vice president elected at-large and eight other vice presidents each from one of the union's industry sectors (e.g., Telecommunications, Health and Education Workers, Publishing and Media Workers). Elections are held at the annual convention.[12] Actors' Equity has only three vice presidents; they are elected annually by mail ballot among the union's membership groups—one (the First Vice-President) from members performing principal work, one from those doing chorus work, and one from those who are stage managers.[13]

Finally, unions have governing boards, often called *executive boards* or *executive councils,* that can have a great deal of power. Typically, governing boards fill officer vacancies until the next convention, propose resolutions to the convention, approve budgets, and levy special fees. They may compel small locals to merge with each other and they may ratify mergers with other unions if those mergers are absorptions or affiliations and do not require changes in the union's constitution. Governing boards have standing committees that meet regularly to decide on such matters as launching regional organizing drives and endorsing political candidates. There may also be special committees to consider such matters as plans for union revival, the expansion of union jurisdictions, and the terms for union merger.[14]

Local Union Government

Locals have presidents, secretary-treasurers, and vice presidents who sit on executive councils and direct union affairs. They also have shop stewards—officers who process the workers' grievances about violations or misinterpretations of the collective agreement—and business agents— officers or staff members, usually paid, who assist the local officers in the negotiation and enforcement of collective agreements and help run the day-to-day affairs of the local.[15] Local officers are elected to their positions although they often run unopposed, particularly in small locals where they are unpaid.[16] Union locals have meetings, generally held each month, that are attended by members (although, unless there is pressing union business such as authorizing a strike or ratifying a collective agreement, it is rare for more than a quarter of the members to attend).

Union Democracy[17]

Although we expect unions to be governed democratically, it is difficult to define union democracy. To many, it simply has to do with elections. It means that members can easily run for office and oppose incumbent officers. Democratic unions have, at the very least, contested elections and, at the very most, challengers often defeating incumbent officers. Undemocratic unions have entrenched officers who face little if any opposition, and elections are more like rituals than leadership contests.

But running for office is never a simple matter even in the most democratic unions. Opposition to incumbents is inherently difficult; established leaders of big nationals or locals have political skills and allies and are well-known by the membership. Serious election challenges happen more often at the small local where campaigning is easier and incumbents are more willing to leave office because their positions are usually part-time and unpaid.[18] More important, the rate of officer turnover at any union level is not necessarily a good indicator of union democracy. If officers run unopposed or easily defeat challengers, it may mean only that the members are satisfied with their performance and see no need for a replacement.[19]

Union members tend to appraise officers' performance pragmatically, supporting those who produce the desired results in bargaining and rejecting those—even if they are long-time incumbents—who they feel are not up to the task. For example, in August 2003, the members of the American Federation of Government Employees rejected the incumbent president and elected a challenger because they felt a need for militant and more effective leadership. The members anticipated some serious problems—the federal government had threatened to reduce its payrolls—so they wanted a leader who would confront their employer.[20] This defeat of the national president, a rare event, was interpreted as a sign that the incumbent "was not fighting hard enough against the Bush administration's labor policies."[21] Similarly, when the members of the 7,500-member local of New York hospital workers defeated the incumbent president in an election in 2002, they were weighing the costs and benefits of keeping a veteran union leader. They were angered by the union's high dues (about 3 percent of the members' pay) and the local president's fund-raising for an extravagant headquarters that was never built. The president was quite militant and powerful in city politics, yet despite this (or perhaps because of it) the locals had suffered many layoffs.[22]

The best measure of union democracy is the members' ability to influence officers on issues that matter to them. To what degree do the members contribute to union decision making on crucial issues ranging from bargaining strategies to cooperative arrangements with management? Are members able and encouraged to participate in their union in a meaningful way, not just by running for office but by debating issues at local meetings, questioning officers, proposing resolutions for the national convention, and questioning delegates for officer positions at all levels? Do members have a good chance of sitting on bargaining and grievance committees? Can members criticize officers and debate union policies without fear of retribution (e.g., by having their membership suspended for disloyalty)? We should look for such signs of democracy mostly at the local level where members can have the closest contact with union officers, can be well-informed about union matters, and can have the best chances of participating in their unions.

But why should we even care whether unions are democratic? After all, we show little concern if corporations are not democratically run and we rarely ask whether interest groups such as those of environmentalists or retired persons are democratic. The answer lies in the nature of unions as organizations *of* workers and *for* workers. Unions are *of* members because most of their effort toward achieving union goals comes from the members, whether they are serving on committees, walking on picket lines during strikes, or debating union policies at local meetings and national conventions. Unions are *for* members because their purpose is to advance the members' interests through organizing, collective bargaining, and political action.[23] Consequently, as Strauss (2001) observed, democracy is important to unions because it enables the union officers to know what the members want and to ensure that unions have "government by the people, not just for them."[24] Democracy makes unions more effective by weeding out officers who cannot perform well or who seem out of touch with the members' needs. Also, the mobilization of members, for example, during strikes or political rallies, is more likely to be successful if members participate fully in the decision for action. Finally, a sense that

unions in general and an organizing union in particular are run democratically can be crucial to the success of organizing drives; nonunion workers
must be convinced that the union is not run by autocratic union bosses, as
their employers frequently claim.[25]

By and large, unions are democratic. In most unions, there are a significant number of activists (although not a formal opposition party), union
officers tend to be responsive to the members' needs (particularly in negotiations), and officers believe that it is possible to be voted out if they
appear consistently uncaring or self-serving.

Corruption in Unions[26]

Union corruption and union democracy are separate issues, although
the terms *honest* and *democratic* are often mentioned as if they were two
sides of the same coin.[27] It is true that in unions where members do not
influence the actions of their officers, there is little oversight of what officers do and there are greater chances of officers being corrupt and getting
away with it. But some forms of corruption, for example, financial malfea-
sance, can occur in democratic unions, just as dictatorial union officers
may hoard power because of their personal style of leadership rather than
any intent to act corruptly.

From 2001 to 2005, more than 500 union officers were indicted on criminal charges.[28] It is not surprising that there is some corruption in many
unions. After all, union officers have the opportunity to steal—unions have
billions of dollars in assets—and the opportunity to extort—some employers are willing to pay to avoid costly strikes and enter into cheap, substan-
dard collective agreements. But there is no evidence backing the common
charge that union leaders are overwhelmingly corrupt. Furthermore, what
there is of contemporary union corruption pales in comparison to the
depth and scope of corruption 50 years ago when some unions were infil-
trated by organized crime (e.g., the Teamsters and many construction
locals), and more than a few union leaders saw the union treasury as their
personal property and routinely responded with violence to any political
opposition. Nonetheless, union corruption, to whatever extent it does exist
now, hurts the labor movement because it lends credence to employers'
antiunion propaganda during organizing drives—the claims that unions
are mob-controlled and the private fiefdoms of union bosses. Corruption
also tarnishes the unions' public image and weakens their claim to be the
progressive voice of working men and women. Unions cannot simply

excuse their leaders' failings by pointing to high-profile cases of corporate corruption. As Douglas Fraser, a former president of the United Auto Workers, pointed out, "Business is about making money but labor leaders are supposed to be about helping workers."[29]

Union corruption can range from simple extortion to complex and sophisticated embezzlement schemes. For example, in April 2003, George Cashman, the leader of a Teamsters' Boston local and one of the most powerful labor leaders in Massachusetts, pleaded guilty to conspiracy charges and accepted a short prison term. He admitted to falsifying time sheets to allow truck drivers to illegally collect health care benefits, and he had extorted a company being sued by the Teamsters—he was willing to reach a settlement in return for a kickback. For several years, movie producers had complained that Cashman pressured them with threats of strikes and production delays if they did not pay inflated wages and benefits to drivers who did little or no work. Drivers connected to organized crime were given work before regular Teamsters.[30]

Some officers simply see their unions' treasuries as their own. For example, Pat Tornillo, the president of the United Teachers of Dade, the chapter of the American Federation of Teachers (AFT) in Miami-Dade County, Florida, and a major figure in state politics, misused a union credit card for personal purchases including clothing and extravagant vacations. He also withdrew cash from his local's treasury and diverted union funds to improve his home and hire servants. An audit revealed that Tornillo had misused nearly $2.5 million and his fellow officers misused another $1 million. In the same teachers' union but in Washington, D.C., local president Barbara Bullock and several officers and staff admitted to embezzling $5 million in union funds and overcharging members for their dues. The embezzlement was fairly obvious; Bullock was making personal charges of $1.8 million on the union's credit card at a time that the local had fallen behind paying its rent and utilities. When she became president in 1994, her local stopped the biannual audits required by the parent union and there were no objections. After the embezzlement cases in Washington and Florida, the AFT decided to tighten its financial controls.[31]

Perhaps the most widely publicized instance of recent union corruption occurred in the Teamsters.[32] It was incredibly ironic because the supporters of Ron Carey, the reform-minded Teamsters president, misused union funds to keep him in power and protect the union against organized crime. This was a classic instance of persons wrongly believing that the ends justified the means.

Prior to the 1990s, three Teamsters presidents had been arrested and convicted for corruption (often extortion and misuse of union funds), including its legendary leader, James (Jimmy) Hoffa. Hoffa was president from 1967 to 1971, and then spent four years in prison for jury tampering. He disappeared after his release in 1975, assumedly the victim of a mob murder. In 1989, the Teamsters agreed to a consent decree in a federal court to settle a racketeering lawsuit brought by government prosecutors. An independent review board was empowered to monitor the Teamsters elections and investigate officer corruption at national and local levels.[33]

In 1991, Carey was elected Teamsters president after promising to rid the union of corruption. He was widely hailed as "Mr. Clean," a dynamic leader whose reform party would clean up a huge corrupt union, set an example for anticorruption insurgents in other unions, and become a major player in the revival of the labor movement. When he took office, Carey hired a reformist staff, reduced his own salary, and eliminated some of the Teamsters' extravagances, such as its private jets, for which it had become well-known. But in his 1996 reelection campaign, Carey was challenged by James P. Hoffa, Jr., the son of past president Jimmy Hoffa. Carey won the election with 52 percent of the vote, but Hoffa's followers charged that union funds had been misused in the election campaign. Federal trustees monitoring the Teamsters investigated the charges and found enough evidence to set the election aside.

Those in charge of Carey's campaign were involved in a complicated money-laundering scheme to illegally transfer funds from the Teamsters' treasury to the campaign fund. In the later days of the campaign, they feared the worst—that Hoffa was gaining support, had access to money from the mob for his campaign, and would win the election and bring back corrupt officers. Carey needed a direct mailing to the membership to energize his campaign, but this would cost around $700,000, more than he could afford. But his supporters found a number of ways to siphon off Teamsters funds. In one scheme, donors to a lobbying group contributed to the Carey campaign and the Teamsters reciprocated by transferring funds to organizations supported by that group. In another, the Carey supporters contracted for work by a telemarketing firm with the understanding that the company would then contribute to the Carey campaign.

Carey's victory was set aside and he was barred from running in the new election. He took a leave of absence from union office. In 1998, Hoffa won 55 percent of the vote compared to 39 percent for Tom Leedham, the reform candidate. Many Teamsters officials who had once backed Carey supported Hoffa because they believed he could unify the union and confront powerful employers in upcoming negotiations. Hoffa claimed that he won because the voters understood that he could run the union. "The members see we are a can-do administration. We took this union that was really in chaos, and we pulled it together."[34] In October 2001, Carey was acquitted of charges that he had lied about diverting union funds (charges that his supporters had admitted to).[35]

After he was elected, Hoffa worked to reduce corruption in the Teamsters and asked the government to end its monitoring of the union. In October 2002, the Teamsters released a report of an internal review by a consultant that concluded: "Organized crime is no longer the problem that it once was in the Teamsters. . . . The Teamsters union is no longer dominated or heavily influence by organized crime."[36] But the evidence was not persuasive enough, and the monitoring of the union continued.[37]

Sometimes, union officers act unethically but in an entirely legal manner. For example, a group of union officers directing Ullico (Union Labor Life Insurance Company), a union-owned company that provides insurance and pension services to union members, enriched themselves by buying and selling the company's stock at just the right time.[38] In 1999, the officers bought shares of Ullico at a price set by the board on which they sat, fully aware that the share price would soon rise. After a year, the officers were able to sell their stock at three times its purchase price. Their timing to sell was perfect; they knew that Ullico stock would soon be set at a lower price because it had heavily invested in Global Crossing Ltd, a telecom firm that went bankrupt. The officers paid less than $54 per share for Ullico stock that was valued at $146 per share before falling. They made $13.7 million in profit; Robert Georgine, the Ullico chairman and CEO and the former president of the AFL-CIO Building Trades Department, made about $6 million from stock sales.[39]

The labor movement was split over the Ullico scandal. Some union leaders thought that Ullico's officers should keep their profits because they were doing nothing illegal. Inside profiteering, they claimed, was common among directors on corporate boards. But others believed that the scandal diminished the reputation of the labor movement at a time when unions were so vociferously attacking corporate greed and dishonesty. The officers' conduct may have been legal, but it was seedy. One newspaper editorial characterized the Ullico affair as "a massive, secretive, self-dealing stock scheme," complete with "labor bosses" reaping "booty," and far worse than corporate scandals because it involved so many top union officers.[40] Under pressure from many labor leaders, Georgine and other directors stepped down and a new group of officers took control of Ullico. The board directed all those who profited from stock trading to return their gains.[41]

Union Administration

Unions and Information Technology

Union officers and staff seem to have unlimited faith in the ability of information technology to make unions more effective. Twenty years ago, computers improved the internal operation of unions, particularly record keeping, but they produced "islands of automation"—union departments had few if any links between them. But now, information technology focuses specifically on connecting, converting information into electronic form (e.g., data storage and retrieval and searchable databases), and distributing it widely and quickly (e.g., through the Internet, web, and e-mail, as well as wireless communications).

Nearly all unions now have web pages (several are listed in the appendix). A typical web page describes the union, its mission and history, news of bargaining and organizing achievements, and the address, phone numbers, and e-mail addresses of officers and staff. The web page rallies support for political candidates supported by the union, and gives a synopsis or the full text of the union's constitution and selected collective bargaining agreements. It can also be used to coordinate strikes, update members on the progress in collective bargaining, and link workers with organizers. Proposals for reviving of the union movement assign a major role to information technology, envisioning the rise of the *cyberunion*—a union that deeply integrates the web and the Internet into its system for communicating with members and potential members.[42] But many lose sight of the ways that information technology may be more of a threat than savior for unions. By creating their own internal Internets, called *intranets,* employers have a fast and low-cost way to communicate with their workforce. In their most rudimentary forms, intranets use websites to deliver the company newsletter and training materials and enroll workers in benefit plans. But they could evolve into forums for workers who want to present their grievances to management for resolution or confer with their supervisors and human resource specialists. In this way, company intranets can provide a voice for workers, the usual role of the union, and foster a closer identification between workers and the company and its policies. At unionized workplaces, they can help employers compete with unions for the loyalty of the workers, and at nonunion workplaces, intranets can reduce workers' interest in union representation. In short, if unions can bring workers closer to them through the Internet, so can employers.

Furthermore, as unions compete with employer intranets, they could end up distancing themselves from their members. Unions that create a strong online presence could be sacrificing personal contact with members and reducing the potential for participation and commitment. The challenge that unions face is how to use information technology to enhance their role as the voice of workers at their workplaces, without transforming themselves into just another website.[43]

Union Effectiveness[44]

Advocates of the applications of information technology to unions often speak in terms of enhanced effectiveness, and effectiveness will also be considered in the later discussions of collective bargaining and union political activities. Effectiveness presents a dilemma for unions. They cannot avoid being judged on their effectiveness or their ability to increase it or to maintain it during difficult times. Members fully expect their unions to be effective representatives. Unorganized workers try to estimate the probable effectiveness of unions before they vote for them as collective bargaining agents. The public constantly appraises union effectiveness when it questions whether unions still play an important role in our economy. But effectiveness is difficult to define and measure, and it may not always be a primary union objective.

Part of the problem is that union effectiveness cannot be measured financially in the same way that we can appraise the effectiveness of companies.[45] The union's goal is *not* to show quarterly or end-of-year profits or to have a surplus on its balance sheet. Rather, unions expend their resources to represent workers in their dealings with employers, to recruit new members, and to use their political clout to influence legislation helpful to members and workers in general. The union's primary source of income is its dues from members, and its main expenditures are officer and staff salaries.[46] Dues income is determined by union size (i.e., the number of dues-paying members) and how much members are willing to pay, rather than by investment decisions of union officers or staff, or the sale of union services. Usually, dues are a fixed amount paid monthly by members or the members' wages for a specified number of hours per month. The Teamsters' and United Mine Workers' dues are a multiple of the members' hourly rate. The Laborers dues are a flat monthly fee. The Steelworkers dues are a fixed percentage of the members' monthly earnings. Actors' Equity, a union that always has many unemployed members and a few well-paid, employed ones, charges a flat monthly rate plus a percentage of gross earnings.[47]

Although union effectiveness cannot be measured by union finances, it cannot be divorced from them either. For unions, the acquisition of financial resources is not an end in itself. If unions have an annual surplus, the members assume that dues were either set too high or the level of services provided was too low. But if unions have many budget deficits, their condition as viable organizations will be jeopardized. We cannot expect unions to be moneymaking ventures, nor can we expect them to be money losers.[48]

Union financial reports must meet accounting standards and can be audited for irregularities by the U.S. Department of Labor.[49] But balance sheets and income statements, however accurate, give us a very limited view of unions. The financial statements of the Service Employees, for example, would show only the huge size of the union (it had cash receipts of about $151 million in 2002), its primary source of income (more than 90 percent of its receipts came from dues collected by locals), and its need for more money (cash disbursements exceeded receipts by about $9 million).[50] But this gives us practically no idea of the effectiveness or even the basic character of the Service Employees—one of the largest and fastest-growing unions; a union that is extremely active in politics and organizing; a major proponent of mergers of small unions into large ones; a union whose president, Andrew Stern, is a leading critic of the AFL-CIO leadership; a bargaining agent that negotiates with 12,000 employers; and an organization with a diverse membership (more than half are women) that includes many low-paid health care and building service workers.[51]

What is union effectiveness? Rose and Chaison defined union effectiveness in the broadest sense as union strength, ability, and improved performance in the three basic union activities of organizing, bargaining, and political action, and the ways that unions optimize the relationships between them. They showed that for the labor movement in general, the decline in union density—the proportion of the workforce in unions—resulted from the unions' inability to recruit a sufficient number of new members to offset declining employment at unionized workplaces. As the unionized share of the workforce became smaller and smaller, unions went on the defensive in bargaining, trying to repel attacks on their past gains by employers who suffered under intense nonunion competition. Union density continued to fall, and unions also found that the only way to exert influence in politics was by working through coalitions; this meant that their emphasis shifted to broader issues such as higher minimum wages or health care reform rather than changes in the labor law dealing with organizing and bargaining. Lacking the ability to pass laws that made organizing easier and bargaining from a position of weakness, the unions' effectiveness was further eroded.[52]

Effectiveness means using strength in one area to build strength in another. For example, the Communications Workers of America has been able to successfully adjust to employer competition, industry deregulation, and company divestiture, by using organizing and union mergers to strengthen its hand in bargaining. It grew at a time when most unions did not, and it used whatever means necessary including organizing outside the National Labor Relations Board procedures and absorbing small unions into its industry divisions. It also leveraged its bargaining power to pressure employers to ease opposition to organizing, and it applied political power in states and at the federal level to extend its collective bargaining coverage.[53] Effectiveness in one area led to effectiveness in another.

Finally, when we examine union effectiveness, we have to consider that unions are always balancing their bureaucratic and political sides. In many instances, acting democratically might be more important than acting effectively. For example, members of a small, declining union might reject the absorption of their union into a larger one because of their attachment to union traditions and concerns about ending the life of a venerable albeit ineffective institution. We might criticize the union members for rejecting a merger that was in their own interests, but we would be aghast if their leaders, believing in the benefits of the merger, signed a merger agreement without the members' approval.

Conclusions

Unions are complex, self-governing organizations with their own officers, governing bodies, constitutions, and conventions. Because they are governed and not simply managed, we expect unions to operate democratically, although union democracy is not always easy to measure. Adding to the organizational complexity of unions, there are possibilities for officer corruption and some uncertainty about the criteria of union effectiveness.

Notes

1. For example, the constitution of the International Brotherhood of Teamsters is 231 pages and the constitution of the Communications Workers of America is 26 pages.

2. American Federation of State, County and Municipal Employees. (2002). *Constitution of the American Federation of State, County and Municipal Employees.* www.afscme.org/about/const_tc.html; International Brotherhood of Teamsters. (2002). *Constitution of the International Brotherhood of Teamsters.* Washington, DC: International Brotherhood of Teamsters; Communications Workers of America. (2002). *CWA constitution as amended.* Washington, DC: Communications Workers of America.

3. For example, the control of the national union over locals is described in American Federation of State, County and Municipal Employees. (2002). Article IX, Subordinate Bodies. *Constitution of the American Federation of State, County and Municipal Employees.* www.afscme.org/about/const_tc.html; United Mine Workers of America. (2000). Article 10—Local Unions. *Constitution of the International Union, United Mine Workers of America.* Fairfax, VA: United Mine Workers of America, pp. 80–95. In regard to control over local bargaining, see United Food and Commercial Workers. (2003). Article 23, Collective Bargaining Contracts. *Constitution of the United Food and Commercial Workers.* Washington, DC: United Food and Commercial Workers.

4. For example, see Communications Workers of America. (2002). Internal Appeals Procedures. *CWA Constitution as amended August 2002.* Washington, DC: Communications Workers of America; American Federation of State, County and Municipal Employee. (2003). Article 2, Bill of Rights for Union Members. *Constitution of the American Federation of State, County and Municipal Employees.* www.afscme.org/about/const_tc.html; United Food and Commercial Workers. (2003). Article 26, Disciplinary Procedures and Appeals. *Constitution of the United Food and Commercial Workers.* Washington, DC: United Food and Commercial Workers. Perhaps the best-known internal judicial procedure is the Public Review Board of the United Auto Workers in which the final decision is made by a panel of neutrals. The procedure deals mostly with officers' violations of the union's code of ethical conduct. United Automobile Workers. (2002). Article 32, Public Review Board, *Constitution of the International Union United Automobile Aerospace and Agricultural Implement Workers of America UAW.* Detroit, MI: United Automobile Workers.

5. Communications Workers of America. (2002). Article VIII—Conventions. *CWA Constitution as amended August 2002.* Washington, DC: Communications Workers of America; United Steelworkers of America. (2002). Article VI, Conventions. *Constitution of the International Union, United Steelworkers of America.* Pittsburgh, PA: United Steelworkers of America; American Federation of State, County and Municipal Employees. (2003). Article 5, The convention. *Constitution of the American Federation of State, County and Municipal Employees.* www.afscme.org/about/const_tc.html; International Brotherhood of Teamsters. (2002). Article III, Convention and Representation. *Constitution of the International Brotherhood of Teamsters.* Washington, DC: International Brotherhood of Teamsters; United Automobile Workers. (2002). Article 8, Conventions. *Constitution of the International Union United Automobile Aerospace and Agricultural Implement Workers of America.* Detroit, MI: United Automobile Workers; United Mine Workers of America. (2000). Article 7—International Convention. *Constitution of the International Union, United Mine Workers of America.* Fairfax, VA: United Mine Workers of America; International Brotherhood of Teamsters. (2002). Article 3—Convention and Representation. *Constitution of the International Brotherhood of Teamsters.* Washington, DC: International Brotherhood of Teamsters; Laborers International Union. (2001). Article V, Convention and Representation. *Constitution of the Laborers International Union of North America.* Washington, DC: Laborers International Union.

6. United Steelworkers of America. (2002). Article 6, Conventions. *Constitution of the International Union, United Steelworkers of America.* Pittsburgh, PA: United Steelworkers of America.

7. For example, see American Federation of Teachers. (2002). Bylaws, Articles 1–9, *Constitution of the American Federation of Teachers, AFL-CIO.* Washington, DC: American Federation of Teachers.

8. The president of the Mine Workers has tremendous power over strikes: "Only the International President can call or authorize a strike. . . . No District or Local Union can call an authorized strike without approval of the International President." United Mine Workers of America. (2000). Article 19—Strikes. *Constitution of the International Union, United Mine Workers of America.* Fairfax, VA: United Mine Workers of America, pp. 132–133.

9. The United Mine Workers of America has only a single vice president but it has an executive board member from each of the union's eight districts. United Mine Workers. (2000). Article 4—International Officers. *Constitution of the International Union, United Mine Workers of America.* Fairfax, VA: United Mine Workers of America.

10. International Brotherhood of Teamsters. (2002). Article IV, Officers, Delegates, Elections. *Constitution of the International Brotherhood of Teamsters.* Washington, DC: International Brotherhood of Teamsters.

11. Laborers International Union. (2001). Article VI, Officers. *Constitution of the Laborers International Union of North America.* Washington, DC: Laborers International Union.

12. Communications Workers of America. (2002). Article 12—Officers and Their Duties. *CWA Constitution as amended August 2002.* Washington, DC: Communications Workers of America.

13. Communications Workers of America. (2002). Article 9—Executive Board. *CWA Constitution as amended August 2002.* Washington, DC: Communications Workers of America.

14. Some union constitutions may even give governing boards the nearly unlimited power to take action as needed to promote and conserve the general welfare and interests of the union. For example, see the expansive authority of the Laborers' General Executive Board in Laborers International Union. (2001). Article 8, General Executive Board. *Constitution of the Laborers International Union of North America.* Washington, DC: Laborers International Union. The Executive Council of the American Federation of Teachers also has broad powers that include "deal[ing] with all the affairs of the federation in the period between the conventions." American Federation of Teachers. (2002). Article VI, Executive Council, section 13. *Constitution of the American Federation of Teachers, AFL-CIO.* Washington, DC: American Federation of Teachers.

15. Geoghegan, T. (1998). *The lexicon of labor.* New York: New Press.

16. Chaison, G., and Rose, J. (1989). Unions: Growth, structure and internal dynamics. In J. C. Anderson, M. Gunderson, and A. Ponak (Eds.), *Union-management relations in Canada.* Don Mills, Ontario: Addison-Wesley, pp. 125–154.

17. The two classic studies of union democracy are Lipset, S. M., Trow, M., and Colemen, J. (1956). *Union democracy: The internal politics of the International Typographical Union.* New York: Doubleday; Edelstein, D. J., and Warner, M. (1975). *Comparative union democracy: Organization and opposition in British and American Unions.* London: Halstead. An excellent review of the research literature on union democracy is Strauss, G. (1991). Union democracy. In G. Strauss, D. G. Gallagher, and J. Fiorito (Eds.), *The state of the unions.* Madison, WI: Industrial Relations Research Association, pp. 201–236.

18. Chaison, G., and Rose, J. (1977). Turnover among presidents of Canadian national unions. *Industrial Relations,* 16, pp. 199–204.

19. Measures of union officers turnover are found in Strauss, G. (2001). The present state of national union democracy. In S. Estreicher, H. C. Katz, and B. E. Kaufman (Eds.), *The internal governance and organizational effectiveness of labor unions.* New York: Kluwer International. Turnover tends to be higher in small unions although Strauss does mention some strong challenges to officers of large unions, notably in UNITE and the Service Employees.

20. AFGE chooses new president. (2003, August 22). *Washington Post,* p. A19; Miller, J. (2003, August 21). AFGE elects new president. *Newsbytes.* www.gcn.com.

21. Union outs president. (2003, August 22). *New York Times,* p. A16.

22. Greenhouse, S. (2002, March 13). Longtime head of city hospital union loses re-election bid. *New York Times,* p. B8.

23. Fiorito, J., Jarley, P., and Delaney, J. T. (1993). National union effectiveness. *Research in the Sociology of Organizations*, 12, pp. 111–137. For a discussion of the members as the key constituency of unions, see Chaison, G., and Bigelow, B. (2002). *Unions and legitimacy*. Ithaca, NY: Cornell University Press, pp. 28–33.

24. Strauss (2001), p. 57.

25. Strauss (1991, 2001).

26. For a historical review of corruption in labor unions, see Hutchinson, J. (1972). *The imperfect union: A history of corruption in American trade unions*. New York: Dutton. Union corruption is primarily addressed by the Landrum-Griffin Act of 1959 (the Labor-Management Reporting and Disclosure Act), specifically those sections requiring that unions file financial reports and maintain appropriate standards for their pension plans. A review of the regulation of the internal affairs of unions is found in Goldberg, M. J. (2001). Union democracy, American democracy, and global democracy: An overview and assessment. In S. Estreicher, H. C. Katz, and B. E. Kaufman (Eds.), *The internal governance and organizational effectiveness of labor unions*. New York: Kluwer Law International, pp. 75–83.

Also, the Racketeer Influenced and Corrupt Organizations Act (RICO) has been used by prosecutors to impose monitorships on national unions (the Laborers, the Hotel and Restaurant Workers, and the Teamsters) as well as several union locals. Monitorships are court-backed compromise agreements under which union leaders and federal prosecutors agree that no charges will be brought against the union officers if control of union elections and financial matters is given to a committee of monitors.

This discussion of corruption does not deal specifically with unions and violence. Although union officers may engage in corrupt activities that entail violence against union members, other workers, and employers (e.g., through extortion or intimidation), most of the violent activities of unions occur during strikes, particularly those directed against crossing picket lines or involving the destruction of company property. For example, see Craft, J. (2001). Union violence: A review and critical discussion. *Journal of Labor Research*, 22, pp. 679–694; Thieblot, A. J., Jr., and Northrup, H. R. (1999). *Union violence: The record and response by courts, legislatures and the NLRB*. Fairfax, VA: George Mason University, Olin Institute.

27. For example, see Goldberg (2001), p. 75.

28. Greenhouse, S. (2005, April 17). Labor Department plans increasing scrutiny of union finances. *New York Times*, p. A20.

29. Greenhouse, S. (1997, October 28). Series of new corruption cases hampers labor's efforts to improve its tainted image. *New York Times*, p. A20.

30. Sullivan, J. (2000, August 19). Records: Cellucci knew of studio's gripes: Memos cite alleged Teamster troubles. *Boston Herald*, p. 1; Sullivan, J. (2000, August 20). Records: Teamsters answered only to Cellucci—Filmmakers complained often to state officials. *Boston Herald*, p. 4; Kurkjian, S. (2000, August 12). Teamsters to probe movie dealings: Union headquarters says inquiry launched at

hub local's request. *Boston Globe,* p. B5; Phillips, F. (2003, April 26). Cashman's guilty plea ends a long flirtation with GOP. *Boston Globe,* p. B1; Lavoie, D. (2003, April 26). Union leader pleads guilty. *Worcester Telegram and Gazette,* p. A13; Ranalli, R., and Murphy, S. (2003, April 25). Hub Teamsters chief seen taking plea deal. *Boston Globe,* p. A1.

31. Greenhouse, S. (2003, June 1). F.B.I. is investigating teachers' union leader in Miami area. *New York Times,* p. A16; Labor, teachers unions probed for corruption. (2003, July 1). *Facts on File,* p. 621D3; Parker, L. (2003, February 7). Along D.C.'s gold and platinum coasts, a wave of outrage. *Washington Post,* p. C1; Leonnig, C. D. (2004, January 31). Ex-teachers union chief gets nine years. *Washington Post,* p. A1.

Union staff can also be involved in corruption. For example, in 2003 the former director of the Massachusetts Teachers Association was sentenced to two years in prison for embezzling more than $800,000. During a six-year period starting in 1996, Richard Anzivino wrote himself 270 union checks and listed them as payments for expenses. Ex-union leader jailed for stealing $800,000. (2003, December 19). *Telegram and Gazette* (Worcester), p. A2.

32. For a report of the scandal surrounding the Teamsters election, see Greenhouse, S. (1997, September 21). Behind turmoil for Teamsters, rush for cash. *New York Times,* p. A1; Greenhouse, S. (1997, November 19). Tarnished knight of a revived labor movement. *New York Times,* p. A28.

33. The independent review board of the Teamsters, established under the federal consent decree, is composed of a member designated by the attorney general of the United States, one designated by the Teamsters, and one chosen by the Teamsters and government designees. The board hires staff to investigate allegations of corrupt union activity. In 2002, the review board had a staff of 13 investigators and 10 other staff and administrators. The total expense for the operation of the review board was $2.7 million. U.S. Department of Labor. (2003). *Form LM-2 Labor organization annual report.* Washington, DC: Government Printing Office, pp. 160–161. The consent decree establishing the review board is *88 Civ 4486 United States v. International Brotherhood of Teamsters et al.* More than 250 Teamsters officials and members accused of corruption resigned or have been expelled from the union, and James P. Hoffa has been lobbying for the end of the federal supervision of his union. Greenhouse, S. (2001, September 9). Teamsters seek to end U.S. oversight. *New York Times,* p. A26.

34. Greenhouse, S. (2001, November 16). Hoffa claims victory in bid to stay head of Teamsters. *New York Times,* p. A14.

35. Chen, K. (2001, October 15). Carey acquitted on all counts in federal trial. *Wall Street Journal,* p. B12.

36. Teamsters winning fight against organized crime. www.teamster.org/ 02news/nr_021003_1. Goldberg (2001) writes that despite the inappropriate fundraising by Carey, "democracy is established more firmly in the IBT [Teamsters] than even the most wildly optimistic observers would have predicted."

37. For a view that pockets of corruption still thrive in the Teamsters and that only the Teamsters for a Democratic Union, a reform organization of rank-and-file activists, can help the union from returning to its old ways, see Goldberg, M. J. (2005). Teamster reformers: Their union, their jobs, their movement. *Journal of Transportation Law, Logistics and Policy, 72*, pp. 13–27.

38. Ullico was founded 77 years ago to help union workers buy burial insurance and is now a retirement annuities and pension fund and group health and life insurance provider with $3.7 billion in assets. For a discussion of Ullico see Edsall, T. B. (2003, February 23). Uproar over stock deals divides labor leaders. *Washington Post*, p. A4.

39. A few years before the most recent case of self-dealing, Ullico was tainted by another episode of questionable dealings. In 1997, it had sold one of its holdings, the Diplomat Hotel in Hollywood, Florida, to the Plumbers union. The leaders of that union then invested $100 million to help create the 998-room luxury hotel—the Diplomat Resort and Spa—which opened five years later at cost of $800 million. The U.S. Department of Labor sued officials of the Plumbers' pension fund, charging imprudent use of funds. The initial sale of the hotel to the Plumbers would have normally violated a federal law prohibiting a large portion of a pension fund from being invested in a single property, but an exemption had been granted by the Department of Labor in 1999. Bernstein, A. (2002, November 18). Labor chieftains' secret stock deal. *Business Week*, p. 104.

40. Big labor's continuing scandal. (2003, April 6). *Washington Post*, p. B2.

41. Bernstein, A. (2003, April 28). It's looking uglier at Ullico. *Business Week*, p. 70; Bresnahan, J. (2003, March 20). Boehner targets Ullico. *Roll Call*. Greenhouse, S. (2002, November 28). Investigation of stock deal leads to criticism of union chiefs. *New York Times*, p. 30; Greenhouse, S. (2003, April 2). Report said creditors of union-owned insurer should return unfair trading profits. *New York Times*, p. A16; Greenhouse, S. (2003, April 8). Stock dealing at union-owned insurer creates a schism within labor. *New York Times*, p. A15; Greenhouse, S. (2003, April 23). Chairman of insurer says he plans to step down. *New York Times*, p. A25; Greenhouse, S. (2003, May 9). Laborers' leader takes over troubled union-owned insurer. *New York Times*, p. A23; Greenhouse, S. (2003, May 18). The Fighting O'Sullivan. *New York Times*, p. 32.

42. For major works on unions and information technology, see Ad Hoc Committee on Labor and the Web. (2001, December 11). Why the Internet matters to organized labor. www.mindopen.com/laborweb; Shostak, A. B. (1999). *Cyberunion: Empowering labor through computer technology.* Armonk, NY: M. E. Sharpe. Also see the case studies in Greer, C. R. (2004). E-voice: How information technology is shaping life within unions. In D. G. Taras, J. T. Bennett, and A. M. Townsend (Eds.), *Information technology and the world of work.* New Brunswick, NJ: Transaction Publishers, pp. 55–75; Barnett, V. (2004). The use of information technology in a strike. In D. G. Taras, J. T. Bennett, and A. M. Townsend (Eds.),

Information technology and the world of work. New Brunswick, NJ: Transaction Publishers, pp. 173–189; Shostak, A. M. (2004). Today's unions as tomorrow's cyberunions: Labor's newest hope. In D. G. Taras, J. T. Bennett, and A. M. Townsend (Eds.), *Information technology and the world of work.* New Brunswick, NJ: Transaction Publishers, pp. 77–88.

43. The argument against information technology is found in Chaison, G. (2004). Information technology: The threat to unions. In D. G. Taras, J. T. Bennett, and A. M. Townsend (Eds.), *Information technology and the world of work.* New Brunswick, NJ: Transaction Publishers, pp. 89–99; Chaison, G. (2005). The dark side of information technology for unions. *WorkingUSA,* 8, pp. 395–402.

44. For discussions of union effectiveness, see Fiorito, J., Jarley, P., and Delaney, J. T. (1993). National union effectiveness. *Research in the Sociology of Organizations,* 12, pp. pp. 111–137; Rose, J. B., and Chaison, G. N. (1996). Linking union density and union effectiveness: The North American experience. *Industrial Relations,* 35, pp. 78–105.

45. Strauss, G. (1975). Introduction: Symposium—Union financial data. *Industrial Relations,* 14, p. 132.

46. Information about union finances is available to union members and the public. Under the reporting requirements of the Landrum-Griffin Act of 1959 (the Labor-Management Reporting and Disclosure Act), unions must provide financial data to the government each year. These data are readily available on the web page of the U.S. Department of Labor: http://union_reports.dol.gov/olmsWeb/docs/index.html. The reporting requirement has been scheduled to be expanded so that unions will have to disclose additional information about trusts and other funds to which they contribute while also itemizing receipts and disbursements of $5,000 or more. Union officers have complained that this would place a tremendous record-keeping burden on them, but the Bush administration said that such reports are much needed because they would reveal the extent of union spending on political campaigns and lobbying. Greater details in financial reports would, the government claimed, act as a deterrent against financial misconduct. The unions saw it as a Republican-inspired attempt to reduce their political power before the 2004 national elections. Valbrun, M. (2003, October 6). Unions to disclose more on finances. *Wall Street Journal,* p. A2. For a description of the new regulations, see U.S. Department of Labor. (2003). Labor organization annual financial reports final rule. www.dol.gov/esa/formrevfinal.

47. For most of their members, the Teamsters dues are 2.5 times the hourly rate. The dues of the United Mine Workers are three hours' wages per month. The dues for the Laborers are a maximum of $23 per month. The Steelworkers charges 1.3 percent of the members' total monthly earnings except that the amount shall not be less than $5 and shall not be more than 2.5 times the members' average hourly earnings. The dues for the members of Actors' Equity are $118 annually plus working dues of 2.25 percent of gross earnings (not to exceed $300,000

annually). International Brotherhood of Teamsters. (2002). Article 10—Payment of Initiation Fees, Reinitiation Fees and Per Capita Tax. *Constitution of the International Brotherhood of Teamsters.* Washington, DC: International Brotherhood of Teamsters; United Mine Workers of America. (2000). Article 13—Initiation Fees, Dues and Assessments. *Constitution of the International Union, United Mine Workers of America.* Fairfax, VA: United Mine Workers of America; United Steelworkers of America. (2002). Article 14—Dues and Fees. *Constitution of the International Union, United Steelworkers of America.* Pittsburgh, PA: United Steelworkers of America; Laborers International Union. (2003). Article 8—Dues. *Constitution of the Laborers International Union of North America.* Washington, DC: Laborers International Union; Actors' Equity Association. (2001). Article 9—Membership and Dues. *Constitution of Actors' Equity.* New York: Actors' Equity.

A portion of union dues is retained by the local union that collects it and the remainder, the *per capita fee,* is remitted to the national union. Per capita fees vary; for example, 62 percent of the dues of members of the Automobile Workers locals is sent to the national union compared to 54 percent for the Steelworkers, 35 percent for the Laborers, and 27 percent for the Utility Workers. www.teamster.org/2002specconv/brcchart10.

48. For a comprehensive discussion of the financial condition of unions, see Masters, M. F. (1997). *Unions at the crossroads: Strategic membership, financial and political perspectives.* Westport, CT: Quorum. Masters argues that unions will be unable to organize to the extent that they must to reverse declining union density unless they dramatically increase the portion of their budgets allocated to organizing.

49. The government increased the frequency of union audits in 2005, allegedly to fight embezzlement, although the unions claim the government is being politically vindictive for their support of Democratic candidates in the 2004 elections (Greenhouse, 2005, April 17).

50. U.S. Department of Labor, Office of Management Standards. (2003). *Form LM-2: Labor organization annual report—Service Employees receipts and disbursements.* Washington, DC: U.S. Department of Labor, p. 4.

51. www.seiu.org; Bernstein, A. (2004, September 13). Can this man save labor? *Business Week,* pp. 80–88.

52. Rose and Chaison (1996), p. 100.

53. Katz, H. C., Batt, R., and Keefe, J. H. (2003). The revitalization of the CWA: Integrating collective bargaining, political action and organizing. *Industrial and Labor Relations Review,* 56, pp. 573–588.

Four

The Union as Bargaining Agent

U nions are engaged in politics, they have social activities and join community coalitions to further workers' rights, and they organize new members, but the very heart of what unions do is represent workers in collective bargaining and enforce collective agreements at workplaces.[1] Quite simply, workers select or form unions to serve as their bargaining agents and to negotiate with their employers over wages, hours, and conditions of employment. Most workers—about four-fifths of private sector workers and about two-thirds of government workers—have legal rights to be represented by unions and to be covered under collective agreements, although we saw in the previous chapter that only about 13 percent of all workers are actually represented.[2] Of course, employers would rather not deal with unions, preferring instead to make all personnel decisions on their own, but the law requires that they recognize their workers' choice and negotiate in good faith.

The Fundamentals of Bargaining

It is difficult to succinctly describe collective bargaining because it is such an incredibly complex process; each set of negotiations has its own history, context, and character. Sometimes unions negotiate their first agreements at workplaces after certification, meeting with employers for months or even years and fashioning contracts with hundreds of clauses. In other cases, the unions and employers meet for only a few sessions to tweak old agreements by revising wage and benefits clauses or changing a word here or there in some vague clauses. Bargaining can be friendly or acrimonious, and it can simply follow patterns established by other recent negotiations in the industry, or it can be highly experimental, exploring, for example, ways of cushioning the impact of new technologies on the workforce or ways to save huge amounts of money with slight modifications in health care benefits.

All bargaining, however, can be either *distributive* or *integrative* in nature. When bargaining is distributive, the union and management negotiate over the distribution of scarce resources, usually pay and employee benefits. What one party gains, the other party loses. For instance, when the employer has to increase its wage offer by 10 percent to have it accepted, the employer has lost 10 percent and the union has gained 10 percent. This is what is called a *win-lose* or *zero-sum bargaining*—the different between one party's gain and the other party's loss amounts to zero.[3]

But there is also integrative bargaining in which *both* parties gain together because they integrate their goals and solve problems jointly. For example, hospital managers and nurses' unions often negotiate over the assignment of overtime. Management wants the greatest amount of flexibility when it assigns overtime and tries to reduce costs by assigning overtime rather than hiring additional nurses. The nurses' union wants fewer hours of overtime so work schedules can be made more predictable for the convenience of the nurses and the safety of the patients. When they carry out integrative bargaining, both parties recognize that it is possible to reach most of their goals together. For instance, under collective agreements for hospitals in Worcester, Massachusetts, overtime work was not entirely eliminated, nor could it be freely assigned. The amount of daily mandatory overtime was limited, nurses could not be assigned overtime more than eight times a year, and nurses could refuse to work overtime when they feel tired or sick.[4]

In all likelihood, the most prominent recent case of integrative bargaining occurred in the 2002 West Coast dock dispute over the introduction of new information technology. The union, the International Longshore and Warehouse Union, tried to protect the jobs of its 10,500 longshoremen and clerks, but management, the Pacific Maritime Association (the multiemployer association operating on the docks), wanted to introduce scanners that could track cargo and eliminate some jobs. Their differences led to an incredibly bitter dispute—the employers locked out the workers when they believed workers were slowing down on their jobs under union orders to create pressure in negotiations. The lockout closed all the Pacific ports from Seattle to San Diego, cost nearly $1 billion a day, and ended only after the president issued a back-to-work order under federal emergency disputes legislation. The union and management knew they could never get all that they asked for, but under the settlement—a six-year contract—management could introduce new technology, there would be no layoffs, by 400 jobs affected by technology would be reduced by retirements or transfers, and the pension plan would be increased to encourage voluntary retirements.[5]

In at least half of collective bargaining agreements, integrative bargaining results in some form of union-management cooperation program or employee participation plan. These range from shop-floor committees that raise quality and productivity, to the restructuring of jobs to increase workers' skills and production, to committees for labor and management consultation over such strategic issues as new production methods and plant relocation.[6] Often these arrangements were introduced when unions and employers saw a common predicament in low-cost competition from abroad. They feared that if they could not work together to raise productivity and lower costs, many jobs would have to be cut.[7]

Distributive and integrative bargaining are both *interorganizational*—they are between two parties, the union and management. Collective bargaining also has an *intraorganizational* side.[8] Before they meet with each other, the union and management must each negotiate internally, usually informally, to identify and balance the priorities of their constituencies. For example, the older workers in the union might want their negotiators to push for what is most important to them—pensions and health care benefits—while younger workers who have less seniority and job protection might be most concerned about the impact of new production technology. On the management side, there might be conflicts when corporate headquarters wants to cut labor costs with lower wages while plant management wants to focus on eliminating unproductive work rules. Intraorganizational bargaining—reaching internal consensus on bargaining issues and priorities—precedes interorganizational bargaining. Negotiators for the union and management must bring offers and proposals to the bargaining table that are backed by their constituencies so they can sign off on them during negotiations. In essence, collective bargaining has two faces; it is about first getting agreement before going to the bargaining table and then getting agreement at the table.

Collective Bargaining Structure

Bargaining structure is the scope of bargaining—who bargains with whom. It can cover a single plant of a company, many or all plants of a company, many companies, all companies of an industry in a geographic area, or an entire industry nationwide. Also, workers can be represented according to their crafts, or all production workers at a plant or company can be represented together.

In some industries, such as construction, there is separate bargaining for each craft (plumbers, painters, bricklayers, etc.) in a city or region. But in the airlines, each company negotiates a nationwide agreement with unions representing the major crafts (pilots, flight attendants, machinists, ramp workers, etc.). In professional baseball, the bargaining structure is industrywide; one union—the Major League Baseball Players Association—represents all players for all teams. But the most common structure in the United States is a decentralized one: Unions usually negotiate for the production workers at a single facility (e.g., plant or office) or with a single company. Industrywide or multiemployer bargaining is rare.

Unions and employers pressure each other to adjust the parameters of bargaining structure. They might do this to recognize the unique character of occupations (e.g., a separate unit for nurses in hospitals); to stabilize competition in an area (e.g., a citywide construction agreement) or in an industry (e.g., a nationwide agreement for actors or athletes); or to make a strike more effective (e.g., companywide bargaining in the hotel industry so a strike will shut down all facilities) or less effective (e.g., single-plant negotiations in manufacturing so some plants of a company will continue to operate if others are struck). Among government workers, bargaining tends to be decentralized because it is at the level of each school board, police department, or city hall that personnel decisions are made and budgets are prepared. Since the 1980s, bargaining structures in the private sector have been shifting downward under pressure from employers who want to minimize the damage from a strike by keeping their plants under different collective agreements while also negotiating for changes in work rules that can increase productivity at the plant level.[9]

Collective Bargaining Agreements

There are about 180,000 collective bargaining agreements in the United States. Their average duration is three years, so every year about 60,000 negotiations take place.[10] Each negotiation is unique. The give-and-take of bargaining and the eventual settlement are shaped by a number of factors. These include the dynamics of the relationship between the union and management (e.g., whether the parties respect each other or are openly hostile), the history of bargaining (e.g., understandings about and commitments to issues from prior negotiations, personal friendships among negotiators), any problems that occurred living under the last agreement (e.g., contract language that proved difficult to enforce because it was so vague), and the bargaining priorities of the parties (e.g., for management, a strong need to reduce labor costs to stay competitive, and for the union, the importance of protecting workers' jobs in a declining industry).

The thousands of collective bargaining agreements have many clauses in common, and these are listed in Table 4.1. Some clauses establish the rules for administering the agreement (e.g., contract renegotiation and grievance procedures), and others describe aspects of the relationship between the union and management (e.g., management's recognition of the bargaining status of the union, management's right to contract out work). But most clauses set out the rules of employment (e.g., hours of work and rest periods) and the compensation of workers (e.g., wages and pensions).[11]

Collective bargaining agreements are *not* contracts for the sale and purchase of labor. Rather, they establish the relationship between the employer and the union by setting forth the terms and conditions under which workers will be employed. Consequently, they are shaped by the unique conditions and concerns of the workers covered. For example, the collective agreement of the National Basketball Players Association has clauses on special salaries for rookies, the league's antidrug program, and team accommodations, among other issues. The clause on team rules states: "Each team may maintain or establish rules which its players shall comply with at all times, whether on or off the playing floor; provided, however, that such rules are in writing, are reasonable, and do not violate the provisions of this Agreement or the Uniform Player Contract."[12] The agreement between United Airlines and the Association of Flight Attendants has sections on flight assignments, expenses and lodging, work on extra sections (flights that are not regularly scheduled but operate to provide additional service), and deadheading (the transport of flight attendants to or from flights). There is even a clause requiring that "a flight attendant who, while engaged in the service for the Company, is interned or taken prisoner of war by a foreign government shall be allowed compensation at the basic monthly rate."[13] The collective

Table 4.1   Clauses in Collective Bargaining Agreements

Establishment and administration of the agreement:
   Bargaining unit and definition of employee
   Recognition of the union as bargaining agent
   Contract duration, and reopening and renegotiation
   Union security[a]
   Special committees (e.g., bargaining, retirement, safety)
   Grievance procedures and arbitration
   No strikes and no lockouts
   Contract enforcement

Functions, rights, and responsibilities:
   Management rights[b]
   Plant closing and relocation
   Contracting out of work
   Union activities on company time and premises
   Union-management cooperation and employee participation plans
   Regulation of technological change
   Advance notice of changes and consultation with union

Wage determination and administration:
   Rates of pay and pay differentials
   Allowances
   Incentive systems and production bonus plans
   Production standards and time studies
   Job classifications and job evaluation
   General and individual wage adjustments
   Reporting pay
   Overtime pay

Job and income security:
   Hiring and transfer arrangements
   Employment and income guarantees
   Supplemental unemployment benefit plans
   Regulation of overtime and shift work
   Reduction of hours or work-sharing to forestall layoffs
   Layoff procedures and recall
   Attrition arrangements, and downsizing the workforce
   Promotion
   Training and retraining
   Relocation allowances
   Severance pay and layoff benefit plans
   Calculation of seniority

Plant operations:
   Work and shop rules
   Rest periods and other in-plant time allowances

(Continued)

Table 4.1 (Continued)

Safety procedures
Plant committees
Hours of work and premium pay practices
Shift operations
Hazardous work
Discipline and discharge
Work clothing and tools

Paid and unpaid leave:
Vacations and holidays
Sick leave
Funeral and personal leave
Military leave and jury duty

Employees' benefit plans:
Health and insurance plans
Pension plans
Stock purchase and profit sharing plans
Bonus plans
Educational and training programs

Special groups:
Apprentices and learners
Disabled workers
Older workers
Veterans
Union representatives
Antidiscrimination policies and programs

Source: Bloch, J. W. (1964). Union contracts—A new series of studies. *Monthly Labor Review*, 87, pp. 1184–1185, as modified.

a. Requirements that workers join the union and/or pay dues as a condition of continued employment.

b. Clauses in which management reserves rights not specifically amended by the agreement (e.g., hiring workers, scheduling work hours).

bargaining agreement between the League of Off-Broadway Theatres and Producers and the Society of Stage Directors and Choreographers, Inc., has clauses on calculating compensation when part of a production is on videotape or live on television, the rights of directors and choreographers to copyright their work, and artistic approval ("The cast, the understudies, the replacements, set designer, costume designer, and stage manager shall be subject to the approval of the Director, the Author and the Producer. The dance captain shall be subject to the approval of the

Choreographer. Such approvals shall not be unreasonably withheld.") Yet each of these collective agreements is built on a common foundation of basic clauses dealing with, for example, the employer's recognition of the union, the duration of the agreement, the pension and health care benefit plans, the promise of the union not to strike and of the employer not to lock out during the agreement, and many of the others listed in Table 4.1.

When a collective bargaining agreement is up for renegotiation, the parties serve notice on each other of their intent to bargain. They also notify a government agency, the Federal Mediation and Conciliation Service, for possible assistance that would be purely voluntary. A settlement cannot be imposed on the employer and union, but a mediator might be assigned to the negotiations to help the parties resolve issues on their own and reach agreement. Quite often a mediator will simply get the parties to talk reasonably to each other, to consider each other's offers and demands in a fair and flexible way, and to be prepared to make counteroffers rather than stubbornly insist on their own terms.[14]

After bargaining is concluded and employers and unions sign collective agreements (this happens when it has been ratified by a vote of the unions' members or delegates to bargaining councils selected by the members), the agreement must be applied and enforced at the workplace. The grievance procedure, set forth in a section of collective agreement, provides a multistage process through which the union or the employer can claim that the agreement has been misapplied or misinterpreted. Unions and their members file around 90 percent of the thousands of grievances processed each year (the exact total is unknown), and 60 percent are claims that workers were disciplined, suspended, or discharged by management without just cause.[15] If the parties cannot resolve grievances on their own through discussions at the grievance committee meetings at various levels (e.g., between the union and management grievance committees for the department and later between those for the entire plant), they can move the case to *arbitration*—that is, they can ask that the grievance be settled by a neutral third party, an arbitrator, who will conduct a hearing and issue a final and binding award. Each year, about 14,000 grievances go to arbitration.[16]

How effective are unions as bargaining agents? In the preceding chapter, we saw how difficult it can be to appraise union effectiveness. In terms of bargaining, the historical record of effectiveness differs greatly from the most recent trend. Historically, unions have been successful negotiators—they have been able to raise the wages of unionized workers by roughly 20 percent over similar nonunion workers while also providing valuable health care benefits, pensions, and vacation plans.[17] But recently, unions have turned defensive in bargaining, devoting their energies to protecting past gains from being rolled back by management. Often unions have had to grant major concessions to employers in bargaining, and employers have used negotiations to cut operating costs.

The Return of Concessionary Bargaining

Unions and employers now negotiate in a climate of intense competitive pressure. Concessionary bargaining, an extremely contentious form of distributive bargaining, has become common. Although bargaining always involves some concessions—there would never be any agreements reached if the unions and employers did not make concessions from their initial demands and offers—in concessionary bargaining, unions agree to terms that differ significantly from past trends, often by accepting freezes or cuts in wages and benefits.[18]

We have not seen concessionary bargaining to the present extent since the 1980s when many employers, reacting to competitive forces, sought to reduce costs and increase productivity by pressing unions to lower wages and change work rules. Management's demands were usually backed by threats of mass layoffs, bankruptcies, and plant closures. Concessionary bargaining was widespread in the 1980s because employers had to deal with a major recession, intense foreign competition, and industry deregulation (in trucking and airlines). They believed their companies' very survival depended on lower wages and benefits and greater flexibility in determining how work should be done. In the early to mid-1980s, nearly a quarter of collective agreements had wage freezes or wage cuts and about a third had lump-sum wage payments—a cheaper way of giving a pay increase because the lump-sum (bonus) increases are one-time-only payments that do not get built into the wage rate.[19] Concessionary bargaining lessened in the late 1980s as companies saw profits return and adjusted to international competition, but it has started anew since the recession at the start of this century.

One news analysis summarized the present bargaining situation as "companies nationwide demanding concessions from organized labor. As corporations grapple with a weak economy, fierce overseas competition and soaring health care costs, they have made concessions a focus of labor contracts, often demanding wage freezes, lower starting pay, stingier pensions and higher health insurance premiums and co-payments."[20]

Demands for concessions come not only from failing employers who threaten, quite credibly, to close plants and move work overseas but also from profitable companies who fear possible low-cost international competition in the future and want concessions now. There is also some evidence that employers in service companies, such as restaurants, see a surplus of unskilled workers, particularly immigrants, and feel this is an opportune time to reduce wages and benefits.[21]

A common thread running through most recent negotiations is the employers' insistence that unions help cut costs by giving back something that they won in past negotiations. Otherwise, the employers threaten, jobs will be lost. Union negotiators agree to concessions if they believe that there is no other choice and that management's claims of present or impending hardship are credible. For example, in a settlement with Verizon, the union agreed to a five-year contract that had a one-year wage freeze (with a lump-sum payment instead of a regular increase) and an increase of only 2 percent in wages for each of the next four years. But the union successfully resisted company attempts to lay off or involuntary transfer workers (although such job security does not apply to new hires), and it would not allow management to shift some of the costs of health care benefits to the workers. Management had made a strong case that without concessions it would have great difficulty competing against lower-cost providers of wireless services.[22]

In another typical case of concessionary bargaining, the United Auto Workers and American Axle & Manufacturing reached an agreement that protects the wages of present workers while lowering wage rates for new workers. In return, the workers received a $5,000 signing bonus, the retention of their health care and pension plans, and most important, a ban on plant closings. The union's leadership said, quite simply, that the union would do whatever it believes necessary to save good industrial jobs.[23]

When the workers at a Wisconsin plant of Tyson Foods went on strike, the company's last offer at the bargaining table was drastic—a four-year wage freeze; a lower wage scale for newly hired workers; the elimination of a profit-sharing plan; cuts in vacation time, sick leave, and pension benefits; and more expensive health care benefits. After striking for nearly a year, the union settled on most of the company's terms and the members ratified the contract. They feared that the replacement workers hired during the strike would be able to soon vote to have the union decertified.[24]

The most extreme concessionary bargaining has been in the airline industry as unions of pilots, flight attendants, machinists, ground crews, and clerks negotiated against employers who were often on their way to or actually in bankruptcy court. Everyone knew that the airlines were in deep trouble. Not only did the larger and older airlines (called the *legacy airlines*) face intense competition from low-cost carriers such as JetBlue and Southwest, they lost customers because of the economic recession and the slowdown in travel after the September 11, 2001, terrorist attacks. Increases in the price of fuel had dashed their hopes of cost reductions in 2004 and 2005.[25] At the heart of all the business plans for turning airlines around was the need to reduce fares and regain revenues, primarily by lowering wages and benefits.[26]

The legacy airlines used bankruptcy and threats of impending bankruptcy to compel unions to agree to concessions.[27] The courts could void collective bargaining agreements if the airlines could prove that the contracts seriously hamper their business.[28] One observer commented about the relative power of airlines in the bankruptcy court: "There is no bargaining after this. The company is going to get [to do] what it wants, whether the union agrees or not."[29]

Typically, concessions included cuts in wages, increased employee copayments for health care benefits, and changes in work rules that allowed greater use of part-time or less-skilled employees, more hours of work, and smaller work crews.[30] Employers also pressured unions into letting them start low-cost carriers with lower wages and less stringent work rules.[31]

Each legacy airline used a different approach; for example, United Airlines cut costs by terminating pension plans, while USAirways presented its unions with a list of demands and threatened to ask for even more from a bankruptcy judge if major wage and benefit concessions were not agreed to.[32] But whatever approach was used, concessionary bargaining in the airline industry was the most extreme ever attempted by employers. As a sign of its intensity, consider that in late 2004 the pilots at Delta Air Lines approved a new five-year contract by 79 percent of those voting. This was far from a usual collective agreement. The pilots had wage cuts of 32.5 percent (or reduction in the salary of the highest-paid pilot of about $90,000 per year) for a saving for the company of $1 billion per year.[33] Delta had lost more than $10 billion since 2000 and needed relief.[34]

An observer remarked that the airline negotiations lacked the give-and-take that forms the basis of traditional collective bargaining. "I've never seen bargaining like this before. The company is just taking a lead and the unions are reacting."[35] Although settlements were reached, union givebacks were huge and there were no guarantees that jobs would be saved, bankruptcy avoided, and no more concessions needed in the future. Moreover, concessions became the norm for labor relations; even Northwest Airlines, which was in relatively good shape, felt it should demand concessions from its unions.[36]

At the heart of most of the recent concessionary bargaining in the airlines and elsewhere are attempts to cut the costs of health care benefits. The costs of health care have been going up by double digits in each of the past four years, rising by 11 percent in 2004, five times the increase in annual wages (2.2 percent).[37] This is a particularly heavy burden on unionized firms. Three-quarters of unionized workers receive medical benefits from their employer, compared to half of nonunion workers. Moreover, about half of unionized workers receiving benefits had theirs paid for entirely by their employers (compared to 14 percent of the nonunion workers receiving benefits).[38]

As they tried to gain some control over health care benefits, employers bargained with unions over increased workers' payments for plans, higher deductibles, and reduced coverage. A survey of employers about their bargaining objectives found that about a quarter of them wanted to reduce or eliminate health insurance benefits (almost two-thirds in manufacturing wanted to do so). In about half of the cases in which the federal government tried to help unions and employers resolve collective bargaining impasses (i.e., mediated a bargaining impasse), the key issue was health care.[39] A review of bargaining in the grocery industry succinctly reviewed the situation: "Contract talks are regularly stalled over health care, as employers seek help with one of their most explosive costs, and union workers cling to generous health benefits, which represent [one] of the greatest achievements of organized labor this century."[40]

Employers' attempts to cut health care benefits through collective bargaining often meet stiff union resistance because these benefits are needed in times of difficulty and uncertainty and workers feel that any reductions might expose them to calamitous expenses. It was not surprising that the concessionary bargaining aimed at cutting health care benefits was behind one of the biggest strikes in decades: the California grocery strike.

In October 2003, about 60,000 workers walked off their jobs at the stores of the three largest grocery chains—Safeway (owners of Vons and Pavilions), Albertsons, and Kroger (owners of Ralphs)—rather than accept management's demands for concessions. Wages and benefit costs at the three grocery chains were at least 50 percent higher than those at

Wal-Mart, the huge retailer that had planned to open several stores in the state. The companies asked the union, the United Food and Commercial Workers, for increased worker contributions to their health care plans, as well as a two-year wage freeze for present workers, and lower pay for newly hired workers.[41] Wal-Mart, which is the world's largest company and operates nonunion, would be a tough low-cost competitor to the grocery chains because of its economies of scale in operations and its ability to pressure suppliers to sell goods at lower prices. Also, Wal-Mart pays 30 percent less for health care coverage than the industry average and the grocery chains believed that they could not compete against Wal-Mart without major concessions.[42]

The California grocery strike was long and bitter—lasting for four and a half months, it cost the companies $1.5 to 2.5 billion in lost revenues while the union and its members lost millions of dollars (there were no unemployment benefits and the employer-paid health care coverage expired).[43] On March 1, 2004, the workers ratified, by an 86 percent vote, a new collective agreement and returned to work. The agreement included a cost-cutting arrangement that was found in the concessionary bargaining of the 1980s—a two-tiered compensation system under which newly hired workers receive lower wages and fewer benefits than workers employed at the time of the signing. The union agreed with much of what management offered and that it had rejected just before the strike. For example, current workers have their health care benefits maintained, but new employees—those on the lower tier—must wait a month for health care coverage and have lesser benefits.[44]

After the California grocery settlement, concessionary bargaining spread through the industry. For example, in a six-year agreement covering 30,000 workers at Safeway and Giant Food Stores in the Washington, D.C., and Baltimore areas, newly hired workers receive lower health benefits. As one newspaper analysis concluded: "The settlement . . . coupled with the aftermath of a harrowing supermarket strike in California, may have reverberating effects for workers around the country" because it shows a new management determination to cut costs, the importance of health care benefits as a bargaining issue, and the unions' willingness to return to two-tiered settlements, with "the present membership voting that the new membership, membership that's not even there yet, should make sacrifices for them."[45]

If the California grocery strike was a sign of the new management assertiveness bargaining, the recent negotiations in the auto industry showed how far unions and employers will go to avoid a mutually damaging confrontation in hard times. Faced with strong competition from Japanese and European manufacturers, the Big Three—General Motors, Ford, and Daimler-Chrysler—and the United Auto Workers broke with tradition and sought to negotiate collective agreements simultaneously. In the past, the union would choose one of the companies as its target, negotiate a contract with it, and then demand that the others agree to a similar bargain. In the latest round, however, the union and the company wanted to wrap up negotiations without a strike because that would only accelerate the decline in the company's market share (the Big Three's share of the automobile market had dropped from 75 percent in 1980 to 63 percent in 2002) and create massive layoffs of union members (the United Auto Workers' membership had fallen to half of its 1982 high of 1.2 million).[46] The union and the companies agreed to moderate wage increases (including no wage increases for the first two years of the contract), lump-sum wage increases and signing bonuses, and increases in copayments on the health care plans. In return for these concessions, the company promised greater job security and fewer plant closings.[47] As one observer characterized the negotiations, "The unions, staring at large-scale layoffs at companies with huge losses and dwindling market share, are discovering that they, like it or not, are in the same boat as management."[48]

Less than two years after the auto negotiations, General Motors cut the health care benefits of its white-collar workers and asked the union to agree to similar cuts, despite the collective agreement still being in force. The company claimed financial hardship because of declining sales, caused in large part by consumer concerns about fuel economy. General Motors had to pay health care benefits for about two and one-half retirees for every worker, or a total cost of about $1,400 per car produced, and this hurt its ability to compete against low-cost imports. Although the head of the Auto Workers dismissed the idea of reopening the agreement for negotiation, pressures continue to build for concessions with news reports that China would soon become an exporter of low-cost cars to the United States.[49]

A sure sign of concessionary bargaining is long-term collective agreements: Management wants to save more by locking in concessions for a longer period than the usual contract duration. In 1990, 79 percent of collective agreements expired in three years or less. By 1997, the percentage had fallen to 63 percent, and the number of agreements lasting five years or more rose from 6 to 18 percent. In 2004, more than a quarter of employers said in a survey that they intended to negotiate agreements exceeding four years; the corresponding figure was 37 percent for collective agreements covering 10,000 or more workers.[50]

Several high-profile agreements have been unusually long. The International Brotherhood of Electrical Workers signed an 11-year agreement with Lucent Technologies, the Machinists signed a 6-year agreement with United Airlines, and the Auto Workers signed an 8-year agreement at a Jeep plant.[51] The Teamsters and United Parcel Service (UPS) signed a 6-year agreement; the workers did very well under the settlement, but as one newspaper account reported, "While it gave away a lot, UPS still got what it wanted: the assurance of a long period of labor peace . . . [which] promises extra stability for UPS customers rattled by two rounds of labor unrest during the past five years."[52]

The Decline of the Strike

Unions strike to compel employers to agree to their terms in bargaining. Their objective is to have workers withdraw their labor to inflict enough economic harm so employers will settle or modify their terms in bargaining. This must be done, however, without causing so much harm that employers can no longer afford the unions' demands or even have to shut down.

Can unions strike effectively? This is always a difficult question to answer because both union successes and failures are always easy to find. For instance, when the Teamsters struck UPS for two weeks in August 1997 and the settlement included nearly all the union's demands, it was widely hailed as evidence of the unions' power to strike and a resurgence of unionism in the United States.[53] But in a much less publicized but equally important case, in 2002 the Teamsters had to end its three-year strike against Overnite Transportation, a large trucking firm and unit of Union Pacific, without a contract. Some observers saw this as clear evidence of the unions' difficulty striking against employers with extensive nonunion operations. The Teamsters failed to define a unifying issue of concern for the striking workers and the company expanded its nonunion work and posted profits during the strike.[54]

Without any doubt, the possibility of a strike with its lost production and further loss of market share made the Big Three automakers and the United Auto Workers settle their 2003 negotiations quickly and easily. But when the Auto Workers struck Saint-Gobain's abrasives operation in Worcester, Massachusetts, in an effort to get their first agreement after the union was certified, they had to return to work after eight days because so many workers were crossing their picket lines and the employer announced its plans to advertise for striker replacements.[55] When the tollbooth workers on the Pennsylvania Turnpike went on strike, the turnpike commission simply imposed flat tolls ($2 per car and $15 per commercial vehicle) rather than the usual rates based on weight of the vehicle and the distance traveled. During the one-week strike, there were no traffic tie-ups and the new rates and lower labor costs resulted in increased revenues.[56]

Union officers always try to portray strikes in the most favorable light, and strikes that are clearly lost are described as defining an important principle for future negotiations. For example, the California grocery workers' strike has been characterized by those outside the labor movement as a failure because the union had to settle on many of the terms offered by the employers before the four-month strike.[57] Yet a top union officer called it "one of the most successful strikes in history" because it showed how far unions will go to protect health care benefits and make sure that low-wage workers do not become the working poor.[58]

Looking beyond the outcomes of individual strikes, the strike picture is dim for unions. Unions are reluctant to strike. The number and intensity of strikes are in a long decline.

Figures 4.1, 4.2, and 4.3 show three dimensions of strikes—the number of major work stoppages (strikes), the number of workers involved in major work stoppages, and the number of days of idleness caused by major work stoppages. The decline is obvious: Although there were a few spikes in the trend (the most notable around 1970), strikes fell through much of the 1970s, continued to drop in the 1980s, and settled into all-time lows.[59]

Some might argue that the lower strike rate might be good news for unions because it could be a sign of either a new age of union-management cooperation (the parties are resolving their differences in peaceful negotiations) or overwhelming union strength (the employers are settling on the unions' terms because they fear a strike). But Rose and Chaison examined strike trends and concluded that diminished strike activity is the result of "the unions' recognition of the increased propensity of employers to hire permanent striker replacements."[60] Employers can permanently replace strikers when their strike is caused by the normal give-and-take of bargaining (e.g., attempts to get higher wages and better benefits), and they can temporarily replace strikers when the dispute is caused by an employer's unfair labor practice (e.g., the refusal to bargain in good faith).[61]

The use of striker replacements is one of the most contentious issues in labor relations. Singh and Jain observed: "The debate on striker replacements is marked by considerable passion and controversy with many unions and workers' rights advocates proposing a legal

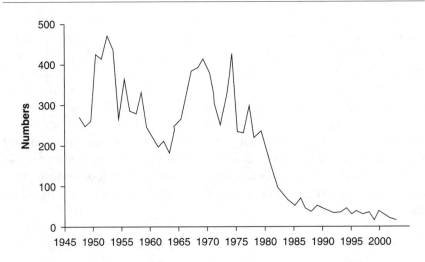

Figure 4.1   Number of Major Work Stoppages, 1947–2004

Source: U.S. Department of Labor, Bureau of Labor Statistics. (2005). *Work stoppages summary.* www.bls.gov/news.release/wkstp.t01.htm.

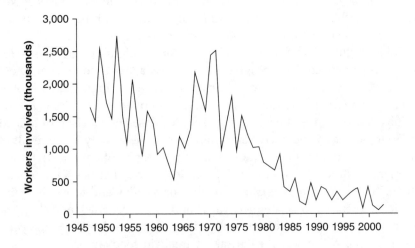

Figure 4.2   Workers Involved in Major Work Stoppages, 1947–2004

Source: U.S. Department of Labor, Bureau of Labor Statistics. (2005). *Work stoppages summary.* www.bls.gov/news.release/wkstp.t01.htm.

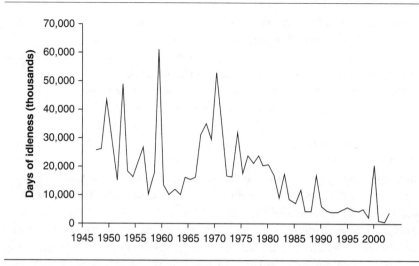

Figure 4.3   Days of Idleness from Major Work Stoppages, 1947–2004

Source: U.S. Department of Labor, Bureau of Labor Statistics. (2005). *Work stoppages summary.* www.bls.gov/news.release/wkstp.t01.htm.

prohibition . . . and employers and 'free-market' advocates generally opposing such prohibitions."[62] A major argument against the employers' hiring of striker replacements is that workers should not lose their jobs because they are exercising their fundamental right to go on strike and withhold their labor. But an argument for the right to replace strikers is that if this right was restricted the balance of power in bargaining would tip toward unions and lead to costly settlements. The companies most hurt would be the smallest ones that can least resist strikes and can ill afford to meet union demands.

There is some validity to the arguments for and against the hiring of striker replacements, and this is why it has become such a thorny issue.[63] It is also an issue with a long and difficult history. In Chapter 1, on the evolution of unions, we saw that American employers commonly dealt with strikers by firing them, replacing them, and continuing to operate and break the union. The unions' hatred of striker replacements has deep roots—they are commonly called *scabs*.[64] When President Ronald Reagan fired and replaced 11,000 striking air traffic controllers in 1981, the unions condemned it in venomous terms, claiming that his act of antiunion and antiworker hatred simply encouraged employers to break unions (there is no evidence to support this). Nonetheless, the use of striker replacements has clearly increased over the years as employers saw that they had nothing to lose by continuing to operate during strikes; consumers generally did not care if goods were made or sold by replacement workers, and workers willingly took the jobs of strikers. Unions became reluctant to call strikes for fear that their members' jobs would be lost, and hence strike activity declined.[65]

But even when the hiring of striker replacements is not practical because so many would have to be hired and trained (e.g., at an auto plant or a steel mill), unions are still reluctant to strike because they know how easily the employer can transfer operations abroad.[66] Globalization has had a tremendous impact on the unions' ability to strike, and therefore their bargaining power, in two ways. First, as noted above, a plant relocated overseas gives an employer a way to continue production during a strike beyond the reach of the union.[67] Second, low-cost goods produced abroad increase competitive pressures on American employers and make credible their argument that unless concessions are granted in bargaining, the company's survival and the workers' jobs will be jeopardized. And if there is a strike, survival and employment will be jeopardized even sooner. As one union officer observed, "The world has changed: globalization. . . .Workers realized that their fortunes were tied to the companies. They couldn't survive unless the company survived."[68]

In the past decade, countries with half of the world's population—China, India, and those in Eastern Europe—entered the international marketplace and had a tremendous impact on trade (e.g., through the "offshoring" (transfers) of technical service jobs from the United States to India or through China's growing dominance of textile and apparel manufacturing).[69] American employers respond to low-cost international competition by restraining labor costs. At unionized firms, employers do this by concessionary bargaining, and back up their demands with threats to transfer work abroad.[70]

Conclusions

The primary objective of American labor unions is to represent workers at their workplaces by negotiating and enforcing collective bargaining agreements with their employers. All signs point to hard times for the unions when they carry out their role as bargaining agents.

As employers react to tremendous competition, they have been pressuring unions for concessions in bargaining. Employers have become assertive, using negotiations to cut costs instead of just responding to union demands. Negotiations are intense, confrontational, and distributive. Unions have fallen back defensively, trying to protect members' jobs and retain past bargaining gains. In particular, health care benefits have become an explosive bargaining issue both because they are so expensive and because workers consider them so important. But for all issues and throughout the general landscape of collective bargaining in America, there has been a return to the concessionary bargaining. To a large degree, this has been a result of the unionized employers' difficult competitive position relative to foreign and domestic nonunion firms.

American employers have always been reluctant participants in the collective bargaining process. Most considered bargaining to be an expensive burden, though one that they could live with. But now they increasingly see collective bargaining as a way to reduce labor costs, get back what was given in the past, and dominate the union-management relationship. Currently, for unions, winning in bargaining simply means not losing.[71]

Notes

1. For example, in his *Lexicon of Labor,* Murray calls collective bargaining the "heart and soul of organized labor." Murray, R. E. (1998). *The lexicon of labor.* New York: New Press, p. 41.

2. About 32 million workers do not have any collective bargaining rights, including 25 million private sector workers (8.5 million independent contractors, 5.5 million employees of small businesses, 10.2 million managers and supervisors, 532,000 domestic workers, and 357,000 agricultural workers). U.S. General Accounting Office. (2002). *Collective bargaining rights: Information on the number of workers with and without bargaining rights.* GAO-02–835. Washington, DC: General Accounting Office.

3. Katz, H. C., and Kochan, T. A. (2004). *An introduction to collective bargaining and industrial relations* (3rd ed.). New York: McGraw-Hill/Irwin, p. 183.

4. Esposito, A. (2001, March 21). University nurses OK 3-year pact; UMass Memorial agrees to overtime-refusal rule. *Worcester Telegram & Gazette,* p. A1.

5. Greenhouse, S. (2002, November 2). Major issue said resolved in mediation over docks. *New York Times,* p. A11; Greenhouse, S. (2002, November 25). Both sides see gains in port agreement. *New York Times,* p. A14. For a detailed description of the technology issue, the events leading to the lockout, and the invocation of the emergency procedures, see Federal Mediation & Conciliation Service. (2004). Pacific Maritime Association–International Longshore and Warehouse Union, AFL-CIO. www.fmcs.gov/internet/itemDetail.asp?categoryID=69&itemID=17678.

6. For example, see the arrangements described in Cutcher-Gershenfeld, J., Kochan, T., and Wells, J. C. (2001). In whose interest? A first look at national survey data on interest-based bargaining in labor relations. *Industrial Relations,* 40, pp. 1–21; Eaton, S. C., Rubinstein, S. A., and McKersie, R. B. (2004). Building and sustaining labor-management partnerships: Recent experiences in the U.S. *Advances in*

Industrial and Labor Relations, 13, pp. 137–156; Schuster, M. H. (1984). *Union-management cooperation.* Kalamazoo, MI: Upjohn Institute.

7. Eaton, Rubinstein, and McKersie (2004).

8. The distinctions between distributive, integrative, and intraorganizational bargaining were first presented by Walton, R. E., and McKersie, R. B. (1965). *A behavioral theory of labor negotiations.* New York: McGraw-Hill. For an excellent comparison of distributive and integrative bargaining, see Budd, J. W. (2004). *Labor relations: Striking a balance.* New York: McGraw-Hill/Irwin, p. 253.

9. Katz, H. C. (2004). United States: The spread of coordination and decentralization without national-level tripartitism. In H. C. Katz, W. Lee, and J. Lee (Eds.), *The new structure of labor relations: Tripartitism and decentralization.* Ithaca, NY: Cornell University Press, pp. 192–212.

10. Katz and Kochan (2004), p. 11; Bureau of National Affairs. (2004, March 15). Employers plan smaller wage hikes and cost-saving benefit changes for 2004 union contracts negotiations, BNA survey finds. *BNA news release.* www.bna.com/press/2004/bargaining 04.html.

11. For a review of collective agreement clauses, see Katz and Kochan (2004), pp. 238–266; Begin, J., and Beal, E. F. (1989). *The practice of collective bargaining* (8th ed.). Homewood, IL: Irwin, pp. 323–445.

12. Article XXVI Team Rules. *Collective Bargaining Agreement.* www.nbpa .com/cba/articleXXVI.html.

13. Article 28: Missing, internment, prisoner of war benefits. *AFA Collective Bargaining Agreement.* www.unitedafa.org/res/cba/2006/section28.htm

14. For a brief description of mediation, see Thaler, D. (2005). *Alternative disputes resolution in the U.S. and the role of the U.S. Federal Mediation and Conciliation Service* (Unpublished conference paper). Washington, DC: Federal Mediation and Conciliation Service. Also, see the description of mediation cases in the agency's web page: www.fmcs.gov.

15. Fax communication from Frank Zotto, vice president of case management for the American Arbitration Association (September 1, 2004).

16. Zotto (2004).

17. Mishel, L., and Walters, M. (2003). *How unions help workers.* Washington, DC: Economic Policy Institute.

18. Chaison, G. N., and Plovnick, M. (1986). Is there a new collective bargaining? *California Management Review,* 28, pp. 54–61; Chaison, G. N., and Rose, J. B. (1991). Continental divide: The direction and fate of North American unions. *Advances in Industrial and Labor Relations,* 5, pp. 169–205. Also, concessionary bargaining is being seen more frequently in Europe. Janssen, R., and Galgoczi, B. (2004). *Collective bargaining in Europe 2003/2004.* Brussels: European Trade Union Institute.

19. Rose, J. B., and Chaison, G. (1996). Linking union density and union effectiveness: The North American experience. *Industrial Relations,* 35, p. 88.

20. Greenhouse, S. (2003, July 11). Employers take a united stand in insisting on labor concessions. *New York Times*, pp. A1, A12. Concessionary bargaining does not occur solely in the private sector. Public employers, such as New York City, have threatened mass layoffs if unions would not agree to cost savings by reducing health care benefits and revising work rules. See, for example, Greenhouse, S., and Steinhauer, J. (2004, May 17). City lays off 2000 as talks grow bitter. *New York Times*, p. B1.

21. Greenhouse, S. (2004, January 26). Seeking an opening at the Oyster Bar. *New York Times*, p. A23; Fabricant, F. (2003, October 29). As contract witching hour nears, restaurant workers talk strike. *New York Times*, p. D6.

22. Greenhouse, S. (2003, September 5). Verizon and unions agree on tentative 5-year contract. *New York Times*, pp. C1, C6.

23. Szczesny, J. (2004, March 1). American Axle strike is over. *The Car Connection*. http://www.thecarconnection.com/index.asp?article=6900&pf=1; Szczesny, J. (2004, March 29). Gettlefinger defends two-tier wages. *The Car Connection*. http://thecarconnection.com/index.asp?n=156,175&sid=175&article=6977&pf=1.

24. Tyson workers reject new contract offer. (2004, January 12). *AP news release*. http://kevxm12adsl.verizon.html; Tyson workers end strike. (2004, January 30). *New York Times*. http://query.nytimes.com/mem/tnt.html.

25. Tatge, M. (2004). Turbulence in the airline industry. *MSNBC News*. http://msnbc.msn.com/id/6434883.

26. Maynard, M. (2004, July 11). Get out the glue for a new business model. *New York Times*, pp. B1, B4.

27. For a short case study of the dynamics of collective bargaining in the context of impending bankruptcy at America Airlines, see Wong, E., and Maynard, M. (2003, April 27). A taut, last-minute stretch to save an airline. *New York Times*, p. B22.

28. As a reaction against their employer's pressure for concessions, some airline workers replaced their unions with one that has a reputation for resisting concessions. In July 2003, the mechanics at United Airlines voted to replace their bargaining agent, the International Association of Machinists, with the Aircraft Mechanics Fraternal Association, a union that had replaced the Teamsters at Northwest Airlines and Southwest Airlines. The Machinists' members were the last of the United employees to agree to concessions in bankruptcy court. They agreed to concessions equal to $794 million per year. Wong, E. (2003, July 15). United Airlines may face deeper challenges. *New York Times*, p. C1.

29. Dash, E. (2005, January 7). Courts side with United and US Airways on labor contracts. *New York Times*, p. C6.

30. Wong, E. (2003, April 9). United and five unions agree on concessions. *New York Times*, p. C2; Maynard, M. (2003, April 29). More than money is at stake in votes by airline unions. *New York Times*, pp. C1, C14; Maynard, M. (2004, June 30). For airlines, a long, argumentative summer. *New York Times*, pp. C1, C6;

Deutsch, C. H. (2004, October 15). For many airline pilots, the thrill is gone. *New York Times,* pp. C1, C4.

31. Wong, E., and Maynard, M. (2003, March 29). Some question bankruptcy role in airlines' cure. *New York Times,* p. C2.

32. Maynard, M. (2004, July 31). Delta wants $1 billion in wage and benefit cuts from pilots. *New York Times,* p. C1; Maynard, M. (2004, September 9). Delta aims to cut jobs 12%, drop a hub and reduce pay. *New York Times,* pp. C1, C8; Maynard, M. (2004, September 25). US Airways plans to seek cuts in pay. *New York Times,* pp. B1, B12; Maynard, M. (2004, September 24). US Airways to ask court to cut union workers' pay 23%. *New York Times,* p. C3; Walsh, M. W. (2004, September 24). United provides an idea of worker pension losses. *New York Times,* p. C3.

33. Maynard, M. (2004, November 12). Delta pilots vote to accept 32.5% pay cut. *New York Times,* p. C3.

34. Maynard, M. (2005, January 21). Delta posts $2.2 billion loss: Continental also reports deficit. *New York Times,* p. B6.

35. Maynard, M. (2004, October 2). Pilots reach tentative deal with US Air on pay cuts. *New York Times,* p. B13.

36. Maynard, M. (2004, October 15). Pilots union agrees to cuts at Northwest. *New York Times,* p. C4.

37. Freudenheim, M. (2004, September 10). Cost of insuring workers' health increases 11.2 percent. *New York Times,* pp. C1, C4. Health care costs increase mostly because of the rising price of drugs, expensive new processes for diagnostic testing, and an insurers' reaction to the lifting of past restrictions on the costs of health care plans. Porter, E. (2004, August 19). Cost of benefits cited as factor in the slump in jobs. *New York Times,* pp. A1, C2.

Health care spending is expected to double from 2004 to 2014. Pear, R. (2005, February 24). Health care costs keep rising, U.S. says, along with government share of paying them. *New York Times,* p. A21.

38. Perotin, M. (2003, May 23). Health care burdens lead union agenda in this year's contract negotiations. *Knight Ridder/Tribune Business News* (item 03143041).

39. Federal Mediation and Conciliation Service. (2004, June 6). FMCS, NLRB and NMB chiefs discuss trends in labor relations. www.fmcs.gov/internet/item Detail.asp?categoryID=39&itemID=18130.

40. Nyhan, P. (2004, March 29). Grocery jobs are not the secure anchors they used to be. *Seattle Post-Intelligencer,* p. A1.

41. The companies paid the entire costs of health care coverage but wanted the employees to begin paying $5 to 15 per week. Madigan, N. (2003, December 17). Striking workers plan Safeway boycotts. *New York Times,* p. A32; Porter (2004, August 19).

42. The average wage at Wal-Mart was $8.50 an hour compared to $13 at the competing unionized stores. Greenhouse, S. (2003, October 19). Wal-Mart, driving workers and supermarkets crazy. *New York Times,* p. C3. For a discussion of the

unions' and local businesses' concerns about Wal-Mart, see Kinzer, S. (2004, July 6). Treading carefully, Wal-Mart enters labor's turf. *New York Times*, p. A12.

43. Greenhouse, S. (2004, February 10). Labor raises pressure on California supermarkets. *New York Times*, p. A12.

44. Appleby, J. (2004, March 1). Calif. Grocery workers go for contract: Overwhelming vote end nearly 5-month strike. *USA Today*, p. B1; Mitchell, R. (2004, October 10). The health care clash moves to the next aisle. *New York Times*, p. B5. The strike has been described as "a total defeat for the union." Sweeny, S. (2005). Industrial relations in the USA 2003–4. European Industrial Relations Observatory Online. www.eiro.eurofund.eu.int/2004/11/feature/Us0411101f.html, p. 6.

45. Hirsh, S. (2004, April 1). Grocery contract a 2-tiered omen. *Baltimore Sun.* http://www.baltimoresun.com/business/bal-bz.groceries01apr01,0,6707786.story.html.

46. Ball, J., Hawkins, L., and Freeman, S. (2003, September 8). Big Three, UAW show rare unity. *Wall Street Journal*, p. A2; Hakim, D. (2003, September 15). Union in deal with Chrysler; Talks with 2 makers continue. *New York Times*, p. A14; Maynard, M. (2003). *The end of Detroit: How the Big Three lost their grip on the American car market.* New York: Doubleday.

47. Hudson, M., Vlasic, B., and Truby, M. (2003, September 21). UAW, Big Three unite to rebuild. *Detroit News*, p. A1; Hakim, D. (2003, September 23). Auto deal or bust. *New York Times*, p. B2; Hartley, T. (2004, March 15). Rush to preserve jobs reduces UAW to tiers. *Buffalo Business First*. http://buffalo.bizjournals.com/buffalo/stories/2004/03/15/story1.html.

48. Greenhouse, S. (2003, September 10). Labor adopts new strategy. *New York Times*, p. A1.

49. Hakim, D., and Peters, J. W. (2005, March 22). Big Three workers give an inch on heath care. *New York Times*, pp. B1, B7; Hakim, D. (2005, March 24). G.M. to seek cuts in health care benefits. *New York Times*, p. C1; Hakim, D., and Peter, J. W. (2005, April 15). Shares of G.M. tumble on issue of health care. *New York Times*, p. C4; Bradsher, K. (2005, April 22). China looms as the world's next auto producer. *New York Times*, pp. C1, C5. For a discussion of the response to GM's demands for contract reopening by Ron Gettelfinger, president of the United Auto Workers, see Hakim, D. (2005, June 23). U.A.W. chief faces shrinking auto industry. *New York Times*, pp. C1, C3.

50. E-mail message (March 17, 2004) from David Thaler, a commissioner of the Federal Mediation and Conciliation Service, citing the results from a survey of the Bureau of National Affairs.

51. Kramer, D. (2000), p. 3: Wong, E. (2003, July 15). United Airlines may face deeper challenges. *New York Times*, p. B1; McKinnon, M. (2003, December 22). Jeep workers weight ground breaking pact. *Toledo Blade*, p. 10.

52. Brooks, R., and Whelan, C. H. (2002, July 17). Hoffa wins with UPS pact. *Wall Street Journal*, p. B4.

53. Rothstein, R. (1997). Union strength in the United States: Lessons from the UPS strike. *International Labour Review*, 136, pp. 469–492.

54. Greenhouse, S. (2002, October 26). Teamsters end three-year strike against trucker without contract. *New York Times*, p. A10; Schulz, J. D. (2002, November 4). *Traffic World*, pp. 10–13.

55. Eckelbecker, L. (2003, November 6). Saint-Gobain workers go on strike. *Worcester Telegram & Gazette*, p. A1; Kievra, B. (2003, November 7). Strike goes on as both sides ponder choices. *Worcester Telegram & Gazette*, p. A1; Kievra, B. (2003, November 14). UAW ends Saint-Gobain strike. *Worcester Telegram & Gazette*, p. A1.

56. WGAL. (2005, January 10). Turnpike commission considers flat tolls. www.wgalchannel.com/print/4068979.

57. For a critical appraisal of the grocery workers strike, see Hiltzik, M. (2004, March 4). UFCW sacrifices workers while declaring victory. *Los Angeles Times*. www.latimes.com/business/la-fi-golden4mar4,1,3861988.column?coll=la-utilities-business.

58. Hiltzik (2004, March 4).

59. U.S. Department of Labor. (2003, March 11). Major work stoppages in 2002. *USDL press release 03-100*.

60. Chaison and Rose (1996), p. 91.

61. U.S. National Labor Relations Board. (1997). *Basic guide to the National Labor Relations Act*. Washington, DC: Government Printing Office. The board draws a distinction between *economic strikers* and *unfair labor practice strikers*. "If the objective of a strike is to obtain from the employer some economic concession such as higher wages, shorter hours, or better working conditions, the striking employees are called economic strikers. They retain their status as employees and cannot be discharged, but they can be replaced by their employer. If the employer had hired bona fide permanent replacements that are filling the jobs of the economic strikers when the strikers apply unconditionally to go back to work, the strikers are not entitled to reinstatement at that time. However, if the strikers do not obtain regular and substantially equivalent employment, they are entitled to be recalled to jobs for which they are qualified when openings in such jobs occur if they, or their bargaining representative, have made an unconditional request for their reinstatement. . . . Employees who strike to protest an unfair labor practice committed by their employer are called unfair labor practice strikers. Such strikers can be neither discharged nor permanently replaced. When the strike ends, unfair labor practice strikers, absent serious misconduct on their part, are entitled to have their jobs back even if employees hired to do their work have to be discharged" (p. 4).

62. Singh, P., and Jain, H. C. (2001). Striker replacements in the United States, Canada and Mexico: A review of the law and empirical evidence. *Industrial Relations*, 40, pp. 22–53.

63. One of the unions' most difficult political fights (and one that they lost) was for legislation proscribing the use of permanent striker replacements. Logan, J. (2004). Labor's "last stand" in national politics? The campaign for striker replacement legislation, 1990–1994. *Advances in Industrial and Labor Relations,* 13, pp. 191–243.

64. Although it is uncertain how the term *scab* originated, there can be no doubt that it implies that a person is despised for taking the job of another. Murray (1998), pp. 160–161.

65. See Logan (2004), p. 224, for a list of high-profile strikes involving permanent striker replacements in the 1980s and 1990s.

66. Ball, J., Burkins, G., and White, G. L. (1999, December 18). Don't walk: Why labor unions have grown reluctant to use the "s" word. *Wall Street Journal,* pp. A1, A8.

67. This can be illustrated by the adverse effect of the North American Free Trade Agreement (NAFTA) on union bargaining power. For example, see Scott, R. E. (2000). *NAFTA's hidden costs: Trade agreement results in job losses, growing inequality and wage suppression for the United States.* Washington, DC: Economic Policy Institute. "Employers' credible plans to relocate plants, to outsource portions of their operations, and to purchase intermediate goods and services directly from foreign producers can have a substantial impact on workers' bargaining positions. The use of these kinds of threats is widespread" (p. 8). Employers' threats during strikes increased, and many employers have indicated a willingness to use NAFTA as a bargaining chip in negotiations to keep down wages.

For a brief review of the impact of globalization on unions and workers, see Newland, K. (1999). Workers of the world, now what? *Foreign Policy,* 114, pp. 52–65.

68. Ball, Burkins, and White (1999), p. A1.

69. Prestowitz, C. (2005). *Three billion new capitalists: The great shift of wealth and power to the East.* New York: Basic Books; Economic Policy Institute. (2005). Offshoring. *CPI issue guide.* www.epinent.org; Blanton, K. (2004, November 17). Offshoring accelerating. *Boston Globe,* p. D1; Barboza, D. (2005, April 4). Stream of Chinese textile imports is becoming a flood. *New York Times,* p. C3; Fong, M. (2005, April 11). Woven in China. *Wall Street Journal,* pp. B1, B4.

70. Greenhouse, S. (2005, April 12). Falling fortunes of the wage earner. *New York Times,* p. C1.

71. Or, as Stephen Greenhouse, the preeminent labor reporter, put it: "Labor's first concern has changed from demanding more and more to making sure that companies and jobs survive." Greenhouse (2003, September 10), p. A1.

Five

Unions in Politics

When we look at the unions' role in politics, we see clear limits to their power. Unions are strongest when they work through coalitions but the results help workers in general rather than unions and their members. They have had some notable victories and near victories, for example, in the area of foreign trade, but their losses have been stunning, such as in the 2004 national elections. They were major forces behind the passage of historic legislation affecting the workplace, such as the Civil Rights Act of 1964 and the Occupational Safety and Health Act of 1970, but for nearly three decades they could not get Congress to reform the basic law of collective bargaining. Unions are greatly respected in political circles for their political savvy and ability to mobilize the membership, yet they are also taken for granted because their allies all know which candidates and legislation unions always support. Unions are also very aware after the 2004 national election that they are no longer the champions of the political "ground game"—canvassing prospective voters and getting out the vote on Election Day. Now, the political parties and nearly all other organizations with political objectives are doing voter registration and getting-out-the-vote drives, and doing it quite well.

In this chapter, I present a broad portrait of the unions' successes and failures in politics. I discuss forms of union political action, the place of politics in the unions' mission, and some of the unions' recent campaigns.

Union Political Action

At first glance, union political action might seem to be a fairly simple matter of endorsing candidates, essentially following the century-old dictum of "rewarding friends and punishing enemies."[1] Unions usually see Democrats as friends and Republicans as enemies, although union officers are always careful to say that they evaluate candidates on the basis of issues rather than party affiliation.[2] In the words of AFL-CIO President John J. Sweeney: "We support pro-working family Republicans wherever we can."[3]

Unions surely want to endorse candidates most friendly to their cause, but they have to temper this with a good dose of realism. They understand they must not only choose candidates they like but also who have good chances of winning nominations and elections. For example, during the 2000 presidential campaign, the unions were initially unenthusiastic about supporting Al Gore because of his strong support of foreign trade policies that cost union members their jobs, particularly the liberalization of trade with China.[4] But they had little choice since George W. Bush's record seemed to them to be so thoroughly antiworker and antiunion. Ralph Nader, the candidate with the strongest pro-union record, could not win and unions believed support for him would only siphon votes off from Gore and hand Bush a close victory. After Gore's endorsement from labor (a late endorsement to show their displeasure with Gore's trade policies), he always saved a prominent place in his speeches for the unions' top issues, for example, increasing the minimum wage and reforming of the law of organizing. He also had to promise that if elected he would sign trade bills only if they included strong labor and environmental standards.[5]

In the 2004 presidential primaries, unions again had to be practical. Senator John Kerry was not the unions' first choice but they supported him because of their intense dislike for the Bush White House and their feelings that they should unite early behind a candidate capable of being elected.[6] Their other choices were Governor Howard Dean of Vermont (supported by many workers and endorsed by two big unions), Senator Richard Gephardt of Missouri (the long-time union favorite, supported by a block of industrial unions because of his policies of restricting international trade), and Senator John Edwards of North Carolina (endorsed by a union and supported many workers because of his eloquently expressed concern for social and economic issues).[7] Senators Gephardt and Edwards did not have the primary victories needed for endorsement from the AFL-CIO. When Howard Dean failed to do as well as expected in the primaries, his union supporters abandoned him.[8] The lesson here for all to see was that the union movement never wants to appear divided in choice and that having momentum and looking like a winner is crucial to getting the union endorsement.[9] As the head of a large public employee union succinctly put it, "Electability is incredibly important."[10]

The AFL-CIO's endorsement can be given only to candidates who have the support of affiliated unions with two-thirds of the federation's members—about 8.8 million members.[11] Each union has its own rules about endorsements, for example, how much support there should be among members, and which union committee decides whom to endorse. Unions invariably endorse the Democratic presidential contender, but there is considerable disagreement among union officers about whether endorsement should be given early—during primaries—or after candidates have been selected. Some union leaders argue that an early endorsement by only a few unions makes the labor movement appear divided, and that any endorsement before all primaries are held gives the impression that unions are unconcerned about their members' preferences. They also oppose an early endorsement because they want to make candidates sweat a little by having them competing among each other for the union's endorsement.[12] Early endorsements can also backfire; if a candidate who was endorsed early does not win the party nomination, the unions will seem politically weak and the winning candidates will owe little to the unions.

But some union leaders believe that their willingness to make an early endorsement gives unions exceptional political power because they can extract concessions from candidates and have greater access to them at a time when their policies are being settled. Successful early endorsements also make union leaders look like kingmakers.[13] Early endorsements instantly broaden the base of support for candidates while increasing the prestige of the endorsing unions by calling attention to them in a matter of great national interest.[14] For example, the leaders of the International Association of Fire Fighters, a small union, seemed powerful and politically astute when the union was first to endorse Senator John Kerry at a time when his presidential primary campaign was faltering, and they could take some credit for reviving it.[15]

Candidates seeking the union endorsement are interviewed by union executive councils about their positions, and they attend local meetings and national conventions to speak on work issues most important to the unions and their members.[16] Endorsements result in greater membership support at the polls, and although this is not an overwhelming advantage because of the small and declining number of union members, it has some importance because union members and members of their households are more likely to vote than others and account for large proportions, often more than a third, of voters in major industrial states.[17]

When they are elected, union-endorsed candidates are expected to fully support worker-friendly and union-friendly legislation (e.g., new minimum wages and new organizing laws). They are sometimes called on by unions to help during organizing drives, for example, by applying political pressure on employers to have unions recognized as bargaining agents, or by speaking or writing to workers and criticizing employers' antiunion tactics.[18]

The unions may not have an easy time choosing the friend to be rewarded with their endorsement, but they are often quite certain who is the enemy to be punished. Their objective in 2004 was clear and simple— to unseat George W. Bush by backing whichever candidate could do it. Bush was characterized as a disaster for the labor movement and workers in general. The unions charged him with conducting a war against them with a "scorched earth policy" that included weakening workplace health and safety regulations, cutting workers' overtime pay, denying the right to unionize for workers employed in the newly formed Department of Homeland Security, privatizing jobs of public sector workers, and proposing regulations that would require unions to file reports on their political expenditures. They accused Bush of favoring the rich and hurting working families with his economic and health care policies. They said that he promoted trade with low-cost producers overseas and, by doing so, not only increased corporate profits but eliminated the jobs of millions of manufacturing workers.[19] The unions of government workers endorsed Senator Kerry despite his past pledges to cut government employment and reduce budgets, because they believed that Bush's election would be far worse for their members' job security.[20]

The unions never missed a public opportunity to make the case against the president. For example, they attacked him for refusing to punish China for gaining unfair trade advantage by denying its workers the basic right to minimum wages and union membership. John Sweeney portrayed the White House as under corporate control: "President Bush proves himself to be, once again, the servant of his corporate donors."[21]

A union political strategist commented: "Another four years of this [Bush] administration will decimate the labor movement."[22] A union leader exclaimed: "What's at stake is the very existence of the labor movement. The movement . . . will be set back for decades if George Bush wins."[23] Under these conditions, anyone who could displace Bush would be endorsed. As a newspaper report succinctly described the situation, "For most unions, Kerry was not the first choice for Democratic nominee. But labor has rallied behind Kerry, united by a visceral dislike of the Bush White House."[24]

One of the unions' great political strengths is their ability to communicate with voters—members and nonmembers, workers and the public in general. Unions perfected the advocacy ad. Under federal restrictions on the funding of advertisements directly supporting candidates, unions became creative, devising ads that advocate points of view and action on issues of political importance, for example, the need for comprehensive health insurance coverage, and then suggest that some candidates have the right approach to these problems and others do not.

Lobbying is another basic political activity of unions. Unions try to convince legislators to propose and support laws that help unions and their members (e.g., reforming the law of organizing or penalizing employers who discharge union supporters during organizing) or that help workers in general (e.g., increasing the minimum wage or restricting imports that cost workers their jobs). Lobbying and campaigning for candidates are often complementary. Delaney and Masters concluded: "Lobbying is fruitless if elected officials are unsympathetic, and failed electoral efforts may make politicians even less supportive of union initiatives than otherwise."[25] The election of union-backed candidates does not guarantee the passage of legislation favored by unions, but the election of union opponents could doom its passage.

Unions also contribute directly or indirectly to political funds. They spent more than $150 million on the 2004 elections, an increase of about 50 percent over the 2000 elections, but they were outspent by companies by a ratio of about 10 to 1. Unions hold seven places on the list of the top 10 political contributors since 1989—the other places were held by organizations of realtors, trial lawyers, and doctors.[26] Recent legislation, however, has forced unions to redirect their giving.

The Bipartisan Campaign Reform Act (McCain-Feingold Act) of 2002 banned contributions to political parties rather than candidates (so-called *soft money*), increased the amount an individual can give to a candidate (*hard money*) from $1,000 to $2,000 per election, and imposed a cap of $5,000 on contributions from political action committees (PACs) per candidate per election.[27]

But the actual limits to union political funding were unclear because of the presence of *527 committees* (so-called because their status is defined under section 527 of the tax code), the advocacy committees that cannot coordinate with candidates' campaigns nor endorse candidates.[28] McCain-Feingold's restrictions on soft-money contributions did not extend to 527 committees, which do not have to disclose their donors or expenditures.[29] The committees became the source of the new soft money.[30]

Most 527 committees were formed by Democrats and their allies who feared that Republicans enjoyed a fund-raising advantage. Although they promote specific issues (e.g., job creation, voter registration, or environmental protection), the 527's support for some candidates and opposition to others is often transparent. For example, a major 527 committee, America Coming Together, had the objective of "laying the ground work for Democratic victories," and was run by a past political director of the AFL-CIO. In the absence of authoritative clarification on the appropriate role of the 527 committees and restriction of their blatantly partisan activities, unions will continue to use them as soft-money outlets and, as they have to compete against industry 527's, they will increase their political contributions. [31]

With all the controversy over union financial contributions (or the rules of campaign funding in general),[32] it is often forgotten that the most desired contribution any union can make to a candidate or political party is the support and enthusiasm of its members. As John Sweeney observed, "Our strength is not really our financial resources. Our strength is our membership and the people power."[33]

Activist union members lobby legislators, staff phone banks, and drive voters to the polls. Candidates endorsed by unions can always have a backdrop of union members at their rallies and televised announcements (e.g., a job creation announcement might be made at a rally of Steelworkers or Auto Workers, a public safety announcement might have a backdrop of unionized police and firefighters). Union members make personal contacts to get out the vote. Studies have shown that the more that unions contact individual members during election campaigns, the greater the likelihood that the union member will vote and vote for the union-endorsed candidate.[34]

Union members were once called the foot soldiers of the Democratic Party because they have been such ever-present activists.[35] In the past, the unions' ability to rally the membership behind a candidate was usually more than sufficient to offset the greater financial power of employers who support opposition candidates. It also made unions welcomed coalition partners because they could contribute their members to coalition activities whether through rallies or lobbying. One news report rightly compared the unions to the religious right. "The two represent key elements of grass-roots activism within their respective parties."[36] However, unions are no longer the champions of the political ground game—mobilizing members, registering voters, and getting out the vote. The 2004 election campaign (reviewed later in this chapter) was tremendously important for the unions for reasons other than the outcome; the ground game for the campaign was done by 527 committees, church and community groups, and the political parties themselves. They did it much better than the unions, and their efforts made the crucial difference in support of Republicans in states where the vote was close (e.g., Ohio).[37]

Unions and Political Campaigns

The Fight against NAFTA

The North American Free Trade Agreement (NAFTA) removed restrictions and tariffs on trade between the United States, Canada, and Mexico. The campaign against NAFTA was the greatest political struggle of contemporary unions, and although the pact was passed in 1993 and the unions lost the fight, the anti-NAFTA campaign showed labor at its most unified, skillful, and dominant in the political arena.

Shoch summarized the basis for the unions' opposition to NAFTA: "The most concerted opposition to a regional trade pact . . . was mounted by the American labor movement. For labor . . . NAFTA was more an investment than a trade issue [for U.S. multinational companies]. Industrial unions worried that by liberalizing not just trade but also investment rules, such an agreement would intensify both the actual and threatened flight of manufacturing capital to Mexico in search of cheap labor, thus eliminating U.S. jobs and undercutting American workers' bargaining power and wages."[38]

Unions fought NAFTA by leading the NAFTA Fair Trade Campaign, a broad coalition of environmentalist, antipoverty, consumer protection, religious, women's, farmers', students', and public policy organizations. Unions had strained relationships with their coalition partners; for instance, they had fought with environmentalists over the damage caused by manufacturing and development, but they now saw a common purpose and were willing to put aside their differences.

The unions took the lead by skillfully crafting communications, emphasizing the themes that NAFTA was not only a labor issue but an environmental one as well (because Mexico had poor environmental standards); NAFTA affected the social and economic well-being of all Americans because of the widespread job losses; NAFTA perpetuated unjust economic policies that benefited big business but hurt workers; NAFTA hurt rather than helped Mexican workers; and finally, voters could support free trade but also reject NAFTA because NAFTA was wrong by providing only investment opportunities for corporations rather than opportunities for economic and social betterment.[39]

President Bill Clinton managed to defuse much of the opposition to NAFTA by proposing that the trade pact have side agreements for labor and environmental issues. The labor side agreement would, for example, promote the principle of freedom of association and the right to bargaining collectively and prohibit forced and child labor. But the commission that enforces the side agreement has no remedial powers. The labor side agreement enabled the Clinton administration to claim that it had repaired NAFTA's shortcomings, and it gave political cover to members of Congress trying to justify their support for the trade pact.[40]

In November 1993, NAFTA was approved in the House by a vote of 234–200 and in the Senate by 61–38. The bill was supported by about three-quarters of the House Republicans and about 40 percent of the House Democrats, and by three-quarters of the Senate Republicans and half of the Senate Democrats.[41] Although NAFTA had strong congressional backing and passed, the unions and their coalition partners were able to blunt the campaign of the NAFTA supporters. Public support for the trade agreement dropped sharply during the campaign. In March 1991, 72 percent of persons surveyed believed NAFTA was "mostly good," but this fell to 55 percent in September 1992. In November 1993, when the House of Representatives voted, only 38 percent of those surveyed supported NAFTA and 41 percent opposed it.

Although they failed to stop NAFTA, the campaign energized the unions and showed them how it was possible to work through a coalition and devise communications capable of changing public opinion.[42] Moreover, as Rose and Chaison observed, "the failed campaign against NAFTA may have actually enhanced the stature of unions because they led a broad coalition and fought with great passion and skill against a treaty that was widely seen as a threat to both union and nonunion jobs."[43] The next time a trade bill came up before Congress, the unions and their coalition partners were ready and much more effective.

Fast Track

Under *Fast Track* authority from Congress, presidents since 1974 have had the power to expedite trade negotiations by requiring that trade treaties be voted up or down by Congress and not amended. Fast Track was defeated in November 1997 after strong opposition led by unions.

In fall 1997, the Clinton administration requested the continuation of Fast Track authority so it could negotiate treaties that would expand NAFTA to include Chile and eventually other countries in Latin America and Asia. It was made clear than new treaties would *not* include labor and environmental standards in their main body, a feature the unions insisted on since the passage of NAFTA with its weak side agreements.

The understanding behind the administration's Fast Track proposal was that labor and environmental standards would be considered "negotiating objectives" and included in future treaties only if they were directly related to trade. In contrast, intellectual property and agriculture were deemed to be commercial issues that should be dealt with in the core of treaties and thus enforceable through sanctions. Convinced that it needed to get Republican support, the White House had weakened the bill's labor and environmental provisions. Fast Track's supporters argued that no country would agree to negotiate a trade agreement if it believed that Congress could restrict it or water it down endlessly to get the needed approval.[44]

Fast Track was the focal point of an intense political fight between opponents and supporters of trade liberalization. The AFL-CIO launched a $1 million broadcast campaign against Fast Track, claiming that it would allow the Clinton administration to negotiate more NAFTA-type agreements and this would reduce wages and eliminate jobs in the United States, all without helping workers elsewhere. Labor took the position that Fast Track should be approved if, and only if, the administration promised that new trade pacts included labor and environmental safeguards in their core rather than as side agreements.

Fast Track became a litmus test for union support. Labor leaders refused to endorse politicians who voted for Fast Track and even promised to work against them.[45] Environmental and citizen interest groups joined the unions in a coalition to fight the bill. Votes on the Fast Track were delayed twice and its supporters were finally forced to withdraw the bill when it became apparent that it would not pass.[46]

The unions and their coalition partners were able to defeat Fast Track because of the rising public opinion against international trade in general and the feeling that NAFTA had helped neither American nor Mexican workers. They organized a broad-based and energetic grass-roots movement against Fast Track, and Democrats, who were eager for the union endorsement, could not vote for it without losing vital labor support. The unions learned a political lesson from the earlier NAFTA defeat; they had to unequivocally oppose legislators who would vote for Fast Track, and they could not let unenforceable labor side agreements deflect the energy of the antitrade movement.[47] They had served notice to the present and future administrations that henceforth any new trade agreements would face intense and well-organized opposition.[48]

Minimum Wage and Overtime Laws

Unions are always lobbying for higher minimum wages. Although very few unionized workers receive the minimum wage under their collective bargaining agreements, the minimum serves as the floor of the wage structure. When the minimum wage is increased, unions can make a stronger case for higher wages when they negotiate. Also, as unions fight for the minimum wage they show they are concerned with the working poor and not solely with their own members.[49]

Although the minimum wage is essentially an economic matter, it has tremendous political importance because it deals with two conflicting and fundamental rights: the right of employers to pay only what the labor market dictates to recruit and retain workers and the right of workers to earn a decent wage (a family earning the present federal minimum wage receives less than a third of its basic budget needs for living in an urban area).[50] Democrats regularly propose minimum wage increases, attaching them as amendments to other legislation. Republicans usually object to increases in minimum wages, arguing that wages should be determined by market forces rather than by law and that the imposition of artificially high wages will result in job losses among the lowest-paid and least-skilled workers.

The Republicans look at minimum wages from the viewpoint of one of their key constituencies—the small business owners who often pay the minimum wage and do not want an increase—while the Democrats respond to unions, community organizations, and workers' rights groups who claim to speak for the working poor. The result is usually a standoff on the minimum wage, with no changes enacted, except on the state level where unions have sufficient influence in legislatures.[51]

The unions' campaign for a higher minimum wage is a perpetual lobbying effort. But recently, the unions became embroiled in an intense political skirmish over a feature of the minimum wage: the right of employers to reclassify workers as managers or professionals and thus exclude them from receiving overtime pay.[52] The Bush administration and congressional Republicans proposed new overtime regulations in 2003. The unions argued that the initial proposal would disqualify about 8 million workers from overtime (not the 644,000 workers estimated by the government) and would cheat workers out of their hard-earned pay. John Sweeney claimed that: "the Labor Department's proposed revisions to the overtime regulations . . . would drastically broaden existing exemptions from coverage, making it easier for employers to demand more work for less pay from their employees. These changes would hurt millions of workers and their families."[53]

The business community had pressed the administration for changes in the overtime rules, arguing that the old regulations were not compatible with the broadly defined jobs and the greater job discretion and responsibilities that were the new reality of the workplace. The unions immediately attacked the proposed regulations, but it proved difficult to maintain a continuing campaign against them, particularly after they were revised in 2004 to protect the overtime rights of police and firefighters and some lower-paid workers. The new overtime regulations were put into force by the Bush administration on August 23, 2004, despite congressional opposition.

Living Wages

Unions also exercise political power and affirm their role as the voice of the working poor through their *living wage* campaigns. They work in coalitions to win the passage of living wage laws that require contractors who receive public funding to pay their workers wages above the local poverty level. For example, in Berkeley, California, the living wage ordinance, enacted in June 2000, requires a minimum hourly wage and employee benefits from employers who hold contracts with the city, lease city property, or receive city financial aid. Employers have to pay

$9.75 per hour with health care benefits or $11.37 per hour without benefits (compared to a state minimum wage of $6.75).[54]

Living wage laws have been passed by city councils in San Francisco, New York City, Cleveland, Denver, Los Angeles, Detroit, and Boston, among other cities, after rallies and lobbying by unions and their coalition partners (primarily community, workers' rights, and religious organizations).[55] The underlying principle of the living wage campaign is "Our limited public dollars should not be subsidizing poverty-wage work. . . . Public dollars should be leveraged for the public good—reserved for those private sector employers who demonstrate a commitment to providing decent, family-supporting jobs in our local communities."[56] Like the minimum wage, the living wage campaigns demonstrate the unions' concern about the plight of the working poor and it enables the unions to lead a broad coalition.[57] But this can only be done on a local level and in the cities where union political power is concentrated. The result is legislative changes that cannot help unions and their members directly, as can the labor law reforms discussed below.[58]

Labor Law Reform

The political campaign most closely tied to relieving the unions' problems has been the fight for labor law reform. Since the 1970s, there have been proposals for amending federal labor laws to make organizing easier, faster, and cheaper. A typical reform proposal includes amendments to the Wagner Act to determine union certification on the basis of membership cards instead of elections; stronger penalties against employers who discharge workers during organizing drives (e.g., the loss of government contracts for repeat violators, automatic certification of the union if the employer misconduct is pervasive); the use of arbitration to settle first agreements if bargaining after certification is deadlocked; and bans on the hiring of striker replacements.[59] Virtually every union officer decries the inadequacies of the labor law, though they disagree whether intensive political action and changes in the law should precede mass organizing or if unions must somehow organize if they are to have the political clout to eventually change the law.[60]

Nearly every year, there is a labor law reform bill before Congress.[61] For example, in November 2003, Senator Edward Kennedy of Massachusetts and Representative George Miller of California filed the Employee Free Choice Act (S. 1925 and H.R. 3619), which was cosponsored by 30 senators and 201 members of the House. It would allow unions to organize without certification elections by determining majority support through signed membership cards. The legislation would also require that employers pay triple back pay to workers they discharged for union support during organizing and it would use mediation and arbitration to get first contracts if negotiations after certification were not successful.[62]

Unions mobilized for the bill during a Voice@Work Week of Action, holding rallies and asking members to wear lapel stickers, distribute flyers at work, and send postcards to the president urging him to support the bill.[63] Like the earlier attempts at labor law reform, the bill could not get enough support to be passed. Its introduction produced a strong counteroffensive. Opponents argued that the present union certification process was working, employer violations were the exception rather than the rule, and the decline in union organizing was not caused by legal shortcoming but the workers' loss of interest in unions—perhaps their distrust of them—which could not be remedied by an amendment to the law.

Despite their frequent defeat, the reform bills enable the unions' supporters to identify themselves for the record and reciprocate for union endorsement. They also help publicize the fact that unions face stiff opposition during organizing and employers often interfere with workers' rights to choose union representation. But the laws that would most help the unions to reverse their decline seem to be continually beyond their political reach.

Two Campaigns in California

California has one of the greatest concentrations of union members (2.4 million union members or 15.4 percent of total U.S. union membership in 2004),[64] so it is not surprising that it was the site of two major political campaigns—one an attempt to repel a voters' revolt against a friendly governor and the other a fight against a ballot proposition aimed at sharply reducing the unions' political funds.

On October 7, 2003, the voters of California recalled Governor Gray Davis, apparently angry at the deterioration of the state's economy—a record deficit of $38 billion. They elected the actor Arnold Schwarzenegger, a Republican, as governor by a vote of 4.2 million to 2.7 million for his opponent, Cruz Bustamante, the Democratic lieutenant governor. The AFL-CIO, the California Labor Federation (the state branch of the AFL-CIO), the California Teachers Association, and the California

State Employees Association led the opposition to the recall, first fighting its legality and than asking prominent Democrats not to run if it should be held. Union leaders labeled the recall as the hijacking of an election by extremist Republicans.

The vote in favor of recall and the election of Schwarzenegger was an indisputable defeat for the unions.[65] Bustamante had courted the unions.[66] Gray Davis had a strong pro-worker and pro-union record including support of a major reform of the workers' compensation system, requirements that small employers provide health care insurance for their employees, and the right of workers to sue for violations of the state labor code.[67] Despite the unions' campaign, nearly half of the state's union members voted to recall the governor, and a strong majority selected the Republican candidate. Their vote was a sign of overwhelming concern for deteriorating economic conditions in the state and the poor performance of the incumbent governor. Eighty percent of the voters thought that the state economy was "not so good" or "poor," and nearly half the voters strongly disapproved of Davis's performance. The unions had lost a high-profile political contest because the person they were defending was so unpopular.[68]

It is revealing when we compare the unions' loss in the governor's recall to their earlier victory in the fight against Proposition 226 (the "Paycheck Protection Act"), a measure that would have required that unions receive annual written approval from their members before they could use dues to support political candidates and issues. The proposition was voted down in June 1998 by 56 percent to 44 percent. Just a few months before the vote, Proposition 226 had been favored in public opinion polls by a 70 to 30 percent margin; about two-thirds of voters in union households supported it. It could not, however, withstand a forceful attack by a union-led coalition. The unions spent about $5 million (outspending opponents by seven to one), recruited 24,000 volunteers for phone banks, and campaigned heavily among their own members.[69] They claimed that the proposition was designed to weaken school reform by cutting the political power of the California Teachers Association and that it was fundamentally unfair because it imposed requirements on unions without matching ones on businesses. Also, since the proposition received most of its financial support from groups in other states, the unions argued that it was an onslaught against the unions by outside antiworker organizations.[70] Those fighting Proposition 226 saw it as nothing less than a fight for the political survival of the state's unions. One writer concluded: "Proposition 226 was a clear sign that Republicans and conservatives want to limit the financial underpinning of unions. . . . Unions have to use their political clout now or lose it."[71]

The unions and their allies turned back Proposition 226 because they were able to frame their arguments in terms of fairness and as the intrusion of outsiders into California politics. In contrast, five years later, public opinion was so strong against Governor Davis that the unions' appeal to fairness (they claimed that the recall was undemocratic because it would overturn the voters' choice) had little impact. Put simply, no matter how well they organize, finance their campaign, and build their coalition, unions cannot win a losing cause.

Stopping Wal-Mart

Wal-Mart Stores, the world's largest retailer, epitomizes the dilemma of America's unions. Wal-Mart is a huge employer with more than 1.2 million employees at its 3,700 stores and sales exceeding $20 billion *each month*.[72] It has withstood all union organizing campaigns.[73]

Wal-Mart has prospered following a business model of offering consumers low prices made possible in part by offering low wages and few employee benefits.[74] The company exerts a downward influence on wages, benefits, and working conditions wherever it opens its stores, forcing its competitors to lower their operating costs. For instance, at the root of the huge grocery strike in Southern California in 2003, described in the previous chapter, were the supermarkets' claims that they had to lower labor costs to compete with new Wal-Mart supercenters.[75]

Unions have used their political clout to halt the spread of Wal-Mart. In Inglewood, California, a suburb of Los Angeles, unions joined with a coalition of business, religious, and community leaders to lead the opposition against a ballot initiative that would have allowed Wal-Mart to open a 60-acre shopping complex without interference from local officials. The unions feared that jobs would be lost at stores unable to compete with Wal-Mart and that the giant retailer would depress wages and benefits at unionized stories. The vote against Wal-Mart was 60 to 40 percent.[76]

In Chicago, the city council voted to postpone hearings on zoning changes that would have allowed Wal-Mart to open two stores. A coalition of unions and religious groups opposed the stores, but neighborhood groups that wanted more local jobs supported them.[77] In Queens, New York, a real estate developer dropped plans to include a Wal-Mart store in a shopping complex after intense opposition from unions, small business owners, community organizations, and environmentalists. This was part of a coordinated effort to keep Wal-Mart out of the New York City area.[78]

Union leaders realize that they cannot use their political power to win the fight against Wal-Mart because new stores can open outside the cities where they are blocked. Rather, they see Wal-Mart as a beacon of union weakness, the ability of a dominant employer in a growing sector to stave off union organizing. Wal-Mart argues that it does not take a heavy-handed approach against organizing, but rather developed a style of participative management that makes unions unnecessary. A spokesperson for Wal-Mart claimed that it was not antiunion; "the reason our associates haven't wanted third-party [union] representation is because they have faith in the company, and it provides them with tremendous opportunity."[79] Such a challenge cannot go unanswered, but the unions realize the limits of their political power: lobbying can only block the building of new Wal-Mart stores; it cannot organize them where they open.

The 2004 Presidential Election

The most dramatic examples of union political success or failure happen during presidential elections. Unions played an important role in the election of President Clinton; they endorsed him, contributed to his campaign, and encouraged their members to join in his rallies and vote for him. About a quarter of Clinton's votes in 1992 came from union households and, as part of the payback, soon after he took office Clinton reversed two Bush administration antiunion regulations. One would have required federal contractors to post notices that informed workers of their rights to refuse to pay union dues, and the other would have prohibited employers on federally funded construction projects from requiring workers to be union members.[80] Later, the unions had a falling out with Clinton over two issues that greatly outweighed his early reversal of regulations—his support for NAFTA and his failure to propose labor law reforms that would make organizing easier. Despite this, the unions supported him in his second election because they saw no alternative.

In the 2000 presidential campaign, unions were extremely active because they feared the consequences of an unfriendly Bush administration (e.g., budget cuts at the labor board, unrestrained international trade, a presidential veto on any labor law reform bills). They registered 2.3 million new voters in union households, made 8 million phone calls, distributed more than 14 million leaflets, and sent out 60,000 e-mail messages urging people to vote. About 100,000 union members worked as volunteers at phone banks and door-to-door canvassing and more than 900 union members ran for office. Unions spent about $90 million in the 2000 election.[81]

As described earlier in this chapter, the unions were energized by their extreme animosity toward President Bush during the 2004 election. If Bush was reelected, unions foresaw continued opposition to higher minimum wages and labor law reform and the accelerated loss of unionized jobs, particularly in manufacturing, due to unrestrained international trade. Although Kerry did not have a particularly strong pro-union record, he seemed most capable of all contenders to unseat Bush. If unions could play a key role in a Kerry victory it might signal a revival—a new relevancy to the political and economic scene and affirmation of the unions' role as the voice of American workers. Many of the "battleground states"— the 11 or so states where the outcomes would be close and had to be won by a candidate for an election victory (e.g., Ohio, Pennsylvania, Florida)— were those with higher proportions of union members, and if there was not a strong union presence, union activists could be sent there to help turn out the pro-Kerry vote. Unions planned to make a crucial difference with their skill and experience in the ground game.[82]

The AFL-CIO announced a political mobilization plan that included (a) registering millions of union household members to vote and assisting them in casting their ballots; (b) launching a communications program on key issues for union members, including the aggressive public advocacy of issues that resonate with working families (e.g., health care reform); (c) creating a corps of volunteer union members for education and mobilization at workplaces; (d) training full-time political field coordinators; (e) communicating with union households through a variety of methods including home visits, telephone calls, and Internet messages; and (f) recruiting union members to run for political office. John Sweeney declared that the objective of the coordinated campaign, the largest political effort ever undertaken by unions, was to "take the country forward again by removing out-of-touch political leaders."[83]

The labor federation formed a new organization—Working America— to communicate with and mobilize nonunion workers who supported issues of concern to workers and their families. Officially nonpartisan, it did door-to-door canvassing to register voters and distribute campaign literature. In past elections, unions focused on registering and turning out new union voters but in 2004 they changed their strategy to one of going after the undecided union household voters in the battleground states that were narrowly won by Bush in 2000.[84]

The unions contributed huge amounts of money to the campaign. It is difficult to calculate the exact union contributions because funds are given indirectly to advocacy groups as well as candidates and parties. But it appears that the unions spent at least $150 million in the 2004 election, including $65 million from the Service Employees and $45 million from the AFL-CIO.[85] They took advantage of the 527 loophole; there were 9 unions among the 50 largest 527 committees and the Service Employees and the American Federation of State, County and Municipal Employees were ranked fifth and sixth, respectively.[86]

Despite the unions' financial contributions and their extensive campaign activity, the 2004 national elections cast some serious doubt on their political ability. In the election postmortem, it was hard to find any positive signs of union political strength.[87] It is true that 65 percent of union members voting supported John Kerry, but this was not much different from the support for Al Gore (63 percent) in 2000, and 68 percent in favor of Kerry in the battleground states is not remarkable.[88] Declining union membership had taken its toll—fewer members meant fewer votes. About 14 percent of the voters in 2004 were union members, compared to 16 percent in 2000. Union household members were 24 percent of the voters, compared to 26 percent in 2000.[89] Perhaps the most important outcome was the challenge to the unions' supremacy at the ground game. The unions' efforts were certainly impressive. Their staff and volunteers knocked on the doors of 6 million voters and distributed 32 million pieces of campaign literature. Their campaign employed 5,000 full-time workers and more than 200,000 volunteers. The unions set up phone banks with 2,322 lines. They moved staff and members from pro-Kerry states to the battlefield states.[90] The Service Employees alone sent 2,000 volunteers to the battlefield states.[91] But the unions' opponents did even better. Since the close election of 2000, the Republicans had organized their supporters into groups that could turn out the vote on Election Day. For example, in Florida, which many thought would be close but which went to President Bush decisively, the Republicans enlisted 109,000 volunteers, ranging from students to members of church groups, who made 3 million voter contacts on Election Day and the five days prior.[92] In Ohio, the Republicans claimed to have 80,000 volunteers on the ground.[93] In total, the Republicans and their allies may have had as many as 1.2 million volunteers on the ground in the election.[94] The unions were clearly no longer the masters of mobilization.

Conclusions

The political activities described in this chapter were selected as representative of the unions' methods and objectives. Others could be cited as well, for example:

- The unions' leadership of the coalition against the awarding of permanent normal trade relations (PNTR) to China, an alternative to China's most-favored-nation trade status that is reviewed on a yearly basis. After a House vote in May 2000 of 237 for and 197 against, PNTR was granted to China—largely the result of strong support by President Clinton and an intensive, well-funded, and sophisticated pro-China trade campaign by business groups.[95]
- The key role of union members and staff in the rallies for Al Gore during the contested election results in Florida in 2000.[96]
- The unions' lobbying against the Homeland Security bill of 2002 because it denied full collective bargaining rights and job protections to government workers in the new Department of Homeland Security. A compromise bill was eventually passed, but the government retained the flexibility to hire and fire workers in the department.[97]
- The unions' lobbying at the Colorado state legislature for laws requiring that work performed by the state be done by Americans. This attempt to curb the state's off-shoring of customer and technical support services failed to pass when business groups argued that it would be very expensive.[98]
- The unions' collaboration with several women's and workers' rights groups in lobbying against a 2003 congressional bill that would have given workers a choice between compensatory time off or time-and-a-half overtime pay when they work more than 40 hours per week. The coalition against the bill argued that employers would pressure workers to take the time-off option, thus denying them higher wages. The Republican sponsors withdrew their bill when they realized they could not get enough votes for passage.[99]
- Union support of candidates who will extend the legal right to unionize to groups of workers previously excluded because they

are independent contractors. The Service Employees organized 39,000 child care workers in Illinois after the governor signed an executive order giving the workers the right to unionize. The workers are paid by the state and take care of children at home. The Service Employees was the single largest contributor to the governor's election campaign.[100]

We could add to these the unions' endorsement of candidates in countless local elections for every conceivable position from school committee member to mayor; the unions' participation in coalitions for workers' rights and workplace issues, including campaigns against sweatshops and pay discrimination; and the unions' continuous lobbying to protect jobs in industries devastated by low-cost imports (e.g., in clothing, textiles, and steel).

With the unions' mixed record in politics and their disappointing performance in the 2004 election, some are asking whether they should cut back their activities and focus on organizing and bargaining. This question is not worth debating because the spheres of union activity cannot be separated and politics is closely linked to everything that unions do. As Delaney and Masters observed, "The power of government to intervene in society invites even the most pragmatic of union movements into the political realm."[101] The most conservative union leader can easily see how political action strengthens his or her union at the bargaining table, makes it more successful in organizing, and enables its voice to be heard above that of the employers and their allies in legislatures. Developing an imposing political presence is not a luxury but a vital necessity to protect the unions' position, whether those unions represent workers in firehouses or steel mills.[102] "Union efforts to elect politicians sympathetic to the labor movement serve as a hedge against the elimination of union rights to bargain and represent workers and as an effort to create an environment in which statutes favorable to unions can be enacted. Collective bargaining and political action are, in other words, tied together intimately."[103]

Union political power is now severely limited. Unions are strongest when working through coalitions, most able to help workers in general rather than their members, and capable of successful political action only with issues and candidates favored by the public. They cannot win alone and they cannot win with losing issues. They were once the best at the political ground game, but now this is being done well by many other groups. No matter how much the unions spend, they will be outspent by companies and organizations.

A recent article in *Business Week* asked: "Has organized labor, with its fabled ballot-box muscle, turned into a 98-pound political weakling?"[104] Of course, the question is not that simple. We should be asking whether the unions' political successes will be scarcer and their failures will be more frequent and deeper if their membership continues to decline. And, paradoxically, we should also ask whether the only cure for membership decline is renewed political influence.

Notes

1.   Nearly a century ago, Samuel Gompers, the AFL president, told union officers to "reward your friends and punish your enemies." Lichtenstein, N. (1999). American trade unions and the "labor question": Past and present. In Century Foundation Task Force on the Future of Unions (Ed.), *What's next for organized labor?* New York: Century Foundation Press, p. 107.

2.   For a brief review of the historical development of the links between the unions and the Democratic Party, see Change, T. Y. (2001). The labour vote in U.S. national elections. *Political Quarterly*, 72, pp. 375–385.

3.   AFL-CIO. (2002, November 6). Remarks by John J. Sweeney, President, AFL-CIO post-election press briefing. www.aflcio.org/mediacenter/prsptm/sp11062002.cfm. For an analysis of the unions' strategies in endorsing candidates, see Dark, T., III. (2003). To reward and punish: A classification of union political strategies. *Journal of Labor Research*, 24, pp. 457–472. For concerns about the appropriate extent of union involvement in politics, see Phillips-Fein, K. (2003). Does that elephant bite? Union alliances with the GOP. *New Labor Forum*, 12(1), pp. 7–16; Fox-Piven, F. (2003). Can labor bite back? A response to Phillips-Fein. *New Labor Forum*, 12, pp. 17–20.

4.   Greenhouse, S. (1999, September 11). Labor is divided on endorsement. *New York Times*, p. A1; Moberg, S. (1999, November 14). New labor; old politics. *In These Times*, p. 9.

5.   Dark (2003); Wilgoren, J. (2004, May 17). Kerry praises Gephardt in effort to win over Teamsters. *New York Times*, p. A16. Dark (2003) describes the strategy of giving an "empty" endorsement, that is, endorsing a candidate without committing union resources to the candidate's campaign. This might be done to signal dissatisfaction with the candidate's policies. It was used, for example, in the 1994 congressional elections to show the unions' anger at Democrats who voted for the North American Free Trade Agreement.

6.   AFL-CIO backs Kerry. (2004, February 19). *USA Today*. www.usatoday.com/news/politicselections/nation/primariescaucus/2004-02-19-kerry-afl-cio_x.html.

7.   Greenhouse, S. (2004, January 21). For labor, a day to ask what went wrong. *New York Times*, p. A19. At first 18 unions (mostly the industrial unions

in a group called the Alliance for Economic Justice) endorsed Gephardt while 2 large service sector unions backed Dean, but all but one (the Service Employees International Union) switched to Kerry on February 11, 2004. UNITE, the clothing and textile union, endorsed Edwards. Bernstein, A., and Sager, I. (2004, February 23). The unions are falling in behind Kerry. *Business Week, 3871,* p. 14.

8.   Cellender, D. (2004, February 11). Loss of endorsement is hurting Dean here. *Madison.com.* www.madison.com; Halbfinger, D. M., and Lyman, R. (2004, February 20). AFL-CIO, calling for unity, gives backing to Kerry. *New York Times,* p. A16. Gerald W. McEntee of the American Federation of State, County and Municipal Employees withdrew his endorsement of Dean, saying that Dean should pull out of the contest. Nagourney, A. (2004, February 20). Labor supporter says Dean ignored his entreaties to quit. *New York Times,* p. A18; Wilgoren, J. (2004, February 8). Major union plans to pull its support for Dean. *New York Times,* p. A15; Hayes, C. (2004, February 2). Endorsement up for grabs. *In These Times.* www.inthesetimes.com.

9.   Greenhouse, S. (2003, November 12). Old loyalist and new face divide backing of unions. *New York Times,* p. A12; Halbfinger, D. M. (2004, February 10). With Gephardt gone, Kerry is lining up labor backing. *New York Times,* p. A18; Greenhouse, S. (2004, August 1). Though united in politics, unions face internal turmoil. *New York Times,* p. 13.

10.   Nipp, L. (2003, May 2). Labor leader: Kerry "best chance" to beat Bush in '04. *USA Today.* www.usatoday.com/news/washington/2003-02-05-kerry_x.html.

11.   Brownstein, R. (2003, May 20). Who will get labor's nod? *Boston Globe,* p. A17.

12.   Greenhouse, S. (1999, September 11). Labor is divided on endorsement. *New York Times,* p. A1.

13.   Dark (2003); Dine, P. (2004, February 20). Kerry endorsement spurs questions about labor's unity. *St. Louis Post-Dispatch,* p. A1.

14.   For example, the unions' support for Howard Dean in the Democratic presidential primary in 2003 helped him enter the mainstream of candidates and expanded his base to include a broad cross section of workers, while denying this status to his opponents during the early running. Baer, S. (2003, November 6). Service Workers support expected to broaden base. *Baltimore Sun.* www .baltimoresun.com/elections.

15.   Marelius, J. (2004, February 19). Once-divided unions unite around Kerry. *San Diego Union Tribune.* www.signonsandiego.com; Merkels, A. (2004, March 15). Kerry's steady flame. *U.S. News.* www.usnews.com.

16.   Nagourney, A. (2003, August 6). Democrats seeking labor's backing call for more health benefits and less free trade. *New York Times,* p. A14; Archibald, R. C. (2003, September 9). Presidential hopefuls courting huge union for endorsement. *New York Times,* p. A14; PBS. (2003, November 12). *Campaign times.* www.pbs .org/newshour/bb/politics/july-dfec03/dean endorsement_11-12.html.

17.   Annenberg Election Center. (2003, October 4). Annenberg election study measures union votes, shows labor, white votes for Democrats. www.upenn.edu/ researchatpenn. Members of union households account for large shares of the voters of the key industrial states; 43 percent in Michigan in 2000, 36 percent in New York and Ohio, 33 percent in Illinois, 32 percent in New Jersey, and 30 percent in Pennsylvania. Labor Research Association. (2000, November 15). Union voters in key states helped Al Gore win popular vote. www.laborreasearch/org/natl_elections/turnout_00.html.

18.   Moberg, D. (2002, July 1). It's payback time: Labor-backed politicians are being asked to return the favor in union fights. *The Nation*, 275, pp. 19–23.

19.   For example, see Greenhouse, S. (2003, February 23). Labor gathers resources to unseat president in 2004. *New York Times*, p. A21; There goes Hoffa (devil in the details). (2003). *American Prospect*, 14, p. 8; Apple, R. W., Jr. (2004, January 18). Gephardt counts on old-style, blue-collar support. *New York Times*, p. A14. A lengthy union critique of President Bush's record is found in the AFL-CIO website *Bushwatch*. www.aflcio.org/issuespolitics/bushwatch.

20.   Lee, C. (2004, June 28). Federal employees' union endorses Kerry. *Washington Post*, p. A19.

21.   Becker, E. (2004, April 29). Bush rejects labor's call to punish China. *New York Times*, p. A4.

22.   Gonzalez, J. (2003, October 23). Union to be out beating the Bushies. *Daily News (New York)*, p. 8.

23.   Greenhouse, S. (2004, August 1). While united in politics, unions face internal rifts. *New York Times*, p. A14.

24.   Strope, L. (2004, March 11). Swing union voters focus of AFL-CIO mobilization efforts. www.sfgate.com/cgibin/article.cgi?file=/news/archive/2004/03/11/politics0311EST.

25.   Delaney, J. T., and Masters, M. F. (1991). Unions and political action. In G. Strauss, D. J. Gallagher, and J. Fiorito (Eds.), *The state of the unions*. Madison, WI: Industrial Relations Research Association, p. 317.

26.   www.opensecrets.org.

27.   Lewis, N. (2003, September 8). Clout shifts with the change in campaign finance rules. *New York Times*, p. A8. For a comparison of the new and old regulations, see Federal campaign laws: New contributions limits. www.opensecerts.org.

28.   Examples of 527 committees are the Moveon.org Voter Fund and the Media Fund. For a brief discussion of 527 committees, see Section 527: A victory for associations. (2003). *Association Management*, 55, p. 10.

29.   For a discussion of the status of 527 committees, see Wertheimer, F., et al. (2004, February 4). Comments on draft advisory opinion, 2003-37 [of the Federal Election Commission]. Unpublished memo. A description of the canvassing activities of a 527 committee, showing how it can be partisan despite its stated objectives, is Rosenthal, E. (2004). Across the nation, a parallel campaign rolls on, neither neutral nor partisan. *New York Times*, p. A10.

30.   Malone, J. (2004, November 7). Elections for federal office cost $3.9 billion. *Atlanta Constitution-Journal*, p. A7.

31.   DeBose, B. (2003, November 21). House panel to subpoena Section 527 fund-raisers. *Washington Times*, p. A4; Justice, G. (2004, January 16). Finance battle shifts to election panel. *New York Times*, p. A16; Mitchell, K. B., Epstein, K., and Byrd, T. (2004, June 14). 527 groups gain political clout. TBO.COM. http://news .tbo.com/news/MGBZ6ER0GVD.html; Justice, G. (2004, May 14). F.E.C. declines to curb independent fund-raisers. *New York Times,* p. A16; Schmitt, C. H. (2004, September 20). A shift in the balance of power. *U.S. News & World Report,* 137, p. 34. For a postelection review of the role of the 527 committees, see Justice, G. (2004, November 8). Even with campaign finance law, money talks louder than ever. *New York Times,* pp. A1, A16. It has been argued before the Federal Election Commission that any restrictions on 527 committees should also apply to the 501c groups that include charities, trade associations, "social welfare" groups, and *labor unions.* For example, in August 2000, the American Federation of State, County and Municipal Employees contributed to the creation of the 501c organization American Family Voices, which was critical of George W. Bush in his run for the presidency. The same union helped create the Partnership for America's Families, to mobilize the Democrats' base, black and Hispanic voters, in the 2004 presidential election, with the stated purpose of going to the battleground states, where the outcomes are close, to register people, tell them about the issues, and turn them out to vote. Under 501c tax status, unions can engage in political activities, including polling, lobbying, and advertising, but they cannot advocate the election or defeat of specific candidates. The 501c groups were defended as doing important advocacy work that should not be restricted because that would have a chilling effect on the people's ability to criticize their government; others say that they are nothing more than a political subterfuge, a loophole to raise soft money that would otherwise be banned under the campaign reform legislation.

32.   Greenhouse, S. (2001, February 16). Bush is moving to reduce labor's political coffers. *New York Times,* p. 14. The U.S. Department of Labor issued a requirement that unions, starting in the summer of 2004, disclose their spending on election activities under the assumption that such a disclosure would help union members decide whether to opt out of paying full dues. The AFL-CIO saw these regulations as a direct attack on its political power and opposed them, arguing that corporations should then also reveal their political contributions in reports to their stockholders.

33.   Strope, L. (2003, November 11). Big labor chief: Anybody but Bush. *CBSNews.com.* www.cbsnews.com/stories/2003/11/11/politics/prinable582918 .shml.

34.   Strope, L. (2002, October 28). Get out the vote? Labor knows how. *Seattle Post-Intelligencer.* http://seatlepi.nwsource.com/business/93074_labor28.shtml. For some examples of major union achievements in getting out the vote, see

AFL-CIO. (2004). Election Day difference—New working family voters. http://www.aflcio.org/issuespolitics/politics/ns10262000.cfm.

35. Greenhouse, S. (2000, February 16). The 2000 campaign: The unions. *New York Times*, p. A21; Esposito, A. (2004, September 6). Unions want say on E-Day. *Worcester Telegram and Gazette*. www.telegram.com/apps/phcs.dll/article; Seelye, K. (1999, October 13). Gore campaign plans to enlist labor and blacks to beat back challenge by Bradley. *New York Times*, p. A23.

36. Feldman, L. (2000, April 12). Labor's new tactics in stumping for Gore. *Christian Science Monitor*, p. 3; Postman, D. (2004, March 13). Firefighters on the front line in Kerry's campaign. *Seattle Times*. www.seattletimes.nwsource.com/cgi-bin. Some unions have managed to develop high public profiles by mobilizing members. The Service Employees' members seemed to be everywhere in the primary campaign of Howard Dean, and the Painters and Firefighters were prominent in the early days of John Kerry's campaign when few unions supported him. The Firefighters' members did not directly endorse Kerry although they were active in his campaign, particularly during the important early stages when the party's nominee had not yet been selected. The Firefighters' officers asked the members what attributes they would like to see in a president, and then considering these the officers selected the candidate they believed had the most favorable stands on issues affecting firefighters. The Kerry endorsement occurred although more of the union's members identified themselves as Republicans than Democrats or independents.

37. For example, see Date, S. V. (2004, November 4). President won Florida with better ground game. *Palm Beach Post*. www.palmbeachpost.com/politics/content/news/epaper/2004/11/04; Verhovek, S. H., and Shogren, E. (2004, November 4). Republicans beat Democrats in Ohio ground game. *Los Angeles Times*. www.latimes.com/news/nationworld/nation/la-na-ohi04nov04, 1,7834861.

38. Shoch, J. (2001). Organized labor versus globalization: NAFTA, Fast Track and PNTR with China. In L. Turner, H. C. Katz, and R. W. Hurd (Eds.), *Rekindling the movement: Labor's quest for relevance in the twenty-first century.* Ithaca, NY: Cornell University Press, p. 281.

39. Chaison, G., and Bigelow, B. (2002). *Unions and legitimacy.* Ithaca, NY: Cornell University Press, pp. 59–72.

40. Chaison and Bigelow (2002), pp. 62–70.

41. Shoch (2001).

42. Chaison and Bigelow (2002).

43. Rose, J., and Chaison, G. (1996). Linking union density and union effectiveness. *Industrial Relations,* 35, p. 95.

44. Bennet, J. (1997, September 25). Clinton urges labor unions not to punish free-trade Democrats in Congress. *New York Times*, p. 28.

45. Greenhouse, S. (1997, September 24). AFL-CIO turns energy against pacts on free trade. *New York Times*, p. 22.

46.   Shoch (2001), pp. 286–288.

47.   Shoch (2001), pp. 294–300.

48.   There was also strong, well-organized opposition in 2001 when the Bush administration tried unsuccessfully to reintroduce Fast Track. Greenhouse, S. (2001, October 17). Labor leaders oppose a trade bill. *New York Times,* p. A14.

49.   Stout, H. (1988, January 24). The economics of the minimum wage: Propping up payments at the bottom. *New York Times,* p. A4.

The federal minimum wage was established at 25 cents (and overtime at time and a half for hours worked beyond 40 per week) under the Fair Labor Standards Act of 1938. Congress most recently increased the minimum wage in 1996 to $5.15 per hour (effective in 1997). The federal minimum wage does not supersede state laws that are more favorable to employees. HR [human resource management website]. (2004, June 24). Minimum wage: An overview. HR.BLR.com, hr.blr.com/article.cfm/Nav/1.40.202.0.5399.

50.   Sonn, P. (2004). The new municipal minimum wage laws. *Perspectives on Work,* 8, p. 44.

51.   Uchitelle, L. (2004, May 16). Economic view: Election-year shuffle on the minimum wage. *New York Times,* p. B6.

52.   AFL-CIO. (2004, March 29). Bushwatch: The complete file. www .aflcio.org/issuespolitics/bushwatch. The proposal also eliminated overtime pay for aerospace, health care, defense, and information technology workers with incomes above a specified level.

53.   AFL-CIO. (2003, October 2). Statement by John J. Sweeney on House vote to bar Labor Department from cutting overtime pay. www.aflcio.org/medfiacenter/prsptm/pr100022003.cfm.

54.   Richman, J. (2004, June 17). Appeals court rebuffs Skates' living-wage suit. *Alameda Times-Star.* http://www.timesstar.com/Stories/0,1413,1251.

55.   ACORN [Association of Community Organizations for Reform Now]. (2004). Living wage campaigns underway. www.livingwagecampaign.org/campaigns.php; Labor Research Association. (2001, September 4). The labor movement and its achievements. www.laborresearch.org. For an analysis of the impact of living wage laws in terms of local wages and employment, see Neumark, D., and Adams, S. (2003). Detecting effects of living wage laws. *Industrial Relations,* 42, pp. 531–564. A study of the implementation of living wages is Luce, S. (2004). *Fighting for a living wage.* Ithaca, NY: Cornell University Press. A special issue of the journal *Industrial Relations* was devoted to living wages in January 2005. See (2005). Special issue: The impact of living wage policies. *Industrial Relations,* 44, pp. 1–192.

56.   ACORN. (2004). Introduction to ACORN's living wage website. www.livingwagecamapign.org.

57.   Living wage campaigns can lead to creation of lasting union-community organization coalitions because they deal with issues of broad appeal. This is shown in the coalition efforts in south Florida described by Nissen, B. (2004). The

effectiveness and limits of labor-community coalitions: Evidence from south Florida. *Labor Studies Journal*, 29, pp. 67–89.

58. For a review and analysis of the living wage movement, see the articles in a special issue (Volume 8, summer 2004) of *Perspectives on Work:* Kern, J. (2004). The living wage movement: Organizing for the long haul, pp. 31–33; Garthwaite, C. (2004). An argument against living wage laws—And in favor of a sound alternative, pp. 34–36; Luce, S. (2004). What happens after the laws pass? Implementing and monitoring living wage ordinances, pp. 37–39; Levin-Waldman, O. M. (2004). The living wage movement: It's significant to urban politics and citizenship, pp. 40–42.

59. Many of these reforms are based on practices and principles of Canadian labor legislation. See, for example, Rose, J. B., and Chaison, G. N. (1995). Canadian labor policy as a model for legislative reform in the United States. *Labor Law Journal*, 5, pp. 259–272.

60. Expressing the prevailing view, John J. Sweeney, AFL-CIO president, said, "Labor must organize without the law so that we can later organize under the law," quoted in Lichtenstein (1999).

61. For a discussion of the early attempt at labor law reform, see Townley, B. (1986). *Labor law reform in U.S. industrial relations.* Aldershot, UK: Gower. The report of the Dunlop Commission, established to promote labor law reforms, is U.S. Department of Labor. (1995). *Final report and recommendations of the Commission on the Future of Worker Management Relations.* Washington, DC: Government Printing Office. The commission made several recommendations, including expedited certification elections and the use of court injunctions to prevent discrimination against union supporters during organizing drives, but the shift in Congress from Democratic to Republican control in November 1994, in the middle of the commission's work, ended the possibility of major change in labor law.

62. AFL-CIO. (2004). Employee Free Choice Act. www.aflcio/org/aboutunions/voiceatwork; Greenhouse, S. (2003, November 14). National briefing: Washington: New unionization push. *New York Times,* p. A14; Green, C. (2003, November 13). Congressional Democrats seek to streamline unionization process with card check bills. LRA Online. www.laborresearch.org/story2.php/334.html.

63. AFL-CIO. (2004, June 7). Work in progress. www.aflcio.org.aboutaflcio/wip.

64. U.S. Department of Labor. (2004). *Union members in 2004.* USDL 05-112. Washington, DC: U.S. Department of Labor, Bureau of Labor Statistics.

65. Murphy, D. E. (2003, August 6). A.F.L.-C.I.O. joins fight against California recall. *New York Times,* p. A11; Broder, J. (2003, August 27). Leaders of California's largest union vote to raise large amounts to defeat Davis recall. *New York Times,* p. A11.

66. Kasindorf, M. (2003, September 2). Countdown begins for recall vote. *USA Today,* p. A4.

67. For example, see the analysis by the following law firm: Ogletree, Deakins, Nash, Smoak & Stewart. (2003, October 27). Davis leaves his mark with new labor laws. *California Employment Law Letter*, p. 13.

68. NewsMax.com Wires. (2003, October 8). http://www.newsmax.com/archves/articles/2003/10/8/03903.shtml. Some unions softened their opposition for pragmatic reasons after Schwarzenegger was elected. In June 2004, the Building and Construction Trades Council of California, an association of construction unions that once fought the recall initiative, publicly supported the governor when he signed a bill permitting the expansion of tribal gambling operations in the state. Many of their members are likely to get jobs in the highway construction projects that would be financed by revenues from new gambling operations. Broder, J. M. (2004, June 22). More slot machines for tribes, and $1 billion for California. *New York Times*, p. A11.

69. Bernstein, A., and Borus, A. (1998, June 15). A bazooka aimed at big labor backfires on the GOP. *Business Week*, p. 55; Terry, D. (1998, May 28). Labor chips away at ballot nemesis. *New York Times*, p. 18.

70. Protection? Rejection! (California Proposition 226). (1998, September). *NEA Today*, p. 10; Cohn, J. (1998, June 29). Grover cornered. *The New Republic*, p. 6.

71. Gary Chaison, quoted in Paige, S. (1998, November 9). How powerful are unions in politics? *Insight on the News*, p. 34.

72. Greenhouse, S. (2005, May 4). Can't Wal-Mart, a retail behemoth, pay more? *New York Times*, pp. C1, C6; CNNMoney. (2005). Retailers rake in healthy sales. www.money.cnn.com/2005/03/03/news/economy/retail_sales.

73. Greenhouse, S. (2004, January 13). In-house audit says Wal-Mart violated labor laws. *New York Times*, p. A16; Greenhouse, S. (2004, December 11). Unions push for better pay at Wal-Mart. *New York Times*, p. A16. In February 2005, the United Food and Commercial Workers lost a certification election by a vote of 17 to 1 among the workers of the tire-and-lube shop of a Wal-Mart in Loveland, Colorado. Campaigns were said to be under way at other stores, but none had reached the election stage. In 2000, the meat cutters at a Wal-Mart in Jacksonville, Texas, had voted to be represented by Wal-Mart but the company replaced all meat-cutting operations in the Southwest with prepackaged meat. Greenhouse, S. (2005, February 26). At a small shop in Colorado, Wal-Mart beats a union once more. *New York Times*, p. A8. For an overview of labor relations and union organizing at Wal-Mart, see Edid, M. (2005). *The good, the bad and Wal-Mart*. Cornell University Institute for Workplace Studies, IWS issues brief. http://digitalcommons.ilr.cornell.edu/briefs/6.

74. Abelson, R. (2004, November 1). States are battling against Wal-Mart over health care. *New York Times*, pp. A1, A13.

75. Goldman, A., and Cleeland, N. (2003, November 23). The Wal-Mart effect. *Los Angeles Times*, p. A1. It is estimated that each new Wal-Mart supercenter

results in job losses for 200 members of the United Food and Commercial Workers. Wal-Mart plans to open 1,000 supercenters nationally that will sell groceries and general merchandise and have more than 100,000 kinds of products in a single location.

76.   Broder, J. M. (2004, April 8). Voters in Los Angeles say no to a big Wal-Mart. *New York Times,* p. A16; Lin, S., and Morin, M. (2004, April 7). The region: Voters in Inglewood turn away Wal-Mart; Bid by the retailer to bypass environmental review and public hearings and open a "supercenter" in the city is soundly rejected. *Los Angeles Times,* p. A1.

77.   Pallasch, A., and Patterson, S. (2004, April 1). Aldermen say "union, yes" and delay Wal-Mart stores. *Chicago Sun-Times,* p. 17.

78.   Greenhouse, S. (2005, February 24). To cheers of opponents, plans for a city Wal-Mart are dropped. *New York Times,* p. A22; Greenhouse, S. (2005, February 10). Foes dig in as Wal-Mart aims for city. *New York Times,* p. A23.

79.   Kinzer, S. (2004, May 6). Wal-Mart's big city plans stall again. *New York Times,* p. 6.

80.   Rose, J., and Chaison, G. (1996). Linking union density and union effectiveness. *Industrial Relations,* pp. 78–105.

81.   Labor Research Association. (2001, September 4). The labor movement and its achievements. www.laborresearch.org; AFL-CIO. (2000, November 8). In the "cliffhanger" presidential election, massive mobilization and high turnout by union members made the difference in key states. www.aflcio.org/mediacenter/prsptm/pr11080200.cfm; AFL-CIO. (2002, November 22). The union difference: 26 percent of voters are from union households. www.aflcio.org/issuespolitics/ns11082000.cfm.

82.   Hayes (2004).

83.   AFL-CIO. (2004). AFL-CIO Executive Council outlines 2004 working family election mobilization. http://www.aflcio.org/aboutaflcio/ns02282003.cfm.

84.   Greenhouse, S. (2004, March 11). AFL-CIO plans to spend $44 million to unseat Bush. *New York Times,* p. A26; Strope, L. (2004, March 10). Labor approves funds to mobilize members against Bush. *San Diego Union Tribune.* www.signonsandiego.com/news/politics/20040310-1403-afl-cio.html.

85.   Glanz, W. (2004, November 4). Unions' all-out effort comes up short. *Washington Times.* www.washingtontimes.com.

86.   www.opensecrets.org.

87.   In his open letter to workers, John Sweeney wrote, "We are deeply disappointed that the presidential candidate we supported did not win Tuesday's election, but we should all be extremely proud of and energized by the work we did together." But his letter has few specific details about election outcomes in terms of votes, voter turnout and mobilization, or comparisons to past election efforts. Also, his claim that the election was "breathtakingly close" is meant more as encouragement to members and a warning to Congress not to pass any antiunion

or antiworker laws than as a factual evaluation of the situation. AFL-CIO. (2004). AFL-CIO President Sweeney: A letter to America's working families. www .afl-cio.org/issuespolitics/ns11052004.cfm.

88.   Glanz (2004, November 4); AFL-CIO. (2004). Survey: Union members back Kerry. www.afl-cio.org/issuespolitics/ns1103 2004.cfm.

89.   Strope, L. (2004, November 4). Despite massive effort and spending, unions couldn't deliver votes for Kerry. www.sfgate.com.

90.   Strope (2004, November 4).

91.   Glanz (2004, November 4).

92.   Goodnough, A., and Van Natta, D. (2004, November 7). Bush secured victory in Florida by veering from beaten path. *New York Times*, pp. 1, 24.

93.   Kiely, K. (2004, November 3). Volunteers work to last minute. *USA Today*, p. 3A.

94.   Barone, M. (2004, November 15). The 51 percent nation. *U.S. News & World Report*, p. 33. For a description of the activities of the campaign volunteers, see Lyman, R. (2004, November 2). In crunch time, racing door to door. *New York Times*, p. A5.

95.   Shoch (2001), pp. 302–312.

96.   Dine, P. (2000, November 28). Labor says it will support challenge of election. *St. Louis Post-Dispatch*, p. A7; Sengupta, S. (2000, November 27). Counting the vote: The demonstrators. *New York Times*, p. A13.

97.   For example, see CNN. (2002, November 13). Compromise reached on Homeland Security bill. www.cnn.allpolitics.com; CNN. (2002, November 26). Bush signs Homeland Security bill. www.cnn.allpolitics.com.

98.   Fillion, R. (2005, February 22). State lawmakers asked again to curb offshoring. *Rocky Mountain News*, p. B5.

99.   Greenhouse, S. (2003, May 10). Bill offers option of compensatory time. *New York Times*. http://www.nytimes.com/2003/ 05/10/politics/100ve.html; On the job. (2003, June 9). *Seattle Post-Intelligencer*, p. C1.

100.   Meyer, G. (2005, April 7). Child care workers vote to unionize. *Chicago Business*. http://chicagobusiness.com/cgi-bin; Hale, C. (2005, April 8). SEIU to represent day-care workers. *The Southern Illinoisan*. http://southernillinoisan.com/articles/2005/04/08.

101.   Delaney and Masters (1991), p. 313.

102.   Lichtenstein (1999), p.107

103.   Delaney and Masters (1991), p. 341.

104.   Dunham, R., and Bernstein, A. (2004, February 16). It's only the primaries, and big labor is losing. *Business Week*, p. 47.

Six

Union Revival

With rising frequency and a clear sense of emergency, union activists and industrial relations scholars are laying out their proposals for union revival. Some call for quick fixes that pay off in the short run while others prescribe major overhauls of what unions do and promise long-term gains. Some proposals focus on changes within unions; others deal with changes in the legal and economic context in which unions operate. It would be presumptuous to try to appraise the proposals in this chapter—each could produce some gains for unions, whether through more members or more influence, and only time will tell what works best and has a lasting impact. Instead, we trace the common threads that run through proposals for revival to get an understanding of the state of the unions in America.

A good majority of the books on labor relations and union reports over the past two decades point to paths to union revival. A few landmark studies have jump-started debates over union revival in union and academic circles. For example, in 1985 an AFL-CIO strategy committee published a report titled *The Changing Situation of Workers and Their Unions* with its controversial recommendation that unions create new categories of membership "to accommodate individuals who are not part of organized bargaining units . . . and consider dropping any existing barriers to an individual's retaining his membership after leaving an organized unit."[1] In other words, a new type of member—the *associate member,* the *nonmajority member,* or whatever unions wish to call them—would be recruited not to be represented in bargaining but to be provided with benefits and protections as an individual (e.g., legal services, low-cost health care benefits, and advice on workplace safety). The recommendation was never widely adopted, and within a decade the need to organize alternative members was overshadowed by the need to organize regular members.[2]

Over the years, individual unions such as the Steelworkers and the Communications Workers published their own recommendations for revival, usually decrying their low level of organizing activity, emphasizing the need for a clear statement of organizing jurisdiction, and urging locals to increase membership participation and improve public relations.[3] A discussion paper released by the Service Employees International Union in 2003, titled *United We Win*, created quite a stir within the labor movement by demanding more disciplined, innovative, and energetic organizing and "organizing rules based on a common strategy to build industry and market strength, not on whomever-gets-there-first."[4] The report also asked that organizing jurisdictions be clarified and that unions with similar jurisdictions be pressured to merge. An overriding theme was that not only should there be more organizing but that it should be smart organizing aimed at increasing bargaining power and building a foundation for future growth. In 2004, that discussion paper formed the basis of the several unions' demands for change in AFL-CIO structure, policy, and leadership.[5]

In response to the Service Employees' discussion paper, the leadership of the Teamsters presented its own proposal for reform. Among the recommendations was the reduction in the size and complexity of the AFL-CIO's governing structures, more mergers of unions in similar jurisdictions, lower dues for the AFL-CIO, and the development of a political plan to elect a pro-labor Congress and White House.[6]

Proposals for union revival deal with each or all three of the fundamental union activities—organizing, bargaining, and political action. In the following sections, we review the recommendations common to most proposals, in a sense developing a generic proposal for revival that gives us a wide view of the health of the unions.[7]

Organizing

If huge membership losses (down about 4 and a half million members in the past quarter century)[8] are the root of the unions' dilemma, then more and better organizing is crucial to union revival. Revival proponents argue that unions must assign a higher priority to organizing by constantly searching for new organizing opportunities and devoting greater resources to them. They must encourage their members to participate in organizing drives, working alongside experienced, full-time organizers. Organizing can no longer be the sole responsibility of professional staff. Unions must recognize the value of workers as an organizing resource, not simply as the target of organizing. Potential members can organize themselves and the present members can organize workers at nearby nonunion plants as well as the nonmembers at their own workplaces. They have an intimate knowledge of working conditions (and the workers' complaints about them) and greater credibility than staff organizers among the nonunion workers.

There should be greater organizing *activity,* not simply greater organizing *success.* In recent years, the union win rate has been roughly 50 to 60 percent, but even if unions won all of their organizing drives, the membership gains would not have been enough to offset the usual membership loses through retirements, job changes, and plant closings. For significant membership gains, unions should increase the number of elections by at least threefold while also organizing larger companies.

The initial organizing goal should be restoring membership and density to the 1980 levels of 20 million members and 23 percent. A longer-term goal could be raising density to its high of 31 percent in 1956, something that would require unions to at least double their present membership. Unions should pledge about one-third of their operating budgets to organizing, with an eventual goal of one-half (most unions presently allocate less than 5 percent).[9]

Unions should explore all ways of organizing. They should continue to organize through the certification procedures of the National Labor Relations Board, particularly when they know that employers will challenge their majority status or try to coerce and intimidate union supporters. Unions should also apply pressure against employers through threats of embarrassing disclosures at stockholders' meetings and consumer boycotts so that employers remain neutral during organizing and accept membership cards as proof of majority support. When they cannot get agreements of employer neutrality and card counts, unions should press for expedited, privately conducted elections.

Admittedly, organizing energy is greatly constrained by the New Deal model of union representation—the legal certification of unions as bargaining agents for employees in units with the sole objective of entering into legally binding contracts covering wages, hours, and conditions of employment. New forms of membership must be offered if large numbers of workers are to be attracted to unions. Workers who want unions but not collective bargaining should be offered the alternative of nonmajority representation. They can become associate members individually, without having to prove to their employers that the majority of workers where they are employed support the union. For too long, traditional organizing for bargaining has been a matter of all or nothing—unions either get a majority of votes and win certification or get less than a majority and lose. Rather than playing by these rules and often losing, unions must create non-majority membership options that offer benefits (e.g., coverage under low-cost health insurance, a union credit card) and protections (e.g., consultation with expert union staff about workplace safety issues). If organizing possibilities are to be fully exploited, unions must be willing to offer this new membership form as a stand-alone option, not just as a bridge to eventual collective bargaining or a way to retain contact with retired members. For example, if many technology workers (e.g., computer and software designers) are hesitant to be represented in collective bargaining, unions should create workplace associations for them that can meet with employers over such issues as training and overtime pay. If low-paid immigrant workers are distrustful of unions in general and fearful of employer retribution if they choose a bargaining agent, unions have to form organizations that can contact them outside of work and provide legal assistance, language and skills training, and information about wage and hour standards.

Organizing can no longer be done on a piecemeal basis; unions must adopt comprehensive strategies that justify where and why organizing targets are selected. They should focus on industries where there is already substantial union presence to maximize bargaining power. Organizers should not just try to increase union membership but also raise union density in selected industries to the point where, first, employers offer less resistance because most of their competitors are unionized, and second, workers are more willing to select union representation because many others have. Unions that are not actively organizing their core jurisdictions should allow other unions to do so. Finally, organizing should not be neglected under the assumption that the law must first be changed. Only a tremendous increase in union membership, even under the present difficult conditions, can create the political clout needed to change the law of organizing.

A renewed emphasis on organizing will surely change the character of unions. Many unions follow the *service model;* they have centralized administrative control, a full-time expert staff responsible for efficiently delivering representational services, and a high priority on bargaining and contract enforcement. Financial and staff resources are used primarily for servicing the membership rather than expanding the membership. But advocates of revival emphasize that if unions are to commit to continuous, large-scale organizing, they must adopt an *organizing model* approach. Growth and flexibility become primary goals, and the membership is invited to contribute to the organizing effort. Control is no longer at headquarters but at the local and regional district levels where organizing occurs. Union officers and members must become accustomed to sacrifice, to having most of their unions' operating budget go to organizing new members rather than only satisfying the present members with effective contract negotiation and enforcement.

Collective Bargaining

Proponents of union revival always insist that unions become much more assertive in bargaining. They should try to regain control of the agenda at the bargaining table and resist the employers' pressure for concessions. They should negotiate job and income security (e.g., restrictions on outsourcing of union jobs, relocation and retraining allowances, and guaranteed pay and benefits when laid off) and protect health care benefits from being diminished or made more costly for workers.

Unions should not allow employers to use bargaining to cut costs by reducing wages and benefits. When unions are asked to negotiate over committees that seem to give workers a greater voice in production and compensation decisions, they should be careful not to dilute their role as workplace representatives by giving employers a way to circumvent collective agreements and deal directly with workers. Cooperative labor-management programs, whether to merely increase productivity or quality or to give workers input into management's strategic decisions, should be complements to rather than replacements for traditional collective bargaining. Proposals for revival typically warn that cooperative relations are not possible with employers who are trying to rid themselves of unions.

Whenever possible, unions should use collective bargaining to improve their organizing prospects. If they can, unions should negotiate clauses that require employers to remain neutral during new organizing and recognize unions on the basis of card counts (or, as a fallback position, on privately conducted elections). Unions should also explore the outer limits of collective bargaining by negotiating clauses that are attractive to the growing numbers of part-time and temporary workers (e.g., by converting their jobs into full-time regular jobs or providing them with special portable pension arrangements). Successful negotiations over these issues will produce the model collective agreement clauses that are vital to organizing.

If there is ever to be a revival in collective bargaining, unions must find a way to deal with globalization. Unrestrained international competition creates a huge, low-cost nonunion workforce that undercuts union-negotiated settlements in the United States. It reduces union bargaining power and stiffens employer opposition. It causes employers to lay off workers and insist on wage and benefit cuts or freezes—outcomes that decrease the attractiveness of collective bargaining to nonunion workers. A revived labor movement treats international competition as just one of many constraints in bargaining rather than accepting it as a controlling factor. Unions, it is commonly argued, should restrict employers' transfers of work abroad by making it expensive, that is, demanding that workers' jobs should not be lost or their compensation lowered without hefty severance pay and relocation allowances.

Political Action

Plans for union revival recognize the importance of political action and demand that unions not squander their remaining political power. There can be revival only if unions can move beyond their political strategy of keeping enemies out of office even if it means supporting candidates that are not proven friends of labor. The union endorsement must never be automatic but should impose obligations on candidates in return for support. Endorsed candidates should actively oppose laws, regulations, and trade pacts that jeopardize union members' jobs.

Unions will find their political power magnified by working through coalitions of clergy, proponents of civil rights and workers' rights, student activists, consumers' rights organizations, and environmentalists, among others. To do this, they must devote themselves to supporting the wide range of legislative initiatives that are valued by coalition partners (e.g., environmental controls and immigrants' rights). Unions have a great deal to contribute to coalitions—the mobilization of thousands of members throughout the country—and they have much to gain from coalitions—greater political power and identification with a broad social agenda.

The top legislative priority should remain labor law reform; the ideal law would have card-check certification, stiff penalties for employer unfair labor practices (including the award of certification to the union if the employer's conduct stifled employee free choice of representatives), arbitration of unsettled issues if the parties cannot negotiate their first agreement after union certification, and restrictions on the employers' use of striker replacements. Another priority should be universal health care insurance with broad coverage, low costs, and the assurance of high quality. This would take one of the most contentious issues (and frequent cause of strikes) off the bargaining table. Better than anything else, the unions' leadership in the coalition for health care reform would demonstrate its concern for all working families. Other legislative goals should be major increases in the minimum wage, the protection of overtime pay, more vacation time, stronger maternity and paternity leave, tax incentives for employers *not* to move their operations abroad, strict enforcement of prohibitions against sweatshops, and stronger workplace ergonomic rules.

Unions must articulate the broad societal goals that attract and energize coalition partners. They should promote the equitable redistribution of income in society, a greater voice for workers (union and nonunion) in corporate decision making, and the protection of the working poor who are on the margins of the economy—immigrants, migrant workers, and part-time and temporary workers.

Changing the Unions' Mission and Structure

Many advocates of union revival argue for fundamental changes in the unions' structure and mission. First, there should be fewer and larger unions because they are usually financially stable and better able to achieve economies of scale in their operations (i.e., afford the specialized staff and services expected by the membership). A second and related goal should be the redesign of union jurisdictions. Unions that are boxed into narrow jurisdiction should merge into those with broad jurisdictions. Unions with similar jurisdictions should be encouraged by the federation to merge. It must be recognized, however, that it is too late to streamline and rationalize union jurisdictions by creating one major union in each industry. Jurisdictional boundaries overlap too much for such simplification.

But a revived labor movement would ideally have about a dozen very large unions spanning major industries such as autos, steel, and telecommunications, perhaps a half dozen general unions actively organizing workers in all occupations and industries, and a few specialized occupational unions in, for example, the performing arts, professional athletics, and health care.

Internal union structures will have to be rationalized. Local unions that are too small and poor to effectively organize and enforce collective agreements could be compelled by their parent national unions to merge with each other or into larger locals. National union headquarters must be careful not to force locals to merge without the consent of the members, otherwise they might find that they have inadvertently lowered the members' participation and commitment because their union seems so different to them.

Most important, the union mission must be reconsidered in ways that increase the legitimacy of unions.[10] Legitimacy is the perception or the assumption that an organization's actions are desirable, preferable, or appropriate as defined by the values and beliefs of that organization's constituencies. Does the organization meet the expectations of key groups (e.g., members, society, and customers) when it acts? Legitimacy is a valuable resource for those organizations such as unions whose outputs are difficult to measure and that have to operate without any simple definitions of efficiency.

There are three basic forms of legitimacy. *Pragmatic legitimacy* is bestowed when an organization is supported because it gives something valuable and gets something valuable in return (this is a straightforward exchange relationship in which an organization is supported because of its instrumentality); *moral legitimacy* is given when an organization is evaluated favorably not because of its specific benefits but because its activities are generally seen as "the right thing to do"; and *cognitive legitimacy* is bestowed on the rare occasion when a constituency accepts the organization as necessary or inevitable—its existence is taken for granted.

Unions are given pragmatic legitimacy from their constituencies (primarily their members but also workers in general, the public, and even employers). This type of legitimacy is easy for unions to get because they only have to persuade their constituencies that they offer something valuable (e.g., a collective voice at the workplace, high wages and good benefits, a legally binding contract with work rights that can be legally enforced). But pragmatic legitimacy forms a weak and unstable foundation.

If constituencies no longer see unions as providing something valuable or if what they value changes over time, then the legitimacy of unions can be lost. Unions would be much more secure if they could somehow gain moral legitimacy—a form of legitimacy not subject to constant review and easy withdrawal—or if they had cognitive legitimacy and their presence was always taken for granted and workers joined them and employers dealt with them without question. The unions' dilemma is that labor laws put them in the position of being bargaining agents and little else, so that expectations of them are based on how well they perform in negotiations and contract enforcement. If they perform well, they are granted or maintain pragmatic legitimacy. If they do not, they could easily lose it.

Proponents of union revival believe that it can occur only when unions simultaneously defend and extend legitimacy. To do this, they must first manage their pragmatic legitimacy by showing that collective bargaining remains an effective way to represent workers and that workers should join or stay in them because they get something valuable in return. At the same time, they must become better entrenched by gaining moral legitimacy—something they can achieve by showing that what they do transcends the limited interests of their members and provides value to society. If unions had moral legitimacy, joining and participating in unions would become a fundamental human right, not just a workers' right that can be extended and modified by changes in labor laws. To do this, unions should present themselves as the moral equivalent of the civil rights movement of the 1960s and compare their organizing drives to the voter registration campaigns of the civil rights era.

In brief, if unions are to revive themselves the changes must be deep and lasting and complex; they must retain their pragmatic legitimacy by improving their performance as bargaining agents, but they must also recruit members and offer services that recast them as a social movement worthy of moral legitimacy. Only in this way can they appeal to workers without traditions of unionization—workers who move from job to job, or are self-employed or work in parts of the country such as the South or rural areas where there is little union presence. And only in this way can they escape the loss of legitimacy if their performance at the bargaining table suffers.

Conclusions

Recently, there has been a flood of proposals for union revival that share the broad prescriptions for the organizing, bargaining, and political action that are briefly summarized in this chapter. But as numerous and comprehensive as they are, the proposals fail to consider two crucial factors. First, revival would have to take place in an environment in which some, perhaps many, employers put tremendous effort into resisting unionization because they see it as fatal to their competitive ability. We can expect these employers to fight union revival on all fronts, for example, by moving abroad (or threatening to do so) to avoid unionization, by pressing for wage and benefit concessions during bargaining, and by making campaign contributions to candidates who will oppose pro-union legislation.

Second, revival calls for some serious changes within the union movement, and most unions do not embrace change. For example, despite exhortations from the AFL-CIO leadership over at least the past 10 years, most unions still do not devote major portions of their budgets to organizing. Also, when nonmajority or associate membership was being debated by unions in the 1980s, it was often met with derision (some critics called it "toy membership"), and when it was adopted it was often reserved for retired members or promoted as a bridge to eventual collective bargaining, rather than accepted in its own right.[11]

Our review of proposals for union revival enable us to develop a portrait of a labor movement in serious decline, searching for ways out of problems of historic proportion. It remains to be seen how far unions are willing to go, how far employers are willing to let them go, and whether all this talk of revival is coming too late. More about this in the next chapter.

Notes

1. AFL-CIO. (1985). *The changing situation of workers and their unions.* Washington, DC: AFL-CIO, p. 19.

2. Chaison, G., and Bigelow, B. (2002). *Unions and legitimacy.* Ithaca, NY: Cornell University Press, pp. 48–57.

3. For example, see Communications Workers of America. (1983). *Committee on the Future report.* Washington, DC: Communications Workers of America; United Steelworkers of America. (1984). *Report of the Convention Committee of the Future Directions of Unions.* Pittsburgh, PA: United Steelworkers of America.

4. Service Employees International Union. (2003). *United we win: A discussion of the crisis facing workers and the labor movement.* Washington, DC: Service Employees International Union.

5. Service Employees International Union. (2004). Unite to win: A 21st century plan to build strength for working people. www.unitetowin.org; Greenhouse, S.

(2004, November 10). Largest union issues call for major changes. *New York Times,* p. A16; Greenhouse, S. (2004, November 18). Unions resume debate over merging and power. *New York Times,* p. A24.

6. International Brotherhood of Teamsters. (2004). Which way for the AFL-CIO? The Teamster view. www.teamster.org/Hoffa/TeamsterViewReport_3.pdf; Greenhouse, S. (2004, December 9). Teamsters offer plan to reshape labor future. *New York Times,* p. A19.

7. Proposals for union revival either tend to be general prescriptions for change (e.g., new union priorities or new ways of representing workers) or focus on specific activities that can lead to revival (e.g., union mergers, labor law reform, or increasing membership participation in organizing). The discussion of revival in this chapter is based on the following general proposals: AFL-CIO (1985); Century Foundation Task Force on the Future of Unions. (1999). *What's next for organized labor?* New York: Century Foundation Press; Harper, M. C. (2001). A framework for the rejuvenation of the American labor movement. *Indiana Law Journal,* 76, pp. 103–133; Heckscher, C. C. (1988). *The new unionism: Employee involvement in the changing corporation.* New York: Basic Books; Hurd, R. W. (1995). *Contesting the dinosaur image: The labor movement's search for a future.* Ithaca, NY: Cornell University, New York State School of Industrial and Labor Relations, unpublished; Kochan, T. A. (2003). *Restoring worker voice: A critical national priority.* Cambridge, MA: Massachusetts Institute of Technology, unpublished paper; Mantsios, G. (1998). *A new labor movement for the new century.* New York: Monthly Review Press; Rogers, J. (1995). A strategy for labor. *Industrial Relations,* 34, pp. 367–381; Nissen, B. (1999). Which direction for organized labor? *Essays on organizing, outreach, and internal transformations.* Detroit, MI: Wayne State University Press; Rose, J. B., and Chaison, G. N. (2001). Unionism in Canada and the United States in the 21st century. *Relations industrielles/Industrial Relations,* 56, pp. 34–62; Shostak, A. B. (1991). *Robust unionism: Innovations in the labor movement.* Ithaca, NY: Cornell University Press; Strauss, G. (1995). Is the New Deal system collapsing? With what might it be replaced? *Industrial Relations,* 34, pp. 329–349; Tillman, R. M., and Cummings, M. S. (1999). *The transformation of U.S. unions: Visions, voices and strategies from the grass roots.* Boulder, CO: Lynne Rienner; Turner, L., Katz, H. C., and Hurd, R. W. (2001). *Rekindling the movement: Labor's quest for relevance in the 21st century.* Ithaca, NY: Cornell University Press; Wheeler, H. N. (2002). *The future of the American labor movement.* New York: Cambridge University Press; Wunnava, O. (2004). *The changing role of unions: New forms of representation.* Armonk, NY: M. E. Sharpe.

Studies that deal with specific elements of revival are Bronfenbrenner, K., Friedman, S., Hurd, R. W., Oswald, R. A., and Seeber, R. L. (1997). *Organizing to win: New research on union strategies.* Ithaca, NY: Cornell University Press; Bronfenbrenner, K., and Hickey, R. (2003). *Blueprint for change.* Ithaca, NY: Cornell University, School of Industrial and Labor Relations; Chaison, G. N. (1986). *When unions merge*. Lexington, MA: Lexington Books; Chaison, G. N. (1996). *Union mergers in hard times: The view from five countries*. Ithaca, NY: Cornell University Press; Chaison, G. N. (1995). Reforming and rationalizing union structure: New directions and unanswered questions. Paper presented at the Second International Conference on Emerging Union Structures, Stockholm, Sweden, unpublished; Chaison, G. (2002). Information technology: The threat to unions. *Journal of Labor Research*, 23, pp. 249–259; Chaison and Bigelow (2002); Freeman, R. B., and Rogers, J. (2002). Open source unionism: Beyond exclusive collective bargaining. *WorkingUSA*, 5, pp. 8–40; Freeman, R. B., and Rogers, J. (1999). *What workers want*. Ithaca, NY: Cornell University Press; Gordon, M. E., and Turner, L. (2000). *Transnational cooperation among labor unions*. Ithaca, NY: Cornell University Press; Gross, J. A. (2002). Applying human rights standards to employment rights in the USA: The Human Rights Watch Report 2000. *Industrial Relations*, 33, pp. 182–196; Masters, M. F. (1997). *Unions at the crossroads: Strategic membership, financial and political perspectives*. Westport, CT: Quorum Books; Rose, J. B., and Chaison, G. N. (1995, May). Canadian labor policy as a model for legislative reform in the United States. *Labor Law Journal*, pp. 259–272; Milkman, R. (2000). *Organizing immigrants: The challenge for unions in contemporary California*. Ithaca, NY: Cornell University Press; Shostak, A. B. (2001). Tomorrow's cyberunions: A new path to revival and growth. *WorkingUSA*, 5, pp. 82–105; Milkman, R., and Voss, K. (2004). *Rebuilding labor: Organizing and organizers in the new union movement*. Ithaca, NY: Cornell University Press.

8. For a review of the decline of union membership, see Lipset, S. M., and Meltz, N. M. (2004). *The paradox of American unionism: Why Americans like unions much more than Canadians*. Ithaca, NY: Cornell University Press.

9. Cohn, J. (1997, October 6). Hard labor. *The New Republic*, pp. 21–26.

10. This application of the concept of legitimacy to labor unions is derived from Chaison and Bigelow (2002) and Chaison, G. N., Bigelow, B., and Ottensmeyer, E. (1993). Unions and legitimacy: A conceptual refinement. *Research in the Sociology of Organizations*, 12, pp. 139–166.

11. Chaison and Bigelow (2002).

Seven

Conclusions

The Unions of the Future

I n preceding chapters, we traced the historical evolution of unions in America and asked how and why they grow or decline. We looked at the complexities and contradictions of union structure and government, the unions' changing influence in bargaining and politics, and the essentials of union revival. At this point, it might seem difficult to speculate about the unions of the future because unions are so diverse and idiosyncratic; each has its own history and traditions, systems of governance and administration, organizing and bargaining practices, and approaches to politics.

While there really is no typical union, all unions do, however, share a singular mission—to represent workers in their dealings with employers and to negotiate and enforce legally binding agreements that establish wages, hours, and conditions of employment. In short, all unions exist to serve as the voice of workers on work-related matters. But unions also share a predicament—they are in a deep crisis. This is the conclusion that led to the proposals for union revival discussed in the preceding chapter. And this is the conclusion that ended each of our chapters on the basic union activities of organizing, bargaining, and political action. It is rare to find a union prospering, and it is easy to find many that are in decline.[1]

We seldom read about great union achievements in negotiations or the deciding role unions played in political contests. But we often read about disappointing outcomes, failed strikes, the unions' steps backward and self-doubts, and their search for relevancy in our economy and society.

Unions are at a critical juncture in their history, and the path that their leaders decide to take will determine what the unions of the future look like. Their future could be any of three possible scenarios—*retreat, rebound,* or *renew.*[2]

Retreat

In the first scenario—retreat—there is continuous and severe union decline. Union leaders decide to simply maintain the status quo—to do nothing extraordinary—not understanding that doing nothing means losing ground. Unions become *ghettoized*[3] or isolated; they continue to represent workers in only a few industries or occupations where they have been traditionally strong, but they are rarely found elsewhere. Their membership is concentrated in shrinking industries or companies. For example, they negotiate in conventional telephone services but not in wireless, with the Big Three automobile makers but not the transplant companies (the U.S. plants of foreign companies) or the auto parts makers, and with the major legacy airlines (e.g., United and American) but not the newer and fast-growing discount carriers (e.g., JetBlue). Unions are still prominent in a few specialized occupations—police, firefighters, musicians, and actors—but they have very few members in health care, finance, service, or retail jobs.

Organizing nearly comes to a standstill. Unions respond to occasional calls from workers who want representation, but there are no comprehensive organizing strategies, no attempts to use collective bargaining to strengthen organizing or organizing to strengthen bargaining. Less than 1,000 certification elections are held each year with unions winning about half and gaining 20,000 new members. But employment contraction, layoffs, and plant closings eliminate nearly 1 million unionized jobs in the private sector each year. Privatization and contracting out of government work cost about a quarter-million union jobs in the public sector. Union density falls sharply, reaching 5 percent within a decade and settling at that level.

Union bargaining power dissipates. Unions are defensive in bargaining, trying only to protect wages, benefits, and work rules from an employer onslaught. Bargaining becomes known as a process in which employers make demands and unions respond, rather than the reverse. Employers recognize the unions' inherent weakness at the bargaining table and they demand cutbacks in pensions and health care benefits, at first for retirees and then for those employed as well. Two-tiered wage systems, wage and benefit freezes, and bonuses in lieu of wage increases become common features of collective agreements as employers see negotiations with unions as a way to cut operating costs and impress creditors and stockholders. Employers let it be known that they will hire replacement workers whenever there are strikes and if strikes last long enough they will consider moving operations abroad. Rather than strike, unions have little choice but to accept most of the employers' demands for concessions. Nonunion workers conclude that unions have become powerless in their dealings with employers. Few workers will join unions, seeing little to gain and much to lose.

Unions also withdraw from politics, with neither the funds nor members to any longer influence candidates. The federal government's relations with unions swing between indifferent and hostile. Members of state legislatures, even in major industrial states, no longer fear union power. Although no overtly antiunion legislation is passed, the unions find few friends and many enemies in Congress and government agencies. Decisions of the National Labor Relations Board (NLRB) restrict the rights of part-timers and professionals to join unions and allow employers wide latitude during organizing drives (e.g., threatening to lay off union supporters and making promises of benefits if unions are rejected). The budget of the NLRB is sharply reduced, resulting in long delays investigating complaints about employer misconduct and in holding certification elections. In the absence of the usual opposition led by unions, the president negotiates and Congress approves trade pacts with Latin American and Asian countries that decimate domestic employment in manufacturing, much of it at older, less-productive unionized plants.

Within a few years of the start of the unions' retreat, it is hard to find a newspaper that even mentions labor unions on Labor Day. Instead, the papers extol the virtues of the growing system of employee representation committees created and controlled by management, restricted to consultation on nonwage issues, and promoted as an alternative to unionism.

A few optimists in the labor movement wait patiently for union resurgence. They argue, following the same line of reasoning as participants at a 1982 conference on the emerging dilemma of the unions, that there must be natural limits on union decline: "Once unions declined to the point of having little impact, discontent would rise . . . the social and personnel problems now handled by unions would no longer be resolved. Union membership and activity would eventually revive."[4] But many others argue that employers are sophisticated at avoiding unions and promoting nonunion alternatives. Resurgence is not inevitable; it is no longer even a possibility. The unions continue to retreat, losing their relevancy and seeming to many workers to be historical artifacts—dinosaurs in the changing industrial landscape, ambling around awkwardly and looking very old and out of place.[5]

Rebound

In this scenario, union officers fully recognize the seriousness of the unions' crisis and choose to make one last stand for unionism. They plan to fully exploit the links between organizing, bargaining, and political action. At a special meeting convened by the new leadership of the AFL-CIO, the officers of nearly every union pledge to donate a third of their budgets to organizing, and another third to political action. They campaign among their membership to convince them that these new priorities must be set. Aiming for annual growth of 1 million members, the officers, their staff, and their marketing consultants design appeals to workers that emphasize how collective bargaining provides dignity on the job for workers, protects against arbitrary management conduct, and gives workers a collective voice. They agree to broad organizing strategies under which unions coordinate campaigns and focus on communities and industries where there is already a major union presence.

The unions rally the membership in support of political candidates and worker-friendly legislation. With greater funding and careful planning, unions regain their role as leaders in the political ground game. They mobilize a million member volunteers for voter registration and getting out the vote. They believe that this is the only way they can offset the huge amounts of money being poured into politics by companies and advocacy groups. In the next election, the Democrats win control of the White House and Congress and they are quick to reward the unions for their crucial support. Congress passes the entire union wish list, including card-count certification, stiff penalties against employer misconduct during organizing, bans on the use of striker replacements, and tax incentives for employers not to move operations abroad and tax penalties when they do. In a series of labor board decisions, large groups of professional and part-time workers gain the protected right to unionize, and amendments to the law extend those rights to supervisors and agricultural workers.

Encouraged by the vastly expanded territory for organizing and the relative ease of achieving recognition for collective bargaining, unions intensify their organizing efforts. More than 1 million new members are brought into the union fold each year. Within a decade, union density is 25 percent, and it continues to rise.

As union membership and density increase in selected industries and areas, employers offer less resistance to the unions' bargaining demands because they see no serious competitive disadvantage in paying union rate wages and they are fearful of strikes (striker replacements can no longer be hired). Under such favorable conditions, unions negotiate major wage gains, more than recouping the concessions of past bargaining. The unions' victories at the bargaining table enhance their reputation, make them more attractive to nonunion workers, and lead to even greater organizing gains. By their sacrifice, energy, and single-mindedness, the unions successfully rebound from their crisis; within a decade they become powerful bargaining agents, important political players, and active and successful organizers.

Renew

Recognizing the tremendous difficulty of reversing their unions' decline, union officers join with staff and members as well as professors and community activists to review and appraise options for renewal. They declare that everything is on the table. All options will be seriously considered, and nothing can be dismissed because it seems too radical, impractical, or against union traditions. After some long and difficult soul-searching about what unions can and should mean to workers and society, they decide that organizing must be the top union priority and everything that could possibly contribute to expanding membership must be tried, even when it is a clear break with tradition. They are committed to the premise that growth can only come from flexibility and experimentation.

Some unions use NLRB certification elections as the main engine for growth, feeling comfortable with the process. Others explore ways to press employers to accept membership card counts as proof of majority status. Still others rely on expedited, privately conducted elections. All unions offer new types of membership. When they get majority support at a workplace, the unions offer workers collective bargaining membership. When they cannot get majority support, they offer nonmajority or associate membership. Sometimes the new forms of membership are offered as bridges to eventual bargaining membership, as a way to maintain contact with supporters until bargaining status is won. But the unions are not reluctant to offer the alternatives as stand-alone options for workers who want union benefits and protections or just union contact but not collective bargaining. Special forms of nonmajority membership are created for immigrants (a key benefit is a system of neighborhood centers with language and skills training), unemployed persons (membership rights include consultation with union specialists about unemployment benefits and job searching), self-employed professionals (unions offer them health care benefits and pensions), and persons such as students and clergy who are interested in workers' rights (unions form them into living wage advocacy and antisweatshop groups). Unions also offer an alternative membership for those who want to maintain contact with the union website and request occasional advice and information.

As they broaden their membership base and redefine their role, the unions transform themselves into the heirs of the civil rights movement— they become the voice of the working poor and the champions of social and economic justice for all working families. At the same time, they remain active in collective bargaining, expanding protections against job losses and strengthening health care benefits and pension plans.

The unions are energetic and imaginative in their political activities. Working with community coalitions that helped them during organizing and strikes, they focus their efforts on voter registration and turnout on the local level. They regain their political power in the cities and leverage it into organizing drives among municipal workers, knowing that they can get and win card-count certification. On the national level, the unions make it clear that they will not be taken for granted by any political party. They endorse candidates only on the basis of legislative records and support for key labor issues, rather than party affiliation. They demand that legislators support issues related to unions (labor law reform) and workers' interests in general (minimum wages, health care reform, protections for immigrants), and they soon become the force behind new, comprehensive antidiscrimination legislation and a federal statute protecting workers from wrongful discharge.

Union membership increases by 2 million each year—fully half of these are workers who joined unions as associate or nonmajority members and are not covered by collective agreements. Within a decade, union density reaches nearly 40 percent, and the unions set a 50/50 target—50 percent of each union's budget should be set aside for organizing to reach a union density (for all forms of membership) of 50 percent. The unions now have many faces—they are strong bargaining agents, valuable representatives for workers who do not have collective bargaining coverage, the voice of working families in the political arena, and a powerful social movement joining together workers and their allies.

Conclusion

The three scenarios might seem extreme, but this is a time of extreme alternatives for unions. We cannot describe the unions of the future until we are able to answer some tough questions. Which scenarios are most probable? Are there any that are not even remote possibilities? Will there be continued decline (as suggested by the first scenario), or can it be avoided by unions doing what they have always done but doing it much better (rebound) or by taking chances and doing many new and different things (renew)? Are union leaders willing to take the risks needed for the two growth scenarios, or will they seek comfort in simply maintaining the status quo without realizing that this is actually a choice, and the wrong one? These are hard times for unions in America, and despite so much talk of the need for unions to move in new directions, it is still not clear where they are heading, or even if it is too late to move at all.

Notes

1. For a rare example of a powerful, growing union, see Greenhouse, S. (June 3, 2004). Local 226, "The Culinary," makes Las Vegas the land of the living wage. *New York Times*, p. A22. This union of hotel employees deals with employers who could not relocate, clearly want labor peace rather than strife, and are extremely sensitive to consumer boycotts and public disclosures. Significantly, the union achieved bargaining status by a membership card count rather than a certification election.

2. For an example of the use of scenarios to illustrate the possible futures of the labor movement, see Freeman, R. B. (1989). What does the future hold for U.S. unionism? *Relations industrielles/Industrial Relations, 44*, pp. 25–46.

3. This term is used by Freeman. (1989); Freeman, R. B., and Rogers, J. (2004). Open source unionism: Beyond exclusive collective bargaining. *WorkingUSA,* 5, pp. 8–40.

4. The future of industrial relations: A conference report. (1983). *Industrial Relations,* 22, p. 128.

5. Chaison, G. N., and Rose, J. B. (1991). The macrodeterminants of union growth and decline. In G. Strauss, D. G. Gallagher, and J. Fiorito (Eds.), *The state of the unions.* Madison, WI: Industrial Relations Research Association, pp. 3–45. Or, in the view of Freeman (2004, p. 19), the study of unionism will be "moving from the province of labor and industrial relations experts into the hands of paleontologists." Freeman, R. B. (2004). The road to union renaissance in the United States. In R. V. Wunnava (Ed.), *The changing role of unions: New forms of representation.* Armonk, NY: M. E. Sharpe, p. 19.

Appendix

Selective Bibliography and Industrial Relations Websites

Bibliography

This is a selective bibliography of books on industrial relations including some classics, specialized studies, and edited collections of research.

Jeremy Brecher. *Strike!* (Revised and updated edition). Cambridge, MA: South End Press, 1997.

A history of the union movement that uses strikes as its focal point.

Kate Bronfenbrenner, Sheldon Friedman, Richard W. Hurd, Rudolph A. Oswald, and Ronald L. Seeber (Editors). *Organizing to win: New research on union strategies.* Ithaca, NY: Cornell University Press, 1998.

An important collection of studies of union organizing with topics ranging from community-based organizing to the determinants of individual support for unions.

Gary Chaison. *Union mergers in hard times: The view from five countries.* Ithaca, NY: Cornell University Press, 1996.

A review of union mergers during a period of union decline, including the causes and consequences of union amalgamations and absorptions in the United States, Canada, Great Britain, Australia, and New Zealand.

Gary Chaison and Barbara Bigelow. *Unions and legitimacy.* Ithaca, NY: Cornell University Press, 2002.

An analysis of the ways that unions gain, maintain, and repair legitimacy— a crucial resource and a key factor in their revival.

Bruce Feldacker. *Labor guide to labor law* (4th edition). Upper Saddle River, NJ: Prentice Hall, 2000.

A comprehensive and easy-to-understand guide to labor law, including organizing, bargaining, and the rights of union members.

Richard B. Freeman and James Medoff. *What do unions do?* New York: Basic Books, 1984.

A classic study of the role of unions in the economy, society, and the company. (A reappraisal of the authors' conclusions is found in *Journal of Labor Research,* 25, Summer 2004, pp. 339–456.)

Richard B. Freeman and Joel Rogers. *What workers want.* Ithaca, NY: Cornell University Press, 1999.

The results of a controversial survey of workers' beliefs about unions, management control, and government regulations, including their impressions of the best approaches to workplace representation and conflict resolution.

Courtney Gifford. *Directory of U.S. labor organizations.* Washington, DC: Bureau of National Affairs, 2004.

An annual collection of information on national unions and the labor federation, including officers, locations, membership, and structures.

Michael E. Gordon and Lowell Turner. *Transnational cooperation among labor unions.* Ithaca, NY: Cornell University Press, 2001.

A collection of essays, research articles, and cases studies of international cooperation among unions including the ways that they confront multinational corporations in organizing and bargaining.

William B. Gould IV. *A primer on American labor law* (4th edition). Cambridge, MA: MIT Press, 2004.

A classic review and critique of labor law, written for a general audience by an eminent legal scholar and past chair of the National Labor Relations Board.

Charles C. Heckscher. *The new unionism: Employee involvement in the changing corporation.* New York: Basic Books, 1988.

A classic argument for an expanded form of unionism that helps and protects workers in ways other than traditional collective bargaining.

Barry Hirsch and David Macpherson. *Union membership and earnings data book.* Washington, DC: Bureau of National Affairs, 2000.

A compilation of data on unions from the Census Bureau survey, including the most accurate union membership figures.

Sanford M. Jacoby. *Modern manors: Welfare capitalism since the New Deal.* Princeton, NJ: Princeton University Press, 1997.

A history of welfare capitalism in the twentieth century, tracing the evolution of plans created by nonunion employers to protect the economic security of their workers.

Tom Juravich and Kate Bronfenbrenner. *Ravenswood: The Steelworkers victory and the revival of American labor.* Ithaca, NY: Cornell University Press, 1999.

A close-up examination of the 1990 dispute between the United Steelworkers of America and the Ravenswood Aluminum Corporation in West Virginia, with details on the causes of the employer lockout, the union's strategies and eventual victory, and the implications for the revival of the labor movement.

Bruce E. Kaufman. *The origin and evolution of the field of industrial relations in the United States.* Ithaca, NY: Cornell University Press, 1993.

A landmark study of the development of industrial relations as an academic discipline and profession.

Thomas A. Kochan, Harry C. Katz, and Robert B. McKersie. *The transformation of American industrial relations.* New York: Basic Books, 1986.

A ground-breaking analysis of the industrial relations system that integrates processes on three fundamental levels—strategy and policy making, collective bargaining, and the workplace.

Nelson Lichtenstein. *State of the union: A century of American labor.* Princeton, NJ: Princeton University Press, 2002.

A history of the labor movement over the past century with particularly strong sections on the rebirth of unionism in the 1930s and union-management relations in the 1950s.

Seymour Martin Lipset and Noah M. Meltz. *The paradox of American unionism*. Ithaca, NY: Cornell University Press, 2004.

A comparison and contrast of unions in the United States and Canada, written to explain the differences in union density in the two countries.

Marick F. Masters. *Unions at the crossroads: Strategic membership, financial, and political perspectives*. Westport, CT: Quorum Books, 1997.

A comprehensive review of union finances with revealing sections on financial performance, resource allocation, and the costs of union growth.

Ruth Milkman. *Farewell to the factory: Auto workers in the late twentieth century*. Berkeley: University of California Press, 1997.

An intensive study of the closing of a unionized automobile factory, including discussions of the nature of auto work, the role of the union on the shop floor, and management's reaction to economic hard times.

Ruth Milkman and Kim Voss (Editors). *Rebuilding labor: Organizing and organizers in the new union movement*. Ithaca, NY: Cornell University Press, 2004.

A collection of articles, essays, and case studies about union organizing written mostly by sociologists and union activists.

R. Emmett Murray. *The lexicon of labor*. New York: New Press, 1998.

A brief collection of labor terms and biographical sketches of labor leaders.

Bruce Nissen. *Which direction for organized labor?* Detroit, MI: Wayne State University, 1999.

A collection of essays on the paths to union revival including greater organizing, coalition activities, and the internal transformation of unions.

George Strauss, Daniel G. Gallagher, and Jack Fiorito (Editors). *The state of the unions*. Madison, WI: Industrial Relations Research Association, 1991.

A landmark review of the state of the unions with important discussions of union growth and governance.

Lowell Turner, Harry C. Katz, and Richard W. Hurd. *Rekindling the movement: Labor's quest for relevance in the 21st century,* 1991.

A collection of articles on the revival of the labor movement that includes studies of innovative organizing, new union priorities, political action, and changes in union structure.

Bruce Western. *Between class and market: Postwar unionization in the capitalist democracies.* Princeton, NJ: Princeton University Press, 1997.

A study of the economic and political factors leading to union growth and high union density in the post-World War II years in several countries, including the United States.

Hoyt N. Wheeler. *The future of the American labor movement.* New York: Cambridge University Press, 2002.

A proposal for the revival of the labor movement based partly on a return to earlier union priorities and forms of representation.

Websites

This is a list of selected Internet websites that have information on industrial relations. In addition to these, nearly all labor unions have their own websites, and newspapers have websites that are searchable for industrial relations topics, although some, such as the *New York Times* and the *Wall Street Journal,* may charge subscription fees.

Labor Unions

www.alpa.org	Airline Pilots Association
www.aflcio.org	American Federation of Labor–Congress of Industrial Organizations
www.afscme.org	American Federation of State, County and Municipal Employees
www.aftra.org	American Federation of Television and Radio Artists
www.afm.org	American Federation of Musicians
www.aft.org	American Federation of Teachers

www.nbpa.org	Basketball Players Association
www.cwa-union.org	Communications Workers of America
www.iamaw.org	International Association of Machinists
www.ibew.org	International Brotherhood of Electrical Workers
www.teamster.org	International Brotherhood of Teamsters
www.ilwu.org	International Longshore and Warehouse Union
www.iuop.org	International Union of Operating Engineers
www.iww.org	Industrial Workers of the World
www.liuna.org	Laborers' International Union
www.nea.org	National Education Association
www.npmhu.org	Postal Mail Handlers
www.sag.org	Screen Actors Guild
www.seiu.org	Service Employees International Union
www.ufcw.org	United Food and Commercial Workers
www.uswa.org	United Steelworkers of America
www.unitehere.org	Union of Needletrades, Textiles and Industrial Employees and the Hotel Employees and Restaurant Employees (UNITE-HERE)

Sources of Information about Unions and Industrial Relations

www.adr.org	American Arbitration Association
www.bls.org	Bureau of Labor Statistics, U.S. Department of Labor

www.bna.com	Bureau of National Affairs
www.ilr.cornell.edu/library	Catherwood Library, Cornell University, School of Industrial and Labor Relations
www.opensecrets.org	Center for Responsive Politics
www.epinet.org	Economic Policy Institute
www.ebri.org	Employee Benefit Research Institute
www.fmcs.gov	Federal Mediation and Conciliation Service
www.nlrb.gov	National Labor Relations Board
www.reuther.wayne.edu	Reuther Library, Wayne State University
www.lib.berkeley.edu/IIRL	Institute of Industrial Relations Library, University of California
www.dol.gov	U.S. Department of Labor
www.unionstats.com	Union membership and coverage database

Union and Worker Advocacy Organizations

www.acorn.org	Association of Community Organizations for Reform Now (ACORN)
www.uniondemocracy.com	Association for Union Democracy
www.labornet.org	LaborNet Labor News Service
www.labornotes.org	Labor Notes: Putting the Movement Back in the Labor Movement
www.livingwagecampaign.org	Living Wage Resource Center
www.tdu.org	Teamsters for a Democratic Union

Professional Associations

www.acrnet.org	Association for Conflict Resolution
www.uwe.ac.uk/bbs/buira	British Universities Industrial Relations Association
www.cira-acri.ca	Canadian Industrial Relations Association
www.ilo.org/public/english/iira	International Industrial Relations Association
www.lera.uiuc.edu	Labor and Employment Relations Association (formerly the Industrial Relations Research Association)

Index

About the Author

Gary Chaison is Professor of Industrial Relations at the Graduate School of Management of Clark University in Worcester, Massachusetts. Before coming to Clark 25 years ago, Professor Chaison was on the faculty of the School of Administration of the University of New Brunswick, Fredericton, New Brunswick, Canada. He has a Ph.D. in industrial relations from the State University of New York at Buffalo. His research has been in the areas of union structure, government and growth, collective bargaining, and international labor relations. He has published extensively on the determinants of union growth in the United States and Canada, and the causes and consequences of union mergers in the United States as well as several other countries. Professor Chaison is the coauthor of *Unions and Legitimacy* (2002) and the author of *Union Mergers in Hard Times: The View from Five Countries* (1996) and *When Unions Merge* (1986), as well as a number of articles in industrial relations journals. Recently, he has written about the impact of information technology on unions, the prospects for union revival, and the behavioral dimensions of union mergers. He teaches graduate and undergraduate courses in human resource management, industrial relations, international labor relations, discrimination in employment, the contemporary workplace, and collective bargaining.